Teaching and Assessing Writing

Edward M. White

Teaching and Assessing Writing

Recent Advances in Understanding, Evaluating, and Improving Student Performance

SECOND EDITION

Jossey-Bass Publishers · San Francisco

Substantial discounts on bulk quantities of Jossey-Bass books are available to corporations, professional associations, and other organizations. For details and discount information, contact the special sales department at Jossey-Bass Inc., Publishers. (415) 433-1740; Fax (415) 433-0499.

For sales outside the United States, contact Maxwell Macmillan International Publishing Group, 866 Third Avenue, New York, New York 10022.

Manufactured in the United States of America. Nearly all Jossey-Bass books and jackets are printed on recycled paper containing at least 10 percent postconsumer waste, and many are printed with either soy- or vegetable-based ink, which emits fewer volatile organic compounds during the printing process than petroleum-based ink.

Library of Congress Cataloging-in-Publication Data

White, Edward M. (Edward Michael), date.
    Teaching and assessing writing : recent advances in understanding, evaluating, and improving student performance / Edward M. White.
      p.   cm. — (The Jossey-Bass higher and adult education series)
    Includes bibliographical references and index.
    ISBN 1-55542-619-0
    1. English language—Composition and exercises—Study and teaching. 2. English language—Composition and exercises—Ability testing. 3. English language—Rhetoric. 4. English language—Rhetoric—Ability testing. I. Title. II. Series.
LB1576.W48628   1994
808′042′071—dc20

                                       93-43200
                                          CIP

SECOND EDITION
HB Printing   10 9 8 7 6 5 4 3 2 1   *Code 9416*

The Jossey-Bass
Higher and Adult Education Series

Contents

Foreword to
the First Edition

Teaching people to write is one of the chronic problems of American education, right next to teaching them to think, a closely related but even more knotty problem. Although hundreds of books at any period in time give instruction in writing, few squarely face the question of how we evaluate writing, clearly a vital part of teaching it well. In this respect, Edward White's book stands with Mina Shaughnessy's (1977) *Errors and Expectations* as testimony that there is something new under the sun even in books about writing. Specifically, both books aim at enlarging the reader's view of what is involved in evaluating writing and what that evaluating can best contribute to a person's learning to write.

The mating of teaching and assessing is not an accidental coupling. In practice, *teaching* writing is an eminently satisfying task. It is the grading of papers that makes it so much a burden. Edward White has not solved that conflict, but he has spoken directly to making the assessing of writing—not the mere grading of papers—an integral part of teaching. Whether for a teacher in a composition class or for the director in charge of evaluating the writing skills of large numbers of students, his book is precise and detailed about the best way to use evaluation toward the aims of developing writing skills.

Chief among the ways in which evaluation has become more sophisticated and useful to the teacher is the development of holistic scoring. At first confined to large-scale testing programs, this method of training readers to do multiple and carefully conducted readings of student essays is adaptable to all teaching situations. Beyond the method itself are the contributions such a method makes not just to identifying the elements that go into good writing but to illuminating what is meant by good writing in the large. What emerges is an analysis that reinforces what the student has achieved while still indicating directions for further development of skills.

Outside the classroom, educators are pressed to provide evaluations that can be trusted as specific measures of basic educational achievements. White has been a leader in the formation and conduct of large-scale writing evaluation programs in California and throughout the country. His years of experience provide the combination of theory and practice that makes this book the definitive one on the testing of writing skills in educational programs.

The author writes with a skill uncommon among teachers of writing and rare among those primarily engaged with educational tests and measurement. One of the simpler ways for improving writing in schools and colleges is to increase the numbers of teachers who write well. Edward White has written a book whose style and substance speak both to stimulating other teachers to write and to ways in which a shared enthusiasm and practice can lead to developing teachers' writing skills.

January 1985   Kenneth E. Eble
                                                   Professor of English
                                                   University of Utah

Preface

Every decade or so in this country, people become aroused about writing performance of students. The recurring complaint that Johnny can't write is documented by egregious examples of student prose, selected statistics, and solemn faculty opinion. Whether or not the concept of writing ability is well defined or responsibly measured, these expressions of concern reflect not simply one more educational fad but the realization that writing ability relates directly to learning and to thinking. The ability to express oneself is so central to education—and to the democratic political theory behind public education—that such attention ought to be expected, even welcomed.

　　Until recently, most of those concerned about student writing, including most educators, have assumed that writing ability is relatively easy to assess. Traditionally, such assessment has been either a haphazard matter of individual teachers grading papers or a supposedly objective compilation of statistics from large-scale multiple-choice tests. Now, however, as teachers of writing have moved more prominently into the area of measurement, the intimate relationship between assessing and teaching writing has begun to emerge with startling clarity. As a result, both the measurement of writing ability and the teaching of writing have begun to change.

This revised and expanded edition of *Teaching and Assessing Writing* is designed for all teachers in the schools and universities who use writing in their classes (including present or future English teachers and teachers in other disciplines) and for writing examiners, administrators, and others concerned about the effectiveness of student writing. Besides presenting recent advances in the theory and practice of assessing writing ability, the book also discusses current theories of reading and responding to writing; program evaluation; and, most prominently, the assignment and grading of student papers as a central aspect of the teaching of writing.

No one should imagine that student writing is the sole preserve of English teachers or that only English faculty should be involved in the measurement of writing ability. More and more teachers in the schools and the universities, and in all disciplines, are becoming aware that writing is a student's chief means of learning. However, faculty outside the field of English often feel insecure when assigning or grading student writing, imagining that a degree in English imparts specialized knowledge about writing that they do not possess. But only rarely do English majors, or even those with doctorates in English, receive instruction in the teaching or measurement of writing. By presenting—without resorting to technical language—current knowledge in both the assessment and the teaching of writing, this book is particularly designed to encourage the use of writing across the curriculum. The materials included should help faculty in all disciplines assign and respond to student writing more comfortably and effectively than they have to date.

Despite recent advances in the measurement of writing, much assessment of writing skill, particularly in the elementary and high schools, still takes place by means of norm-referenced multiple-choice testing of usage or mechanics. Many teachers are convinced that such measurement devalues writing itself and is destructive to their best work, but they feel powerless to deal with decisions (made "downtown" or "upstate") on which they are never consulted. Besides, the information about the testing of writing contained in this book has usually been confined to fairly small circles and is only slowly coming to be known. How, the question arises at every turn, can informed teachers convince those in power to use and develop better types of writing-assessment procedures?

As teachers at all levels have begun to discover, with some astonishment, knowledge in this area is power. Although some principals, assistant superintendents for instruction, school boards, chancellors, regents, and the like, are impervious to argument, most are not. When concerned faculty have marshaled the evidence and shown themselves ready to take responsibility for a writing-assessment program that supports the teaching of writing, they tend to find much more support than they ever imagined. This book gathers in one place the theories, arguments, and practices that will enable teachers to present a convincing case for such a program where it is appropriate. Many of those who employ multiple-choice tests as the only measure of writing ability will be ready to include writing if they can be shown that essay tests and portfolio assessments can be properly constructed, reliably scored, and cost-effective.

Public outcry about literacy will recur, whatever teachers may do. But schools and colleges that can show they have helped their students write well will have replies to such concern. Such schools will value teachers who can use assessment to improve as well as judge student work and who can help the institution develop assessments to demonstrate that improvement.

Background

This book is the product of more than two decades of practical experience and theoretical speculation on the subject of the assessment of writing ability and its relation to the teaching of writing. Most of the materials here were developed from talks, presentations, and workshops I have given in the years since I was appointed the first director of the California State University (CSU) Freshman English Equivalency Examination in 1972. Much of what is here printed in book form for the first time has become generally known and practiced among the dozen or so English faculty members and test specialists who have been working intensively in the area of writing and its evaluation. The first edition (1985) sought to move this knowledge and experience from the oral tradition and from journal articles into a more accessible and unified form. This new edition includes the major advances in both teaching and assessing writing that have taken place in the last decade.

My first action upon my appointment in 1972 was to survey the field in order to build on current knowledge. I was a rather rare bird at the time, an English department chair with all the usual credentials (a doctorate in literature and publications about literary figures) but with a deep interest in the teaching of writing. My fellow CSU department chairs asked me to administer a writing test, not because I was a test specialist (I was not) but because I had shown a slightly disreputable concern for freshman composition. My surveys of other "experts" (I had become one by appointment, not by knowledge) were most surprising: virtually no one in the field of English claimed to know much about large-scale assessment of writing, although I was frequently referred from one person to another and back again. My search for literature on the subject was almost as barren. Aside from one book published by the College Board (Godshalk, Swineford, and Coffman, 1966) and a series of unpublished research reports from the Educational Testing Service (ETS), almost nothing useful turned up.

I did happen to have some experience as an essay reader for the Advanced Placement (AP) program, which is administered for the College Board by ETS, and I immediately set out to learn all I could from those in charge of essay testing at ETS. I received gracious and valuable help from the AP team, and I also had the great good fortune to spend time with several ETS specialists in essay testing—Evans Alloway, Paul Diederich, Alan Seder, and Albert Serling—all of whom taught me a great deal about the issues and problems of the field. Although this book is not particularly complimentary to ETS, my debt (shared by virtually everyone working in assessment) to the basic work done by and at ETS is substantial.

As the English Equivalency Examination program began, it became clear that the assessment of writing and the teaching of writing were intimately related and that many of the abuses in assessment and teaching resulted from the separation of the two. As our committees attempted to develop essay tests, we found ourselves dealing with basic questions about the goals of writing instruction. As we included more and more faculty members in our holistic scoring sessions, we noticed that changes in the teaching of writing were beginning to occur on many of the CSU campuses. The workshops I conducted at the Bay Area Writing Project in Berkeley (and then at many of its satellite projects as it grew to become the National Writing Project) proved that teachers in the grade and high schools also found the connection between assessment and teaching interesting and important. Increasingly, faculty came to me after my workshops at schools and universities, asking where the materials and ideas of the workshop could be found in print. For some years, the first edition satisfied such questions. In recent years, those requests have resumed, as the first edition became less current and as I kept adding new material to the workshops. When, the question became, will a new edition appear? This book is my attempt to meet that need in the larger context of general concern about student writing performance.

The major change in viewpoint in this new edition is in my approach to essay testing and holistic scoring for measuring writing. I was relatively partisan and uncritical in the first edition, but it has now become clear that essay testing has some serious problems and that holistic scoring of essay tests is an important way of measuring writing but not the only one. Thus this edition offers a more balanced approach to assessing writing, with cautions as well as practical advice about all the methodologies of measurement. Portfolio assessment was not mentioned in the first edition and now figures prominently throughout the book.

The new edition also considers much more broadly the ways assessment affects teaching, with much new material on developing writing assignments and responding to them. I have also added new chapters on the way language affects assessment and on the politics of writing assessment as I have seen them in action over the last twenty years and as they may occur in the future.

Plan of the Book

The first six chapters (Part One) of the book discuss the relation of teaching to assessment in current practice (with some attention to teachers' hostility toward assessment), the history and meaning of "basic skills" in reading and writing, and the use of assessment to support writing instruction. Chapters Two and Three attend specifically to one of the most neglected of teaching responsibilities, the designing of writing assignments and test questions; Chapters Four, Five, and Six look closely at another neglected issue, responding to student texts. Chapter Four demonstrates how theories of reading (especially poststructural literary theory) influence our reading of students' written work. Chapter Five makes practical suggestions for teachers, many of whom view grading papers as the most problematic part of their profession. Chapter Six discusses the strengths and weaknesses of the newest method of assessing writing—the use of portfolios; this method holds great promise for the improvement of teaching but presents even greater problems in measurement.

Part Two moves beyond the classroom to a wider scene where assessment has principally to do with measurement, often in large groups. Here assessment is not so much *formative* as it is *summative,* providing information on student performance for various institutional purposes. Chapter Seven points out that different "discourse communities" in the university have different ways of speaking about and hence envisioning writing assessment—and gives examples of the practical difficulties that ensue when such visions collide. The next three chapters (Chapters Eight, Nine, and Ten) provide theoretical and practical information about large-scale writing assessments. An underlying message throughout these chapters is that large-scale assessment is too important to leave in the hands of assessors: faculty, particularly those with a special interest in writing, need to be heavily involved if the assessment is to be useful. Chapter Eleven shows readers how to avoid the most common pitfalls in conducting large-scale assessments. Chapter Twelve moves beyond student assessment to program assessment, another crucial task fraught with theoretical and practical problems; this chapter describes more and less effective procedures, resources, and plans.

The final chapter of the book, Chapter Thirteen, looks back at the historical and political issues in writing assessment over the past two decades. Since I have wound up either at the center or as a close observer of these issues, the discussion tends to be both a personal and an analytical essay, enriched by anecdote. Assessment is not, in itself, a truly stirring topic, I must confess; but its implications are powerful for society as a whole as well as for education. The chapter ends with some speculations about the future of writing assessment.

The four resources at the back of the book provide guidelines and sample evaluation and scoring guides.

The reference section that concludes the book is selective rather than comprehensive, designed for the teacher, evaluator, or other reader looking for further information on the issues and practices dealt with in the book. Anyone comparing this section with the one from the first edition will be struck, as I have been, by the extraordinary energy expended on the subject over the past decade.

Acknowledgments

Anyone who seeks, as I do here, to integrate diverse information into a comprehensive view of a whole is bound to deal with special fields of study, such as statistics, in a way that some specialists may find elementary. But these fields have made important contributions to the improvement of writing instruction, and their contributions need to be recognized and made more common property. While I have tried to make my own writing nontechnical and free of jargon, I have also tried to be responsible and accurate. The various specialists with whom I have worked over the last two decades will recognize their ideas embedded throughout the book and will, I hope, accept this general acknowledgment of the education I received from them.

Early versions of several chapters and parts of chapters have appeared in various publications, which have given permission for their use here. Chapter Seven is adapted from an article in *College Composition and Communication,* and materials from Chapter Nine appeared in *College English;* both of these journals are published by the National Council of Teachers of English. Parts of Chapters Two, Three, Five, and Six are adapted from *Assigning, Responding, Evaluating: A Writing Teacher's Guide* (White, 1992); I thank the publisher, St. Martin's Press, for permission to adapt those materials here. Chapter Thirteen is slightly revised from Chapter Three of *Validating Holistic Scoring for Writing Assess-*

ment (Williamson and Huot, 1993) and is reprinted here with permission of Hampton Press. Donald Daiker and Gail Hughes have given permission for use of their materials in the Resources section, as has the Council of Writing Program Administrators. The holistic scoring guide in that section is the product of committees of my friends and colleagues in the California State University English departments, whose ideas are no doubt to be found in many other places in the book. We all, to paraphrase Isaac Newton, stand on the shoulders of others so that we may see as far as we can.

I also owe a special debt to the late Kenneth Eble, who, as consulting editor for Jossey-Bass Publishers, was a constant source of wisdom and encouragement during the production of the first edition of this book. I wish he had been here to help with the new edition.

San Bernardino, California   Edward M. White
January 1994

The Author

Edward M. White is professor of English at California State University, San Bernardino, where he has served for prolonged periods as English Department chair and coordinator of the Upper-Division University Writing Program and where he received the Outstanding Professor Award in 1993. He received his B.A. degree (1955) from New York University and both his M.A. (1956) and Ph.D. (1960) degrees from Harvard University, focusing on literature. Statewide, he has been coordinator of the California State University Writing Skills Improvement Program, and for over a decade he was director of the English Equivalency Examination program. On the national scene, he has directed the Consultant/Evaluator service (for colleges and universities) of the Council of Writing Program Administrators for five years and has been elected to a second term on the Executive Committee of the Conference on College Composition and Communication.

He is author of more than forty articles on literature and the teaching of writing, has written three English composition textbooks (most recently *Inquiry*, 1993, coedited with L. Z. Bloom), and has one more in progress. His other books include *Developing Successful College Writing Programs* (1989) and *Assigning, Responding, Evaluating* (1992). He is also a coeditor (with W. Lutz and S. Kamasukiri of a book scheduled for publication in the Modern

Language Association's series on scholarship in composition, *The Politics and Policies of Assessment in Writing*.

White is a frequent speaker at conferences and has been a consultant to more than seventy-five educational institutions in the area of writing and evaluation. He was principal investigator for Research in the Effective Teaching of Writing, a project funded by the National Institute of Education, 1980–1985. He has given many workshops on measurement, the improvement of teaching, and writing across the curriculum. The first edition of *Teaching and Assessing Writing* (1985) was widely reviewed and has been called "required reading for the profession."

Teaching
and Assessing
Writing

Part One

Assessment—
A Critical Tool
in the Teaching
of Writing

Assessment plays an important part in every class that asks students to write. Every teacher who uses writing as part of teaching must devise tasks for the students; explain the assignments; help students draft, revise, and complete them; and respond in some way to the students' work. All these activities involve assessment. While much of the discussion in this part of the book focuses on teachers of writing courses, for whom these matters constitute a major and continuing concern, most teachers in most fields of study and most of those who work with teachers will find material here of immediate use.

The first chapter looks directly at the hostility many teachers feel toward assessment, which usually appears as an outside intrusion into their work with students. Without excusing the abuses of assessment, this chapter shows teachers how to defeat its threat and take advantage of its promise to improve instruction and the quality of teachers' working lives.

The next two chapters concern the design of writing assignments: class papers in Chapter Two and essay examinations in Chapter Three. The chapters include examples of writing assignments that should produce better writing and more student learning than most teachers now elicit.

1

Chapter Four discusses poststructural literary theory, recent innovative ideas about the reading of texts. Since every teacher reads student texts according to *some* theory of reading, this chapter seeks to make explicit the ways in which some competing theories lead to different kinds of responses to student writing. The chapter concludes with a consideration of the theory behind controlled holistic scoring, an example of a specialized interpretive community.

The last two chapters in this part focus on responding to student writing, a subject much more complicated than grading or writing comments on papers. Chapter Five examines the responding options available to teachers and the concepts behind them. Chapter Six discusses the recent adoption of portfolios from the fine arts to writing and suggests that the use of writing portfolios might expand the definition and scope of writing assessment.

Not all writing should be graded, but assessment of some sort is an inevitable part of all learning. These chapters should help teachers with this troubling and pervasive activity and support their efforts to improve student writing.

CHAPTER 1

Assessment as
Threat and Promise

Assessment of writing can be a blessing or a curse, a friend or a foe, an important support for our work as teachers or a major impediment to what we need to do for our students. Like nuclear power, say, or capitalism, it offers enormous possibilities for good or ill, and, furthermore, it often shows both its benign and destructive faces at the same time.

Most of my academic friends shudder at the mere sound of the word *assessment*. They equate *assessment* (a large term, referring to the gathering of all kinds of information) with *testing* (a much narrower term); they hate tests, at least other people's tests, and often their own, and they hate the idea of people looking over their shoulders to see if work is getting done. Most teachers at all levels work hard at their teaching, and they regard assessment as an intrusion into their lives, for no good purpose. These attitudes about tests in particular and assessment in general, which are widespread among teachers, reflect experiences with bad assessment and a well-founded awareness that assessment can and often does function as the enemy of instruction.

Most of my nonacademic friends have trouble understanding why teachers get upset about assessment. In their view, it seems perfectly reasonable and fair to ask teachers to find out whether their students are learning. And most nonacademics, particularly public officials, regard academic arguments about the difficulties of assessment as bald admissions of incompetence. Those of us who deal with the public or with political bodies must be extremely careful not to appear to reject *all* assessment when we protest bad assessment, for then we are ignored as self-serving and inept.

Assessment as Threat

Assessment is a threat to instruction under the following conditions: when it is imposed from outside the classroom; when it is insensitive to the students, to learning, to teaching, and to the discipline; when it is done on the cheap; when its results are misused. Let me give you an example. My wife used to teach sixth grade in an inner-city school, a school whose students bring with them the usual social, economic, nutritional, family, and (of course) educational problems of the slums. It is a major task to teach children to read and write under the best circumstances, but the job becomes Herculean when many students have no homes, no breakfast, no experience seeing anyone read. She gave up sending notes home to the parents because, even when there were parents around, they might not know how to read English or any other language. A central part of her job, then, was to help her students discover that reading is a legitimate and rewarding activity and that writing is a source of pleasure and power, to encourage them in the creative use of language. She carried out this task with an energy that I found admirable and with considerable success. But the school district measured her success by an elaborate multiple-choice test in correct usage of Edited American English, a test of dialect that virtually all her students were doomed to fail. The test defined basic skills in a particularly narrow way that negated the really important work she had done. In order to help her students score well on that test, she had to stop teaching what is most important to teach. The test is a serious threat to instruction.

There seems to be a perverse law of motion to educational innovations: the best ideas creep forward in geological time, while the worst ideas spread like forest fires before a gale. Some of you will remember a reductive idea that became popular a few years ago: education through testing "behavioral objectives." Teachers were required to provide detailed statements of goals for instruction in the schools (for example, "90 percent of my students will spell correctly 90 percent of the words on this list") and frequent testing to see whether the goals had been met. The theory behind the measurement was a narrow version of behavioral psychology, which insisted that the only educational outcomes that mattered—indeed, the only ones that really could take place—would be manifested by changes in behavior. Thus, the goals, whatever the subject, had to be "behavioral"—that is, readily observable and measurable. The hard-headed Skinnerians behind the movement declared that less obvious gains, such as attitude changes or general improvement in cognitive ability, would appear as measurable behaviors if they had in fact occurred. To be sure, there was a certain amount of good common sense in requiring teachers to state what they were trying to do and how they would measure success. But a first-grade teacher, delighted with the concept, unwittingly pointed out its serious deficiency when I asked her how she could write behavioral objectives for much of what (in my naiveté) I took to be the first-grade curriculum: story telling, poetry, art, or music appreciation. "No problem," she told me cheerfully. "We just don't teach those things anymore."

Despite the obvious reductiveness of the concept, it spread rapidly from the schools to the colleges, and numbers of university presidents and legislative committees adopted the idea. All over the country in the 1970s, puzzled professors were struggling with the constricted language and concepts of behavioral objectives. One reluctant Elizabethan scholar, required to write behavioral objectives for his upper-division Shakespeare course (during the heights of the fad), responded with appropriate cynicism. His goal for teaching *Macbeth*, he wrote, was that 90 percent of his students, 90 percent of the time, would not kill a king.

Happily, only vestiges of the "behavioral objective" fad remain, often in sensible goals statements on course syllabi. But bad ideas remain in the system like dormant viruses, and this one has come back in the form of "value-added" assessment.

In value-added assessment, an attempt is made to measure the direct gain from a particular curriculum. The term comes from the world of commerce, most directly from the European value-added tax on goods. Thus, raw rubber has a certain value when it reaches the tire plant, but much more value after it has been turned into tires; that added value can be identified, measured, and taxed. No European arguments for applying this metaphor to education exist, to my knowledge; it is the American genius for practical applications that has made this leap. Entering freshmen, the argument goes, may be seen as the raw rubber of the mind, and college composition (for example) then becomes the processing plant. The freshman program adds value the way the factory presses tread lines and shapes sidewalls. If the program, or the factory, is doing its job, the added value of the processing must be made manifest. The task is not hard, or unreasonable, for the tire plant; but when we start applying that language and its concepts to liberal education, we run into difficulties. For such assessment, "gain scores" from parallel tests (usually called pretests and posttests) must be obtained. Improved scores on the posttests show that the program, or the individual, is doing what should be done. *Outcomes assessment* is the guiding term, and once again a crude behaviorism provides the underlying psychological theory and language.

The concept as it has developed has a certain superficial and political appeal, in particular to those for whom commercial metaphors are a dominant means of perceiving reality. Behaviorism makes a powerful claim: if education has brought about changes of any sort, as every educator asserts, those changes should appear in measurable behaviors that can be tested. The changed behaviors then become the "value added" to the student from the educational program. If a teacher or an entire discipline cannot come up with measures that produce results, the argument continues, either no real change has taken place or the teachers are unclear about instructional goals and therefore cannot tell whether the goals have been reached. Arguments about gains that are qualitative rather than quantitative, or about insensitive measuring tools, are dismissed as smoke screens, rather in the same tone that Skinner used in dismissing the concepts of freedom and dignity in his famous book (Skinner, 1972).

In addition, for once, this measurement concept favors the *less* privileged students and institutions, since those who begin at a very low point are most likely to show gain scores on tests. Selective institutions, on the other hand, are hard pressed to come up with measurement devices that readily and economically show measurable gains for students already functioning at high cognitive and skill levels. Such institutions are no longer spared these demands; indeed, their high tuition spurs demands for value-added assessment to prove that the education they offer is worth the price. The concept also favors vocational and technical curricula, which lend themselves to the concept of learning as simple accrual of skill and information, over the liberal arts.

Unfortunately for those of us who have had to confront the behaviorist perspective, we have yet to come up with writing tests sensitive enough to measure the value added to individual writing skill (out of a lifetime of language use) by a single writing course. Despite great gains in reliability for holistic scoring over the last twenty years, there is still only slim evidence that a direct writing measure (such as an essay test) can yield sufficiently precise data to provide clear gain scores. Of the more than five hundred experimental studies on written composition reviewed by Hillocks (1986), only a few tested anything anything more elaborate than sentence skills. As with other kinds of advanced arts and skills, simple numerical positivism devalues the meaning of writing. The problem is not that the writing community has failed to attempt measurement; we have had measurement of writing of every sort almost beyond counting in the last decade. Behind the problem is the language and worldview of the behaviorists, who measure the value of education in crudely simplistic ways. They are looking for value in all the wrong places, as the song has it.

Pretesting and posttesting thus promise little for writing teachers; instead, such testing threatens all liberal education, since it necessarily puts a premium on low-level skills that can be easily examined, through inexpensive multiple-choice tests, and readily improved by short-term learning or drill. This kind of testing may work in some fields, but it is particularly dangerous in writing and other liberal arts fields, where outcomes are complex and not necessarily manifested immediately. Even so behavior-oriented a team as Benjamin Bloom and his colleagues (1971) caution against simplified testing, which often works in opposition to the important goals of education; they warn, for example, that an emphasis on knowledge about literature (which can be readily tested) can destroy the love of literature, which is far more important but much more difficult to assess.

In short, at its worst, assessment forces teachers to use bad or inappropriate tests that demean everyone involved and trivialize learning. The results of such tests can be used to show that teachers are not doing their job, that their students can't learn, that their budget should be cut, and that simple-minded solutions should be imposed on teachers and their students from the outside.

Assessment as Promise

I have dwelt on this unpleasant picture of bad assessment not only because it exists in reality somewhere and is possible everywhere but also because many teachers regard it as an assessment model. Unfortunately, this negative picture is the only assessment model that many of us have. My intention in this book is to add to that model a wholly different one—that is, to suggest that we can supplement our awareness of the threat of assessment with a comparable awareness of its promise. For at its best, assessment can improve our teaching, make our jobs easier and more rewarding, and demonstrate the value of what we do. This kind of assessment enables us to define clearly what we are doing as teachers, what we expect our students to do as learners, and how they should be different as a result of study. Then it helps us find ways to discover whether our students have learned what we want them to learn. It changes our teaching, since we wind up with better writing assignments, more constructive responses to student writing, and less (not more) grading. Serious and promising assessment does not require all this to happen easily, cheaply, or by means of a single test; it asks us to look closely at the results of a variety of assessments, to see whether they suggest ways of improving what we do. Such use of assessment is worth the effort and the expense, which are often considerable. Incidentally, it also offers outsiders evidence they have a right to ask for, just as we have the right, actually the duty, to ask for evidence that our students have earned passing marks. In many cases, the rule, far from golden, becomes "Do assessment yourself, or it shall be done unto you."

When we step back to look at ourselves as teachers, we must admit that almost all of us are engaged in some forms of assessment most of the time. Every thoughtful person knows that assessment is absolutely necessary for learning. "How'm I doing, teacher?" is the question on every learner's lips. An analogy to learning in sports is appropriate, if not perfect. The batter in a batting cage, or the tennis player at the base line, hits the ball and gains an immediate response; if the ball goes awry, he or she will make immediate corrections, working, with steady practice, until the ball begins to go straight and true. The coach closely observes the performance and offers suggestions, sometimes modeling the most productive behavior, but the player is the only one who can make the changes needed. It is patently absurd for the batter to blame the coach for his strikeouts or for the tennis player to ignore her game and strive only to please the coach. And with sports, as with writing, assessment needs to be sensitive as well as honest if students are to internalize it. No coach, however kind and supportive, can pretend that bad play will win; nor can an irascible and competitive coach bring about improvement by continuous harassment if the players wind up hating the game. Furthermore, the game sometimes is played merely for fun, without the coach's assessment; and at these times the players can develop self-assessment. My point is that learning in sports—as well as in writing—is a matter of steady and clear assessment, which learners must internalize before they can make any real improvement.

In the field of composition, in particular, evaluation is crucial. The problem of teaching students how to revise, for example, is essentially an assessment problem. The unwillingness of students to revise is really an odd paradox: no professional writer would dream of publishing work without many revisions, but the least skilled writers in America, the students, almost invariably hand in first drafts, usually produced the night before the due date. Writing teachers constantly implore students to revise, without much effect. And why do students see no point in revising? Certainly one reason is perfectly plain: they see nothing wrong with what they have written. They look at their work, however filled with original sins, and, like another Creator, pronounce it very good. The teacher may fuss about this or that, and diligent students will fix things up to please the teacher and get a better grade. But no real revision of writing can take place unless the *writer* sees what needs to be changed and how to change it. Professionals revise all the time because they are careful readers and evaluators of their own work and therefore know how to make it better. In contrast, most students do not revise because they have not learned how to evaluate what they write; they have not internalized any consistent set of criteria or standards to which they can hold themselves. Teacher evaluation is normally so idiosyncratic and its criteria so hidden that students see most grading and commentary as merely personal reactions by this or that unique teacher, not clear or generalizable enough to be used for the writer's own purpose. Think of what it would mean if our students saw us as coaches intent on helping them reach their own goals, instead of as inscrutable judges with our own agendas.

Assessment, then, can be a powerful teaching tool that offers us an opportunity to lead more satisfying professional lives. It is not only something we do to students as part of our jobs but also something we must teach our students to do for themselves, so that they can become better writers and thinkers. Self-assessment is a crucial skill that we must teach our students, whatever they may be attempting to learn.

How can we develop assessment procedures and devices that will support our teaching and our discipline and, at the same time, meet our students' needs and outside demands for accountability? I propose to pursue this question through two familiar measurement concepts: validity and reliability.

Developing Valid Assessment Procedures

Although validity is a complex issue—colleges offer advanced courses in it—one simple concept lies behind the complexity: honesty. Validity in measurement means that you are measuring what you say you are measuring, not something else, and that you have really thought through the importance of your measurement in considerable detail. This sounds simple enough, but violations of validity are routine in assessment all the time.

For example, the standard college aptitude tests—the Scholastic Aptitude Test (now renamed Scholastic Assessment Tests but still the SAT), administered by the Educational Testing Service (ETS), and the parallel test offered by the American College Testing Service (ACT)—are designed to offer certain limited information to admissions officers about the likelihood of a student's finishing the freshman year of college. The SAT has a Standard Error of Measurement of some thirty points on the verbal portion (and, interestingly, about thirty-five points on the mathematical portion); that is, the test is an approximate measure, although it does seem to relate closely to student persistence. (No one knows quite why: perhaps the key talent necessary to make it through the freshman year is the sheer ability to cope with long and random multiple-choice tests.) Some items look very strange indeed, but, as the test makers tell us, the students who get through the freshman year are those who got them right and those who are gone the next year tend to have got them wrong. The tests are designed particularly *not* to show effects from short-term coaching.

Yet some institutions persist in using these approximate aptitude tests for purposes that are simply invalid. For example, sometimes they appear as pretest/posttest measures, as if they could measure the effects of freshman-year learning, something they are expressly designed not to do. Again, some politicians like to use the SAT results as scorecards for the nation's schools, a gross simplification that borders on simple dishonesty. Some English departments will use these (or other) multiple-choice tests by themselves for placement into freshman English, as if they measured the ability to produce writing, which they do not. It is not valid—that is, it is simply dishonest—to use a test that depends heavily on the dialect spoken by a student's parents as if it actually measured writing ability. We no longer need argue, I hope, that social class is not necessarily the same thing as academic ability.

I don't mean to suggest that validity is an easy issue to deal with, though the examples I have just used seem easy to me. The difficulty comes from the questions behind validity—that is, the questions about what we want to examine. The only way to deal with these questions is to think through what we really want our students to learn, and that immediately lands us in a quagmire. The English curriculum remains more of a battleground than a field of dreams or a place of consensus. Validity is important as a concept because, by forcing us to ask what we are really measuring, it forces us to ask what we are really teaching, and why.

The difficulty of coming up with a valid assessment of writing derives from the double role of writing as a *socializing* discipline (enforcing and confirming student membership in an educated community) and as an *individualizing* discipline (demanding critical thinking and an active relation of the self to material under study). Although both of these functions are important, the second one is more significant for American education. That is, writing instruction becomes a *liberating* activity, and hence properly an essential part of the liberal arts, when it demands and rewards thinking for oneself. When we look closely at the school and college program most American students pursue, with its fragmented view of knowledge and its emphasis on the accumulation of information, writing emerges as a unifying and integrating force. Writing, as an active form of critical thinking, demands that students make sense of what they think they know. But such writing never comes easily to students and is much harder to teach than the conventions of discourse. The problem of developing a valid writing assessment reflects this root problem in teaching.

The teaching of creativity and independent thinking has never been easy or comfortable (as Socrates could attest), and in contemporary America it has become particularly controversial and risky. Social critics point to the refined management and manipulation of popular opinion in our time, government secrecy, and incredible armaments as signs that a truly informed and independent populace is the last thing our society now demands, although it is the first thing society really needs. Sometimes the version of "literacy" that meets with general approbation, and is usually tested, is so conventional that it actually interferes with critical thinking. The social and literary critic R. P. Blackmur (1955, p. 16) spoke to this issue when he described what others were calling literacy as "the new illiteracy"—that is, the minimum amount of reading and writing skill for a trained population to be effectively controlled: "Ignorance is a permanently urgent problem in any society. The new illiteracy is the form that ignorance takes in societies subject to universal education." Schools and colleges have never been eager to support students who decide to question authority, to challenge the religious and sexual patterns of their parents, to undertake much creative thinking and writing, to read a variety of political views so that they can evaluate political statements themselves. Today, in many communities, even the teaching of archaeology and biology severely strains the social fabric, and standard reading (such as *Romeo and Juliet* or *Huckleberry Finn*) leads to censorship battles. For many of our students, and for even more of their parents, an attempt to open questions, rather than provide information and answers, seems dangerous and subversive. As the Orange County parent said, in a rage at inventive teachers, "We're paying you to educate our kids. Stop messing with their minds!"

The schools, to be sure, in all societies, have an overriding social goal: to "sivilize" (as Huck Finn saw it) students into accepting their society and their place within it. Schools are in large part devoted to normalizing creative thinkers and troublemakers, training workers to accomplish efficiently what they are told to do, making things go smoothly. In this context, it is not surprising that the mind-stunning teaching of so-called grammar and mechanics often replaces writing instruction in the schools and on tests that purport to measure writing ability.

All of us who are English teachers, at whatever level, know that terrible moment at social occasions when some stranger innocently asks what we do to earn our living. After we confess our profession, there is an awkward moment when the eyes of the questioner reveal panic and a desperate need to escape. "Er, I guess I'd better watch what I say," we hear over a departing shoulder. Those young to the profession develop bitter or obscene replies to the unintended insult, while those of us who have heard it over and over again just smile wanly and turn to more vodka. I was even able to grin when my fifteen-year-old daughter's boyfriend stared in acute disbelief when I told him I was an English teacher. "What kind of job is *that*," he asked, "for a grown man?"

It is surely an unhappy irony that teachers of literature and writing—the carriers of the world's entertainment as well as of revolutionary thought and ideas, the instigators of creativity and originality—should be universally seen as picky pedants interested only in correcting trivial errors. The insult is particularly oppressive because it so fully misunderstands the important aspect of what we do, so badly reduces and narrows—even reverses—the creativity of our working lives. But we rarely take the insult personally because it reveals a kind of emptiness in the questioner, as well as a history of bad encounters with English teachers; here is someone who failed to experience the excitement of reading and writing in school, or perhaps anywhere.

Some of us in higher education might be willing to smile grimly from a distance at this description of the social imperatives that define and restrain the teaching of writing in the schools. Yet a significant portion of American higher education defines itself in similar ways, and an even larger portion of the student body sees its goals only as harmonizing with (rather than examining) the values and practices of the society. Those who contend that higher education must serve democratic political purposes as well as conforming social ones, those who argue that the coming "information society" will require a much larger number of independent thinkers than we now prepare, and those who support the traditional goals of the liberal arts are (as they have always been to some extent) swimming upstream against a heavy current. And the same issues apply in virtually all fields; the simple imparting of information and inducting of students into the dialect and culture of a field seem to dominate college and even graduate study.

But, you are saying, it is part of my job, and every teacher's job, to help students learn the school dialect and become comfortable using the social codes, the linguistic etiquette, the ways of doing, that define an educated person in our society. And you are right. We must do that. Much of education is not really concerned with stimulating individual thought and furthering democratic political concepts. Nor are most of our students particularly interested in such matters. And we ourselves, although we may and usually do welcome original ideas, are not hospitable to original spelling and punctuation—mainly because we must help our students acquire the "right" language, the language of the rich and powerful. If we neglect that task, even in the name of equality and creativity, our students will rebel, for they are seeking the linguistic tools that will help them fit into and advance within, not challenge, the social structure. We can—and should—also help them examine and question the social structure, but no teacher working within a writing program can be separate from the socializing institution. Thus, even the most politically and socially aware writing teachers are always forced to socialize their students, even as they urge them to become more fully themselves through their writing.

But education at any level in a democratic society can not rest content with teaching and testing conformity and good manners, useful though they are for the society and for the students eager to fit into that society and into their profession. When Thomas Jefferson and his colleagues in the founding of this nation (five of whom founded universities) spoke of the need for public education, as they frequently did, they were not concerned about spelling, or job skills, or the ability to think like a lawyer or to compete with the Japanese for world markets. They were concerned with maintaining a government whose powers derived from the consent of the governed. The problem for democratic political theory is that an uninformed consent is not consent at all. Behind all the volumes talking about school and college curriculum lies that simple fact: education in a democracy must prepare an informed and independent electorate. Despite the necessary conformity and socialization that must go on in any school, we have the particular obligation to foster critical thinking, questioning, and creativity. And writing, so defined, is the single most effective way to develop these most essential basic skills, at all levels. Any definition of skills in writing that leaves out thinking is undemocratic, insubstantial, and unprofessional. Thus, the attempt to improve assessment of writing—to remove its threat of repression, conformity, narrowness, and bias—turns out to be a social issue with important political dimensions.

Furthermore, since none of us—teachers or students—really exist outside of our temporal, social, ethnic, sexual, and family contexts, we need to recognize that those contexts help shape our own and our students' individuality. Instead of trying to repress or ignore difference, we have begun to understand that we should treasure it. Behind the arguments about multiculturalism rests the indisputable change it has wrought in education: we can no longer see all subjects, including writing, from our own standpoints and imagine that we are being somehow objective or neutral.

English teachers delude themselves when they argue, as many do, that they are not bringing political or social issues into their classrooms. Such a delusion actually makes one more, not less, political. A teacher insensitive to the social and political role of dialect is likely to tell or suggest to a student that her many "mistakes in English" are the result of ignorance, derived from an uneducated home. A more politically aware teacher is likely to tell such a student that the home dialect is perfectly fine in its context but will not lead to success in the school context; students who want to succeed in school have to learn the language of the school, have to be able to "switch codes," as the linguists say. In both cases, the teacher is upholding standards, but only the second teacher will be able to teach effectively by maintaining the self-esteem of a socially disadvantaged student.

In the light of its dual role as a socializing discipline and an individualizing discipline, what will a valid assessment of writing include? Clearly, it must test the socializing skills, but it must do so as part of the critical thinking skills. We want student writers to reveal how they think and express what they know, but they can do so only in the context of who they are. Even the best multiple-choice tests have obvious problems with validity, since they do not measure most of the skills we are attempting to teach. Would an essay test be preferable? Perhaps, unless we are defining the thinking skills in part by use of the library, or by the practice of revision, or by complex and reflective problem solving. Would a portfolio assessment be a better choice? Perhaps, unless we want a measurement of writing under pressure, or we have too many students and too little time.

Thus, consideration of validity is not only the starting point for discussion of an assessment device. It leads to a definition of what we are about in our discipline and to some reconsideration of what we are really doing in class. This is a tough job, hard enough for us to do with our own classes. As soon as we move away from our own classrooms toward a departmental, or schoolwide, or statewide assessment, we must painfully work toward a temporary agreement, filled with compromises, on what a valid assessment must measure. Such demanding committee work forces us to confront different definitions and practices than our own, different goals for teaching, and, hence, different ways of developing a valid assessment.

Developing Reliable Assessment Procedures

If validity has to do with honesty, reliability has to do with fairness and consistency. No measure, however valid it may seem, can be used for assessment if it is not fair. You may appear to have a perfectly valid final examination; that is, it may perfectly reflect what you have been teaching. But if you score it by throwing the papers down the stairs, your grades are meaningless. Statisticians tell us that reliability is the upper limit for validity, that no assessment device can be more valid than it is reliable. And that makes perfect sense. Your measure must give consistent results as well as honestly measure what you say it measures. If the first problem is validity, the second one is reliability, which is also a thorny and complex problem.

Until we become administrators or involved with large-scale testing, we can ignore the inconsistency of grading and response that students routinely encounter. Most of us are content with our own standards and procedures, and the odd privacy code among teachers allows us to remain unaware of or indifferent to the fact that down the hall or next door very different standards and procedures are being used. But if we admit that reliability is a serious issue, we need to bring the issue into the open.

One of the most interesting grade appeal cases I have been involved with occurred when I was chair of a university English department. A student who received an F on an appalling term paper claimed that it was really worth an A. As evidence, she brought two different statements of praise accompanied by the grade of A that the paper had previously received from two other teachers in other courses, one taken at another university. While there was a certain grim comedy involved in this case of the much-used all-purpose term paper, it was, of course, just a local example of what Paul Diederich (1974) demonstrated to be generally true when he began research into essay scoring; without clear grading criteria, all papers will receive all possible scores. Our students in general believe, on the basis of their experience, that grades for writing are unpredictable, arbitrary, inconsistent, and normally a matter of luck more than skill. Most observers of teacher grading agree that in this respect the students are absolutely right. There-

fore, since students do not, and often cannot, know what we want
or value, they tend to confuse plagiarism with research, passivity
with seriousness, neatness with quality of prose, and fulfillment of
the word count with fulfillment of the assignment. The thriving
market in commercially or fraternally produced term papers is mute
testimony to the interchangeability of our assignments and the lack
of clarity or consistency in our grading standards. Nancy Sommers
(1982), in another context, notes that vagueness is routinely forbidden to student writers but remains the property of their teachers.

Those of us who have worked with others to develop large-
scale essay tests have learned that reliability can be achieved with
some effort, and we have carried that lesson back to our own classrooms. Such consistency begins with a well-developed assignment,
distributed in written form to students and thoroughly discussed in
class. Tutors in a university writing center will confirm that such
care with an assignment is a rarity; the most common complaint
they hear is that the student does not understand the assignment.
Involvement in developing essay test questions is an eye-opening
experience for most faculty in this regard. We examine proposed
questions for clarity, validity, intrinsic interest to students, and
manageability. And we find that most questions are clear only to
the writer, have only vague connections to what is supposed to be
examined, drive readers to distraction with boredom, and cannot
possibly be answered in the time allowed. Most of us return to class
chastened, and wind up spending much more time helping our
students understand what we are asking for and why. We may even
hand out examples of student responses to our assignments, with
explanations of why some were successful and some not. And we
find that we get much better writing from our students when they
can get to work on a clear task, instead of guessing what we want
and trying to "psyche out" the teacher.

We have also learned a great deal about consistent grading
of student work. A teacher will typically pass through three stages
in the process of applying in class what we have learned from reliable holistic team scoring. During the first stage, the teacher becomes aware of the need for consistent grading and draws up a set
of criteria (or a scoring guide) for use while reading and grading
student papers. Since fairness is not a trivial matter, some teachers

also try to eliminate the variables that may keep them from grading student work according to the standards on their scoring guide. For example, some teachers will find ways to conceal the student's name on submitted work, since they suspect that previous grades will influence the scoring of the present paper. (I do not go to this extreme, since my comments on student papers serve as a kind of continuing dialogue with my students; I try to find ways to compliment them on improvement.)

This concentration on a scoring guide for the assignment leads quickly to a second stage. Once the scoring criteria have become clear enough to the teacher to be set down in writing, why not share them with the students? In fact, why not share them with the students early in the writing process, so that they can know from the outset the standards for judgment to which they will be subject? Indeed, why not involve the students themselves in the *creation* of the scoring guide, so that they can see the quality standards as partly of their own devising? Teachers who use scoring guides in this way spend more time working with students as they write their papers, since the standards for performance are clear and public and the students are more ready to seek help in meeting them.

A third stage then beckons. Since the standards of judgment are both clear and public, and since they have at least in part been developed by the class, we can now ask the class members to respond to and score the essays written by their peers. Since the students now have both a vocabulary and a scale to use in discussing and evaluating the writing they examine, they need no longer deliver only the positive and unhelpful comments common to peer groups. Instead, they can (and in fact do) hold the other students' essays to the standards set out in the guide. Moreover, by learning how to read and evaluate the papers written by other students, they learn how to read their own. This procedure has the magical double value of increasing student learning at the same time that it decreases the teacher's paper load. Although few teachers will want to use peer grading for final drafts or for crucial decisions on course grades, many teachers find that students write better drafts for peer groups than for the instructor and that they gain more from a peer group's critique (when it is related to a scoring guide) then from the instructor's comments.

In this way, the general assessment concept of reliability delivers its promise of helping us teach writing: first, by supporting simple fairness in teacher grading; second, as a means of restoring credibility to grades by making the criteria clear and public; and, finally, as a way for students to internalize standards for their peers and themselves. We would be most unwise to dismiss such a powerful concept as only an external testing technicality or as a threat to our teaching.

Assessment remains both a threat and a promise for writing teachers. In many states, and at the national level, politicians are now promoting assessment as a substitute for instruction rather than as support for instruction; it is hard to fund education, but easy to fund reductive tests. We need to respond forcefully to such threats. But we must not allow the threat to obscure the promise. Although not all student work needs to be assessed, students know we assess what we most value; we need to integrate meaningful and authentic assessment into our own teaching and talk seriously about it with our colleagues.

The assessment of writing has something in common with the monster Orillo in Matteo Boiardo's interminable romance, *Orlando Innamorato*. When the hero's sword lopped off any part of the monster, the member immediately rejoined the body, and the monster was as formidable as ever. Only by an astonishing feat of dexterity could the monster be vanquished: the hero slashed off the monster's arms and immediately flung them into the river. But assessment is a still more formidable threat than Orillo; neither fire nor water nor scorn will suffice to defeat its power, however we may hack away at it. We must devour the monster, piece by piece; and by making it our own, we make it serve our own purposes. Mythology warns that we may become partly monstrous ourselves in the process, but that is a danger we must confront or even welcome. The teaching of writing is a job for monsters, as our students keep telling us, and we need all the help we can get.

CHAPTER 2

Assessment
and the Design
of Writing Assignments

Devising writing assignments for students in writing courses is one of the most taxing and least understood parts of the teacher's job. The extraordinary compression of the form, the need for clarity and exactness of communication, the requirement that the assignment elicit a response from students with disparate interests and varying levels of creativity, and the pressures of grading and the curriculum—all contribute to the difficulty of the writing of writing assignments. At the same time, we need to keep in mind that designing writing assignments is an aspect of *assessment*: we are setting tasks for students, to whose work we—or someone else—will respond in some way. Although not all writing needs to be graded (we probably ought to grade less and respond more), it should be written for some audience. Most assignments fail to meet these challenges. Yet we need to offer the best assignments we can devise in order to stimulate our students' creativity and willingness to learn what we teach.

This chapter suggests some concepts to guide the development of classroom writing assignments and then presents and discusses an exemplary series of assignments designed to achieve specific goals.

Elements of Classroom Writing Assignments

Erika Lindemann, in a fine book for writing teachers (1987), has suggested a series of questions for faculty members to ask themselves

21

about their writing assignments; the following version of that "heuristic" (adapted from p. 196) suggests the kind of thinking that ought to go into the making of assignments that can support constructive writing instruction.

1. What do I want the students to do? Is it worth doing? Why? Is it interesting and appropriate? What will it teach the students—specifically? How does it fit my objectives at this point in the course? What will the assignment tell me? What is being assessed? Does the task have meaning outside as well as inside the class setting? Have I given enough class time to discussion of these goals?

2. How do I want the students to do the assignment? Are students working alone or together? In what ways will they practice prewriting, writing, and revising? Have I given enough information about what I want, so that students can make effective choices about subject, purpose, form, mode, and tone? Have I given enough information about required length and about the use of sources? Have I prepared and distributed a written assignment with clear directions? Should I include a few good examples? Have I given enough class time to discussion of these procedures?

3. For whom are the students writing? Who is the audience? If the audience is the teacher, do the students really know who the teacher is and what can be assumed about what the teacher knows? Are there ways and reasons to expand the audience beyond the teacher? Have I given enough class time to discussion of audience?

4. When will students do the assignment? How does the assignment relate to what comes before and after it in the course? Is the assignment sequenced to give enough time for prewriting, writing, revision, and editing? How much time in and outside of class will students need? To what extent will I guide and grade the students' work? What deadlines (and penalties) do I want to set for collecting papers or various stages of the project? Have I given enough class time to discussion of the writing process?

5. What will I do with the assignment? How will I evaluate the

work? What constitutes a successful response to the assignment? Will other students or the writer have a say in evaluating the paper? Does the grading system encourage revision? Have I attempted to write the paper myself? What problems did I encounter? How can the assignment be clarified or otherwise improved? Have I discussed evaluation criteria with the students?

These guidelines for examining assignments must, of course, be adapted to the specific students, the curriculum, and the individual assignment. Not every question need be asked about the typical short assignments or in-class writings that are part of most writing classes. But the heuristic is particularly valuable for longer assignments and for courses in the disciplines. For example, the questions listed under point 4 speak directly to a deadline schedule for submission of stages of the work, if the writing is to be developed over a significant period of time. Depending on the assignment, this schedule could call for notes, bibliographies, abstracts, plans, outlines, sections, drafts, or whatever is most appropriate. A simple deadline schedule for each assignment has two important benefits: (1) it enforces the need for the student to get going quickly and to work steadily at the task, instead of trying to handle the assignment the night before the final due date; and (2) it largely defeats plagiarism, since early stages of the bought or borrowed paper are unlikely to be available.

As these questions suggest, constructing classroom writing assignments involves planning, presentation, discussion, prewriting, writing, and revision.

Planning Assignments for Discovery and Revision

Writing courses should undermine the student attitude embodied in the night-before all-night typing orgy, which is the normal means of production for most student essays. Sometimes known as the McPaper, this fast-food version of writing offers little of nutritional value to students and is frequently indigestible for the reader. Nonetheless, few students really expect, as they begin college, that more than one draft should be produced. At most, even good students will retype an initial draft with an eye to neatness, spelling, and footnote format, the principal criteria for good grades according to folklore (and much experience). I wish I could say that this pattern no longer satisfied most assignments.

Virtually all professional writers (as opposed to novices) spend substantial amounts of time revising their work. Similarly, a useful writing course—and writing assignments in all courses—will seek to emphasize revision. The most effective writing assignments establish a continuum of drafting and revising, which begins when the assignment is distributed and concludes at the end of the term—if then.

Distributing Assignments in Written Form

The first step in eliciting good writing from students is the distribution of a written assignment. Many teachers fail to hand out such an assignment; instead, they simply tell the students what they want or jot something on the chalkboard for students to copy. Such casual treatment of the assignment suggests that a similarly casual response is called for. Experienced teachers have learned that they must write out, distribute, and discuss their assignment directions if they are to be taken seriously. Teachers who are unwilling to take this extra step are constantly being surprised at the misunderstandings that occur despite their painstaking oral explanations.

Some teachers prefer to let students choose their own subjects for writing, on the grounds that such openness will encourage creativity and a greater sense of ownership of the writing. With undefined assignments, however, a large part of the energy available for writing must go into selecting and defining and redefining a topic. If more than one or two such exercises are included in the writing course, students have less opportunity than they should have to learn other aspects of the processes involved in writing different kinds of papers, such as development and demonstration of ideas, use of sources, and revision. Open assignments, in my experience, are more likely to signify an unclear course design than a commitment to independent and creative thought; such assignments also give an open invitation to the unscrupulous to purchase their essays from the supplies available everywhere.

Despite these problems, some superior writing teachers remain committed to open assignments; they are convinced that students will write better when they are free to choose what they will write about. If the assignment is, say, a brief open response to a reading, or a personal narrative, the unstructured assignment should pose no problems—as long as the purpose of the assignment is clear. But more complex writing tasks call for extra efforts to overcome the problems I have been describing. The students should receive a description of the purpose of the assignment, its format, and the criteria that the teacher will use in responding to it. Much class time has to be spent discussing topics and helping students define, limit, and focus what they expect to say. Class time alone is insufficient for many students, who will need individual attention during (and after) office hours. During the writing process, the students should be required to submit plans, outlines, drafts, bibliographies, and the like, because the open assignment makes it easy for students to leave out portions of the complex task; meanwhile, the teacher and the student need to develop a common set of standards, and the teacher needs to know, by the frequent submissions, that the student is actually doing the work.

No doubt, this system helps students write more effectively; it represents an ideal of teacher involvement with student writing that some institutions support for all assignments. But this elaborate and labor-intensive pedagogy is not what we often see; few writing teachers have the time available, and open assignments are more often a symptom of lack of time than a commitment to intensive extra time with individual students. If you use open assignments, your job of helping students develop individual topics is continuous.

Discussing the Assignment in Class

The written assignment should be discussed carefully with the students. For example, since submission of plans or drafts is foreign to most students' experience, some will ignore a draft deadline unless it is explained in detail and its importance is stressed. The class discussion should lead students to envision what the entire task calls for. I often hand out duplicated scoring guides (or develop one with the class) and samples of successful previous papers, so that students can see what a good job looks like and what standards it should reach. If enough time is allowed for discussion of the assignment, students will leave the class session with an understanding of what is required and why, and also of various possible ways to approach the job. And they will know that a last-minute first draft will not fulfill the task. A good assignment will always reinforce the need to draft and revise drafts and will distinguish the cognitive work of revision from the editorial work of correcting errors.

Class discussion of an assignment, throughout the time the students are working on it, will help the teacher find out where the students are having problems; reflection about these problems will often lead to a revised assignment for future classes.

Prewriting

Students will write better if they are required to think systematically before they put pen to paper. Although scholars debate about the most effective kind of prewriting, there is a clear consensus that active engagement with the assignment before the start of writing improves the quality of the work to be done. Some composition teachers use formal methods derived from logic or problem solving (sometimes called heuristics); other teachers use various forms of brainstorming, cognitive mapping, or clustering of ideas. Still others ask students to do unstructured "five-minute writes" or freewriting or aptly named "discovery drafts" as ways to uncover or develop ideas. These are all forms of what classical rhetoric called "invention": the finding of topics for development. The very word *topic* comes from the Greek word for "place," suggesting that the thinking process is a kind of geographical quest, a hunt for a place where ideas lurk.

Any assignment worth doing is worth regular discussion. As students hear what their peers are planning to do, they begin to envision new possibilities for themselves. And when they express their own thoughts on the subject, they begin to acquire ownership of their topic. Some teachers will break the class into small groups on the day that topics or initial writing plans are due, so that all students will need to present their ideas to others in the class. The pressure of such a presentation is healthy, since some students don't mind being unprepared for the teacher, but few students are content to look foolish to peers.

Some teachers believe that grading of early stages of the writing process not only is unnecessary but actually interferes with the student's development by distorting the goal of prewriting. Certainly, prewriting should encourage discovery rather than the production of finished drafts; it should enable students to explore possibilities instead of closing potentially rewarding byways in the interest of focus or grade. If prewriting is assessed, the criteria should reward risk taking, originality, creativity, and promise. At this stage, responding is more important than grading; the most helpful activity for the teacher is to give comments that encourage what is most promising in the student's plans.

Assignments Designed to Meet Specific Goals

I am well aware of the difficulties involved in applying theoretical knowledge to an individual teacher's day-to-day work. As John Barth says, "An excellent teacher is likely to teach well no matter what pedagogical theory he suffers from" (1984, p. 200). In my own case, it took five years for me to begin to apply what I had learned as a test director to my own composition classes. I am not presumptuous enough to imagine that my own way of teaching composition should be set out as a model for the world to emulate. The approach to assignments and the particular assignments that follow make up one way of teaching, my own. There are many other excellent approaches to the teaching of writing, each responsive to particular situations, student needs, and teacher personalities. The assignments that appear in this section have worked well for me at the beginning of my writing classes and have helped my students achieve appropriate goals. I hope they may help teachers with similar goals and students, though I know that every teacher must come to his or her own way of teaching and that most teachers will adapt rather than adopt other teachers' materials.

Nor do I include here all writing that my students do, since they also produce work that is not assessed; there is plenty of room for freewriting, journal writing, and ungraded exploratory writing. Nonetheless, certain kinds of problems are common to composition teaching, whatever the approach, and most teachers are interested in ways of coping with these problems. I have chosen to focus here on one problem that will be familiar to every teacher of composition courses: helping students move from personal experience and expressive writing to expository and analytical writing. I have found that incorporating what I have learned in assessment into my teaching practice has made this problem more manageable and my teaching more effective.

A Descriptive Writing Assignment

Although, as Chapter Three points out, not every student finds personal experience or even descriptive writing easy, most students do write more successful papers in such modes than in the expository or analytical modes. Since I want my students to have a feeling of accomplishment at the start, I normally begin my writing courses by asking students to write on the following assignment:

> Describe as clearly as you can a person you knew well when you were a child. Your object is to use enough detail so that we as readers can picture him or her clearly from the child's perspective. At the same time, try to make your readers understand from the tone of your description the way you felt about the person you describe.

Discussion of the topic usually takes a full class hour. In the first place, we need to talk about the language of physical detail: concrete language, such as "her crooked smile and her cigarette never left her lips," differs sharply from abstract or general language, such as "she was a friendly person." Students need to notice in their reading and understand through discussion the importance of well-observed detail—and not only for this assignment. Concrete detail in a description is *evidence* for its meaning, and one important connection between the two modes of writing I am concerned about is the use of evidence to support conclusions.

Once we have established the importance of concrete detail in the assignment, we then discuss the differences of tone created by different kinds of language. The writing task has a special problem built into it: the description must convey feelings, but only indirectly, by way of the details selected by the writer and conveyed by the writer's language, since particular words communicate different emotions. That is, a writer's "tone"—his or her choice of words and manner of expression—establishes a relationship between writer and reader as well as between writer and subject. So we speak of the different attitudes implied by various terms that describe roughly the same kinds of detail: "fat," "well built," and "husky," for example, or "slim" and "skinny." Their job, I try to make clear to the students before they go home to write, is to communicate an emotion about the person described by choosing exactly the right language for their audience and their subject.

Of course, one reason students have trouble with the concept of tone is that they often do not know just who their audience is supposed to be in school writing. Since we do so much small-group work in class, that problem is easy to define and solve: we define the audience as a group of the most interested and diligent students in the class, an audience both knowable and accountable.

Finally, we talk about the role of the observer in this descriptive assignment. The writer as child needs to be present in the description, somehow, without becoming the central subject. There is an important difference between "I loved her very much," which describes only the child's reaction, and "When she walked into the room, I always noticed first the unraveled hem of her dress." Many students think they are describing others when they are describing only their reactions to others. On the other hand, many students believe that it is simply wrong to use the pronoun "I" in an essay, although few of them know why they have been told a rule that most of their reading contradicts. Many writing teachers enunciate that supposed rule in order to keep beginning writers from turning every assignment into a personal narrative. This assignment helps students control the "I" in their writing, using it when appropriate but not turning the writing into simple subjectivism. It also helps introduce the concept that all writing has a voice of some sort.

This assignment illustrates in classroom terms many of the issues dealt with in this book. The assignment has a clear purpose: it is not only interesting and accessible to students beginning a

college writing course but also serves the curricular design—to help
students move successfully from personal to analytical writing. The
class discussion clarifies both the writing task and the criteria for
scoring the assignment. The students leave class well prepared to
write to a specific demand whose goals are clear. And I know, since
I have given this assignment in various forms for many years, that
it works; it has been fully pretested and will allow students to do
their best work. The topic not only works well in class for a first
writing assignment but also happens to fulfill the requirements set
out in Chapter Three for an essay test.

I have no apologies for using personal writing to begin my
course in expository writing. Personal writing is sometimes attacked as trivial, an invasion of privacy, too subjective for college,
or too distant from the world of work. A poorly designed assignment may be guilty of such accusations, but not because it is based
on personal experience; a poorly designed course curriculum may
never get beyond personal writing and hence will fail to realize the
advantages that skill at such writing brings to other forms of writing. But a well-designed personal assignment, such as this one,
moves beyond the trivial, allows students to select manageable experiences from a wide range of possibilities, meets goals for the
reader as well as the writer, and teaches matters important to all
writing. In addition, good personal assignments ask for deepened
self-knowledge and an examination of the assumptions and contexts that shape who we are and what we do. Such relating of the
self to the subject is important, even crucial, for the student. As
Richard Haswell points out in his important study of student development, *Gaining Ground in College Writing,* "gain in development always begins with reflection on development" (1991, p. 2).

My files are rich with creative and moving descriptions composed in response to this assignment. The demand for childhood
memories is one that every writer can meet and that most writers
find eminently satisfying for many and subtle reasons; the best writers will take up the challenge to convey complex emotions through
subtle language.

When the students appear with their papers for the second
class of the term, I hand out copies of a paper written by one of their
predecessors and ask them to begin to compose a scoring guide to

measure success in meeting the assignment. Perhaps they will receive this paper:

Looking back, practically the first thing I think of when I remember her is her behind. It was a ponderous specimen to the fourth grader that I was; always an impossible obstacle thrust out into the aisles of our desks as she leaned on her elbows, absorbed in the smudgy penciled work of one of her students. I would stand contemplating it, wrapping one white knee-socked leg around the other, waiting. It was not that she intimidated me—she that sat in the dirt of our playground as if she were one of us—I could have made my need to pass known, but where, where to poke or tap her? Her shoulders were bowed over the desk, her face beaming not two inches away from her pupil's.

Her face was an entirely different matter. The precision of her nose brought to mind the image of a pert little bird, a sparrow perhaps. Her eyes were a crisp blue, literally framed by scholarly brown glasses. Her hair might have reminded a student or two of the pictures of the thatched roofs in Norway that she enthusiastically waved at us during geography hour. (She once confided to me that she looked in the mirror but once a day, exclaiming, "God, you're gorgeous!" and then abandoned vanities for the rest of the day.)

Despite her decrepitude—she must have been over forty years old—she was a real Bohemian, complete with bean bag chairs and tie-dyed blouse. She had a deep affection for my father. She was widowed or divorced, I suppose, with three teenaged children, and when she asked me how my father was and told me that he had the most beautiful, happy eyes, I wanted to hug her and let her move into my room with me. She must have been very lonely.

She was generally a soft-spoken person, but was capable of an awesome bellow that would stop any taunting boy in his cruel tracks. How often I wanted to

bury my head in her polyester lap, my friend, my pro-
tector, but she was my teacher. I respected her not
only wholly, but voluntarily.

The discussion of this descriptive piece is always very lively.
Some students, trained to expect negative examples in class and
used to picky grading, immediately start finding fault; they point
out the punctuation error in the first paragraph, say, or the coherence problems in the last two paragraphs. They do not like the
disrespectful beginning, and they complain that the last sentence
gives the game away in contradiction to the specific requirement of
the assignment. I try to get past this phase of discussion very
quickly, by agreeing with these complaints (there is no reason to
deny them) but suggesting that there are more important things to
say about the piece of writing.

Eventually, someone ventures, usually timidly, that the piece
is wonderful. I agree, with some enthusiasm, and ask what makes
it effective. Well, comes a reply, you can *see* the fourth-grade teacher
and the child observer as well. As we discuss this point—that the
writing makes us see what the writer wants us to see—we notice the
precision of the detail: the teacher bending over the desk, sitting in
the dirt, or looking in the mirror and talking; the child, on one
"knee-socked" leg, responding, in a child's way, to the teacher's
loneliness. Someone may suggest that the child is described as much
as the teacher and that the classroom setting seems real through the
use of detail.

As discussion proceeds, the class will begin to shape a scoring
guide for the first assignment. If the class is unusually worried
about grades, I will use a two-point scale: satisfactory or unsatisfactory, depending on whether most of the assignment has been fulfilled. But usually I use the six-point scale (see Resources A and B)
for scoring first submissions (reserving letter grades for revisions),
and so ask the class to begin by defining the characteristics of upper-
half (score of 5) and lower-half (score of 2) papers. The following
guide begins to take shape on the chalkboard:

Score of 5: These papers give enough detail so that the
reader can visualize the character. They also describe

the narrator and give enough interaction between the two to allow the reader to understand an aspect of their relationship. Writing errors do not distract the reader.

Score of 2: These papers give little or no detail, telling us about a person instead of describing one. The focus may be almost entirely on the narrator or a situation, the language may be vague, and there may be more than an occasional spelling or grammatical error.

It is not hard to expand these statements or to fill in the scores on either side of them. For example, my classes will give the paper about the teacher a score of 5, not 6, since it defines the attitude of the writer instead of allowing the tone of the description to convey that attitude. The writer could not resist the last sentence, which is not only unnecessary but too limited: what we have seen in the description is more than "respect." The score of 4 may be reserved for a paper that accomplishes the task without the vigor or style of the sample paper we discussed.

The brief reference to mechanical and grammatical matters at the end of the scoring descriptions is practical and necessary. As Chapter One points out, our function in a writing class is to combine somehow both the socializing and the individualizing aspects of writing. Our scoring guides cannot ignore errors in spelling and grammar that every reader will notice, but we can order priorities so that the more substantive matters come first.

Finally, the students group themselves into clusters of three or four to read and score the papers written by their group's members, in accordance with the scoring guide in front of the room. After quietly reading and scoring the papers, they compare scores and reconcile differences. The author of the paper will record the group score and the group reasons for that score on the paper. If there is time, I will ask each group to select its best paper to be read aloud.

If the class is capable and responsible in the group activity (I circulate from group to group during their discussions, so I have a good sense of what is going on), I do not need to collect and grade the papers myself. The students have received considered responses

from three readers, using criteria for scoring developed publicly and
by consensus. The group work tends to be on task and helpful (as
simple subjective judgments are not) because the scores must be
justified by reference to the scoring guide. Most students find the
expanded audience for their work a major incentive to do good
work, and most of them are ready to revise their work and submit
it for a letter grade after the group discussion.

Writing Assignments That Combine Description and Analysis

If the class is still tentative in its descriptive ability, I may follow
my first assignment with one that builds directly upon it:

> Describe and analyze the relationship you had with
> someone you knew well as a child. The person should
> be the one you described in the first paper. Your aim
> is to show the reader what things were like between
> the child you were and the person you decribe, how
> you got along with each other, and what the relation-
> ship meant to you then and means to you now.

This assignment allows the students further practice in the
use of description as evidence, adds a requirement for some analysis
of the relationship, and further asks students to make clear the
meaning of the relationship from two different perspectives in time.
Usually, the scoring guide we develop will require that upper-half
papers (that is, scores of 4, 5, or 6) include both perspectives: the
relationship as it appeared in the past and as it looks now upon
more mature reflection.

However, the class may be ready for more speedy movement
toward analytical writing. The following assignment still asks for
description but calls for increased attention to evaluation of
meaning:

> Describe and analyze an institution or a group that you
> knew well as a child: a school, a school group, a scout
> troop, a dancing class, a summer camp, a club, a Sunday

school—any group with an internally consistent set of values. You have two specific jobs to accomplish: a clear description of what it was like to be a member of the group at the time, and an assessment from your mature perspective of the meaning of the group's values.

As always, we spend the greater part of a class hour discussing the new assignment, considering its creative possibilities, and drafting appropriate scoring procedures. We are also reading examples of professional writing on the same topic: excerpts from George Orwell, Marcel Proust, John Stuart Mill, Frederick Douglass, Richard Rodriguez, and so on. For textbooks that include such materials, see Bloom and White, 1993; White, forthcoming. Many other composition anthologies offer examples of this kind of personal evaluative writing, drawing on the writer's experience of some group out of his or her past.

The quality of writing on this assignment, when the students are clear about what is called for, is generally high. I may distribute this paper from my files as an example of one that meets the requirements nicely:

Cotillion

Cotillion convened once a week in a large rectangular and undecorated room, and was an event which was both exciting and dreadful. It was, for my girlfriends and me, far more complicated than a waltz in our first pair of high-heeled shoes. We were thirteen-year-olds, struggling to make the transition from childhood to being teen-agers, a period of time marked by wonderful and sometimes frightening experiences. Cotillion was the socially correct, socially condoned organization which taught young teen-agers the graces of social dance by way of the waltz, fox-trot, cha-cha, and swing. I don't recall the duration of Cotillion, but I imagine we endured it through enough seasons to celebrate any holiday with a special dance party. This group of would-be dancers was comprised of about twenty or thirty nervous and curious teen-agers.

My immediate fantasies and fears became known to me through this group of privileged adolescents, not at all in touch with Cotillion's fundamental goal, to teach dancing. My awkwardness was great, for I had never walked hand in hand with a boy, much less danced with one! But eager I was to be close to one, as his arm encircled my waist and his sweaty hands grasped mine. The boys, clustered along one wall, wore looks of concentration and strain, whereas we girls, clinging with giddiness to the opposite wall, exchanged glances of anticipation as Miss Dorothy made her record selections. Concentrating on each step became a difficult task, as I was preoccupied with the details of dress and character, particularly those of the boys. My girlfriends and I had to look neat at all times. Being close to a boy was special, providing my hair didn't become messy or my knee-length dress wrinkled. Invariably I was stepped on, which wasn't a disaster unless I was wearing new shoes.

I can still remember the smell of men's cologne on shaved and unshaved, fuzzy faces, and how the perspiration mixed with my hair spray matted my carefully arranged hairdo. That scent of cologne prevailed long after the dances had ended, only to remind me of what I thought to be an intimate exchange between boy and girl. The physical contact we encountered through dancing was different for me than for my partner, it seemed. It was as if he focused mainly on the careful precision of his every step, where I found myself enthralled with his touch. This romantic perception was only hampered by the truth that I was taller than most of the boys (and girls too!). This interfered with my desire to wear the stylish, pointed high heeled shoes and bouffant hair styling I so admired.

We were instructed to share dances with each other equally so that everyone could become acquainted and form friendships. This meant that sometimes I was forced to dance with those boys who were not on my list of good-looking nice guys about whom I dreamt. Dancing with Greg Harrah, whom I had chased around the playground in third grade, was not my idea of enchantment. Boys with whom I had gone through elementary school were, in my opinion, undesirable. The more attractive and alluring boys attended our junior high from other school districts, and had probably been chased around other playgrounds by other girls. I was convinced that these boys were more exciting and interesting.

Camaraderie was vital, and we girls frequently shared personal feelings about boys, especially ones who were our favorites. We worried much of the time and pondered such questions as, "What if I never get asked to dance?" or "What if that icky guy with the greasy hair who makes me sick asks me to dance?" and "Suppose this big pimple doesn't vanish by Cotillion night?" The girls and I harbored these and similar anxieties, which in part we attributed to our participation in this reputable gathering which taught us ballroom dancing.

I know my parents were pleased that I was engaged in a healthy, maturing exercise, and probably looked upon me with pride and amusement. But we felt an air of arrogance. We were the children of parents who concerned themselves with rights and wrongs and thought our experience would enrich our lives and prospects. My mother was careful to remind me that I should always be refined and lady-like, and she would have been shocked at the feelings that mingling with these nice boys provoked.

I am sure that the girls and I took delight in the adventure more than the boys did. They did not seem as if they enjoyed dancing or even smiling, but I liked just being held. I often fooled myself into thinking that these boys really wanted to dance with me, and I was never sensitive to their feelings since most of my thoughts were introspective. That seems all right to me because at that stage in life, self-oriented attitudes were normal.

The significance of Cotillion was not only in its effort to teach youngsters to dance, but to bridge the gap between the sexes during the crucial time of puberty. This was not an easy mission with a collection of young people who were just becoming aware of their feelings and who were trying to manage those feelings. We, in fact, were youngsters who, with a tincture of time and skillful neglect, would grow into nice young adults—eventually. I am inclined to believe that Cotillion was not only producing good dancers, but proper ones as well.

Students notice immediately the effective detail in this delicate and pleasant paper, as well as the careful management of time, so that we always know when she is re-creating the past and when she is commenting on the past from the perspective of the present. The writer shows several levels of values, including learning the dances and the social customs associated with being "proper," and gives us the views of the proud parents, the boys (with their looks of concentration and strain), and the girls (worried about their appearance and enjoying being held). We are given glimpses of sexual feelings, under tight control, and of the social barriers protecting the "privileged" class. Usually some student will wonder why the writer has nothing to say about those children who were *not* in Cotillion and why they were not there. I will reply that this question could lead to a creative revision of the paper; I then call for discussion of how the paper might be revised.

If the class is relatively sophisticated, I will distribute another paper from my files as an example of one that takes substantial risks and meets the requirement creatively:

Memories of a Catholic Girlhood

I was brought up a sort of a Catholic and as such was required to take religious instruction in preparation for two solemn events: my First Communion, when I was six, and my Confirmation, when I was twelve. The two classes are intertwined in my memory, probably because I was as terrorized by them at twelve as I was at six. Most of the other children in my catechism class were Catholic school students and received daily religious instruction. My religious education came from my mother, who imbued her teachings with an inspired confusion of Catholic traditions, pantheism, and agnosticism, depending on how she felt at any given time. As a result, I wasn't sure who or what to believe, so I just generally felt guilty about everything. I didn't know it then, but this was the first step in becoming a good Catholic.

The purpose of the class was to convince an assemblage of formerly cheerful six-year-olds that they were sinners headed for eternal damnation. Since the preface to the First Communion was the First Confession, we had to find something to confess. This was much easier than we thought. Nearly everything, we soon found out, was a sin or a potential sin. There was original sin, venial sin, mortal sin, and endless variations of each. Even considering a sin was a sin.

The nuns who taught the classes were not a nurturing group. My earliest memories of them are hazy, blurred no doubt by my sheer fright. I remember how, with a sinking stomach, I had tightly gripped my mother's reassuring hand as I passed through the imposing black iron gates of the school for the first time. I was greeted (or rather, my mother was greeted; I was ignored) by a faceless, forbidding figure all in somber black and white with a huge black wooden rosary dangling from her ample waist. There I was abandoned. My stomach sank to my knees. Saturday, previously my favorite day, instantly became an occasion for dread.

In class, we were required to answer a series of questions from the Baltimore Catechism. It was simply rote memorization, and since I was a good student, this posed no problem. The problem was that I attended Mass only when I was coerced; and I soon learned that this was definitely a terrible sin. The dismal realization that I was a sinner was underscored by the feeling that the nuns just didn't like me. That they didn't seem to like *any* of us much didn't help to make me feel any better.

One time I successfully managed to fake a stomach ache on a Saturday (a previously unheard-of occurrence). When I returned to class the following week, they had already assigned places in line for the ceremonial procession to the church. I hesitated, waiting for someone to tell me where to stand (now I really did have a stomach ache). Soon I was roughly seized by a very cross nun who deposited me near the front of the line with a firm painful pinch to my upper arm. Tears came to my eyes. I had never been pinched by anyone over the age of eight before, and the shock and humiliation drove away any remaining possibility of religious curiosity. I didn't doubt that I had sinned: I had lied to avoid coming to class. Of course the nun had every right to pinch me so cruelly. Or did she? I knew someone was wrong. I suspected it must be me, but I wasn't quite sure. Angry guilt replaced my willingness to learn. I sullenly made a silent vow never to become conspicuous again.

I continued to attend Mass as seldom as possible for the next six years until, when I turned twelve, my mother was again overcome by the spirit of tradition and launched me into Confirmation classes. Back through those miserable black iron gates! Saturdays were ruined again. And again the nuns devoted themselves to cataloguing our infinite variety of sins. I remember identifying with one sad tale of a chubby girl who became so obsessed by vanity that she finally refused to eat at all. Not even the priest could force her. I was impressed. How I would have loved to have had the courage to defy a priest! Now *there* was an inspiring thought. The punch line to this story was delivered by an immense nun who had apparently read my mind. With a forbidding gaze directly at me she intoned sepulchrally, "She looked quite beautiful in her coffin." I flushed guiltily. Of course I knew where that immortal soul had gone!

The only other instruction that I can remember well concerned baptism. Anyone, we were told, can perform the sacrament of baptism if the un-baptised person's life is in immediate danger. This is accomplished by pouring a small amount of water on the forehead of the sinner and saying, "I baptise thee in the name of the Father, the Son, and the Holy Ghost." A big loud-mouthed boy who always sat near the back of the room, surrounded by admiring friends, waved his hand wildly:

"If you don't have water, but you've got orange juice, can you use that?"

"Yes," came the resigned answer, "you can use orange juice."

"How about milk?"

"Yes," a little less patiently this time, "you can use milk."

"Coffee?"

"Yes."

"Tea?"

"Yes."

"Seven-up?"

"Yes!"

"Coca-cola?"

By this time sister had had enough.

"NO! NO! Never! Absolutely not! You can't use Coca- cola!"

Roars of laughter from the back of the room.

End of discussion.

Yet I admired and envied those delinquents for their refusal to be intimidated. Obviously they were terrible sinners, much worse than I, but they were so dauntlessly self-assured; whereas I had elevated humble guilt to a fine art. Maybe the stern unforgiving tactics were necessary to keep in line the students who were immune to guilt after years of Catholic training, but they had devastated me. I have since learned that there *are* religions that do not rely on fear and guilt for salvation; that even the Catholic Church has miraculously eased up a bit, but it's much too late for me. Once I had confirmed my religious vows, I promptly abandoned them. For years the thought of entering a church, any church—even voluntarily—filled me with dread. I knew God saw right through me. He knew I had no business there.

The successful papers from former students illustrate the components for a scoring guide for the assignment. Three tasks are required: description of the group, including its people and its location; an evaluation of what it meant to the writer in the past, while a member of the group; and an evaluation of the group and its values from today's perspective. Papers scoring 6 or 5 need to accomplish all three tasks in a coherent or even dramatic way, while the 4 paper will be less well organized and less interesting. Scores in the bottom half will represent increasingly serious failures to meet one or more of the demands of the topic, lack of clarity in distinguishing past from present evaluations of the group, and distracting mechanical and grammatical problems.

Most students find this assignment challenging and interesting, but difficult. They are not accustomed to organizing their personal experience or to developing it as evidence for an idea. But I am convinced that one valuable benefit of writing about personal experience is to gain an understanding of it—through the kind of organization and evaluation this assignment demands. The students also learn the most important skills for writing expository papers: to think systematically about aspects of their topic and relate careful description to a central controlling idea.

If the class needs another assignment with this same general purpose, I will assign the following topic, based on a reading passage:

Write a short essay examining what the anthropologist Jules Henry means in the following passage and showing the extent to which the passage applies to your own schooling.

"Another learning problem inherent in the human condition is the fact that we must conserve culture while changing it; that we must always be *more* sure of surviving than of adapting—*as we see it.* Whenever a new idea appears our first concern as *animals* must be that it does not kill us; then, and only then, can we look at it from other points of view. . . . In general, primitive people solved this problem simply by walling their children off from new possibilities by educational methods that, largely through fear (including ridicule, beating, and mutilation), so narrowed the perceptual sphere that other than traditional ways of viewing the world became unthinkable. . . .

"The function of education has never been to free the mind and the spirit of man, but to bind them. . . . Schools have therefore never been places for the stimulation of young minds" [Henry, 1963, pp. 284–288].

This is a much more difficult writing task for students than it appears to be. They generally have a hard time understanding how anyone, even an anthropologist, can say such a wicked thing about the schools they have often come to love. So, instead of noticing the complexity of Henry's idea that schools everywhere must conserve their culture before challenging it, they write essays defending school spirit and their prom committee's creative choice of colors to decorate the school gym.

The ability of the class determines how much prewriting time I give to this assignment. If the class is very able, I may wait for submission of the first draft before discussing it, even though I know very well that only the best students will respond well to the assignment. Some of the first drafts will be good enough to illustrate the way to respond to a quotation that seems to attack values one treasures. The best writers will both understand and discuss the Henry passage, and bring some experiences from their own schooling to demonstrate the degree to which the passage helps them understand those experiences. Such papers will allow us to construct a scoring guide. Small-group evaluation of each group member's paper, following that scoring guide, will provide enough useful comment for revision to take place. Note that the scoring guide at this point is not so much a grading device—I don't record the scores—as a shorthand to help the writer evaluate the success of the draft. Before writers can revise, they must be able to see clearly what they have done.

A weaker class will need more help. I will ask such a class to read the chapter from which the passage derives and to write a summary of its argument. When these summaries are brought to class, we analyze the chapter as a group and construct on the chalkboard an outline of the principal assertions in it. From that outline, we develop a scoring guide for the summaries: top-half papers must include at least three of these principal assertions, for example. Small-group discussion and evaluation of the papers follow, and students leave the class ready to revise their summaries and prepared to write the essay.

An Expository Writing Assignment

By the time we come to a straightforward expository paper, the students in this writing class find it no surprise. They have been analyzing their personal experiences, organizing complex materials, and learning to use evidence to demonstrate their assertions. In addition, they have been learning how to relate themselves to the material they discuss, so that their writing remains interesting to themselves and their readers. They have also learned to look for the goal of a writing task and to expect an audience beyond the teacher alone to assess its success according to a clear set of scoring criteria. Thus, they take the following assignment as similar to what they have been doing, even though it no longer calls for personal experience.

> Choose an advertisement from a popular magazine for careful analysis. An ad is, of course, designed to urge hasty readers to buy a producet. Your concern, how-

ever, is not with the ad's selling power but with its concealed message. What does it assume and imply about its readers? What does it suggest about their needs, desires, motives, and so on? How does the ad define the self and the world for its readers?

The prewriting discussion of this topic usually focuses on the problem of seeing, the difficulty of moving past the surface of an advertisement to the concealed message most ads convey. Advertisements are particularly good material for this exercise, because they are often designed to appeal to patterns of belief below the surface as a powerful way to sell products. I continue to be surprised at the innocence of even good students about this fact; exposed to selling techniques from their earliest days before a television screen, they tend merely to accept advertisements as a source of information (sometimes, amazingly, as a source of truth) without attending to the picture of their world and of themselves that advertising presents.

If the class is relatively inexperienced with the concept of seeing below the surface, I will spend at least one class hour discussing various advertisements projected on the screen in front of the room. "How are the people dressed?" I will ask, or, more generally, "What is their social class?" We will talk about the use of illustrations that sometimes send more subtle messages than does the text, about the design of the advertisement as art (with its use of color and perspective), or about the use of words to create a "world" sympathetic to the product.

We also attend to the problem of tone in responding to the assignment, since many students will assume that all advertisements are evil simply because they seek to manipulate an audience into buying something. It is no discovery, I need to remind the class, to point out that an advertisement is seeking to sell a product, nor is it necessarily wicked for the ad to do its job well. The goal of the assignment is to discern the concealed, not the obvious, message and then to develop an attitude toward that concealed message. Is the worldview of the advertisement biased, or amusing, or sensible, or what? Analytical writing calls for clear and perceptive examination of detail, the use of that detail to develop generalizations of some interest, and the management of tone to convey a consistent attitude toward those generalizations.

When the students have written their papers, I bring, as usual, a good example from my files to begin development of a scoring guide. I often use this one:

Rick Ate the Whole Pot

I found an interesting, rather disturbing advertisement among the slick pages of *Good Housekeeping*, a magazine dedicated to mild fashion, conservatively good marital sex and white-teethed children. The ad, covering an entire page and appearing perfectly harmless at first glance, features an ecstatic, thirty-ish woman beaming out at us from her beautiful upper-middle class dining room that is both immaculate and crowded with food that would make Julia Child's mouth water. Everything in the decor of the room is color-coordinated and in its place; even her countertop gleams.

Yet we are still convinced that she is a real woman, for she is plump, rather plain and actually has a name: Darlene Hyrb. She even comes from a real place: Wixom, Michigan. She appears in one of the most widely read woman's magazines with her award-winning Brunswick Stew recipe, but most importantly, she has a husband. We learn this first and know that it is paramount because under Darlene's photo, in huge letters is her proclamation: "I knew Rick loved it. He finished the whole pot!" In finer print, we are told that because Rick "had polished off an entire pot of her Brunswick Stew," she knew it had to be a worthwhile, meaningful recipe, and consequently entered it in a recipe contest. Rick's overzealous and masculine appetite proved correct, of course, and the little missus received "French's Prize Recipe Award." To the right of the ad we see Darlene's recipe and underneath that are pictures of French's seasoning mixes that turn "ordinary chicken" and lowly hamburger into a meal fit for a husband.

French's advertisement is very shrewd. Placed in a magazine read by millions of middle class, married women, the ad's assumption hit the bull's eye of their target market. The ad assumes that its readers are average American women who strive to be the Ideal American Homemaker (who else would read *Good Housekeeping?*). We identify with Darlene at first glance. In striking contrast to the cat-eyed, flawless panty hose model a few pages earlier, with legs from the neck down, Darlene is ordinary, like us. With her sparingly applied make-up, lenient waistline and short haircut that is a Xerox copy of millions of other housewives, she looks like a neighbor from whom we'd borrow the proverbial cup of sugar.

The advertisement assumes (and correctly so for all of us that call ourselves red-blooded American housewives), that all of us would like to have a house like Darlene's, that looks as though the interior decorator just deposited his check. Of course, we know, however, that it was Darlene who planned the decor, for the Ideal American Homemaker is naturally a talented designer.

French's ad also assumes that American society considers women admirable when they (1) keep an orderly, attractive household, (2) are interested in cooking, and (3) care about what their husbands think. These are not wicked assumptions and if they are true, they are certainly not things of which to be ashamed. Personally, I think keeping a nice home, cooking well and being sensitive to one's mate are wonderful qualities. What I find unsettling are the implications of these assumptions, for there is a catch in them, exemplified in French's motto "for cooking that could win a prize." The motto is not "for cooking you'll enjoy" or "for cooking you'll find personally satisfying." In short, the overall implication of the ad is that American women base their self-evaluations and esteem on external opinions, and I think, sadly, this is the case in our society. Darlene is not joyous because she knows she is a good cook or because she enjoyed her Brunswick Stew, but because "Rick loved it. He finished the whole pot!" (In passing, I'd just like to say that if someone had eaten my entire pot of stew, I would have called him a pig and gone out for steak and lobster.)

Darlene does not enter her recipe in French's contest because she is confident of her talents, but because Rick demonstrated his personal approval. She depends upon him to validate the expertise of her culinary skills, of her worth as a human being. In this so-called "liberated age," women in our society still define themselves not by who they are, but by who they are to other people: daughter, wife, mother. Certainly, today's "career woman" is not only widely accepted but admired— as long as she maintains top performance both on the job and at home. We still have that primal need to be a woman as defined by the role she has traditionally played in humankind. I think that all women, at varying depths of soul, believe that at the foundation of humankind are the inherent, biological and inescapable roles called "male" and "female." The French's advertisement plays upon this subconscious level by surrounding the Ideal Woman with the rudimentary appeal of food; real food on the the table and in her hands and pictures of food hanging on the walls.

In spite of all our puffing away at Virginia Slims, keeping maiden names and running for office, we as the childbearing sex are forever as essential to human survival as food. It is only natural that we would—however subconsciously—cling to the self-denying traditions of our gender, to strive to fulfill all that a woman is "naturally supposed to be." What I feel is lacking in our society and made apparent in the seasoning mix ad is the complete acceptance of people, male and female, as individuals. Darlene should have had her recipe in *Good Housekeeping* because she liked it, not because Rick ate the whole pot.

Although most students like this paper very much, as I do, those who are studying the social or natural sciences are quick to argue that such a personal tone would be inappropriate for analytical papers in their fields. I usually have on hand some paragraphs from the physician Lewis Thomas, the biologist Barbara McClintock, the economist John Galbraith, and the sociologist David Riesman, to demonstrate that (depending on audience and purpose) such a tone may well be appropriate whatever the field. A research report, however, or a even a term paper in any field might require a much less personal approach to the analysis. The writer's job, we will agree, is to discover the appropriate tone to take for the topic and audience at hand.

As we begin to devise a scoring guide for essays written on this topic, the students list the features of the sample essay that are most important. They see the precision of language and use of detail, the clarity of organization, and the arrangement of evidence to demonstrate an interesting conclusion. They admire the carefully balanced tone, amused and unfanatical about the advertisement's attitude toward women, yet absolutely serious about its concern for an inner-directed validation of individual worth. While many students will be less than fully convinced that cooking—which is nothing much without the eating—is the right subject to make that case, most will agree that the argument is worth making. Certainly, no paper that merely describes an advertisement, or that has nothing to say beyond the fact that an advertisement seeks to sell a product, can be given a score of 4 or above.

After the scoring guide is drafted and the students divide into small groups to read each other's papers, they find that most papers fail to move much beyond description. They also discover that many of the best papers, including "Rick Ate the Whole Pot," seem to come to their topic only toward the end of the essay, and hence need considerable revision, particularly of the early paragraphs. Good writers, who may have been able to deal with the less complicated topics earlier in the term without serious revision, sometimes discover at this point that revision is not a matter reserved only for the incompetent. By this time, the small-group members are accustomed to giving specific advice, usually by referring to the scoring guide: there are too few details to let us visualize the advertisement; your anger at the advertiser is not justified by the evidence in the paper; your attitude toward the advertiser is different at different places in the paper; the spelling and other mechanical errors make the paper hard to respect; you don't seem to have anything much to say. At the same time, the group members try to find good things to say, even about the weakest papers, since nobody wants to revise work that has no redeeming qualities.

Responses to Revised Assignments

In my response to the second drafts, I normally prepare and distribute a revised version of the scoring guide that the class developed for group discussion, and I often direct my written comments to a forthcoming third draft, which may or may not be required. I find that the careful work in class with scoring criteria and the extra commentary the writer has received from the small group free me to spend time on the most substantive matters in each paper. If the writer seems to have little to say, I try to find passages in the paper that indicate potential ideas for development; often, an apparently empty paper will arrive at interesting concepts only at the very end, where they are easy to overlook. I try to link my comments and my grade to the original goals of the assignment, the criteria for writing established during the prewriting class discussion, and the scoring guide. I also attempt to be consistent with the ideas expressed in Chapters Four and Five—that is, to respond to and value the potential of the paper as a whole as well as its present form, and to refrain from taking ownership of the paper from the writer.

The sequence of assignments I have just described brings students to analytical and expository writing through a series of gentle steps from the personal experience papers they are accustomed to in the schools. Each new assignment adds a new component and incorporates matters dealt with earlier. While the writing tasks do not free the students to do anything they may want, the topics offer a wide range of choices within a specific and clear set of goals and criteria. By the time students have completed and revised these assignments, they are ready to handle such subsequent phases of the writing course as a research paper or literary analysis.

A student who has learned in the composition course to develop writing from the personal experience tasks that open this chapter to the analytical paper we have just examined has learned a great deal indeed. If each step along the way is accompanied by small-group discussion of early drafts, based on scoring guides for assessing responses to the particular topics, the student has also learned enough about the writing process to keep improving. Assessing the quality of early drafts should become so much a part of the writing process that revising and grading lose much of their terror and uncertainty. When our teaching leads students to clear definitions of topics, well-stated criteria for assessment, and understandable procedures for revision, we can feel comfortable about our classroom teaching. Not all writing, of course, needs to be revised or graded. But the more we know, and the more we help our students know about assessing writing, the more confident their revisions will be and the more effective our teaching will become.

CHAPTER 3

Using Essay Tests

Even good students have difficulty with the usual essay test question, which often is badly written; sketchy, vague, and confusing; and ill suited to the age, capacity, or background of the students who must take the test. This chapter will summarize the most useful experience and findings about writing assignments from large-scale testing programs. It then looks at ways to help students improve their writing on essay tests. Since more effective topics will lead to more effective writing, faculty willing to plan their tests with some of these points in mind are likely to find their time spent grading more satisfactory. In addition, the findings reported here should enable those responsible for developing tests or testing programs to construct tests that will be more valid because they allow all writers to do their best.

Designing Essay Test Topics

The student confronted with the usual forty-five-minute impromptu test of writing skill must have a particular set of skills beyond an understanding of the material to be tested. He or she must comprehend the question in all its parts (particularly the underlying assumptions), understand the mode of discourse called for, search his or her memory bank for details and other material, conceive and organize the response, fit the response into a given time or length span, and, not least by any means, tailor the response to the primary audience—teachers grading writing. Finally, the student who is writing the test needs to edit the work to remove the spelling errors and other scribal mistakes that appear in almost every writer's first drafts. The student who can get through these matters with considerable dispatch will write as well as he or she can to the topic and use the time allowed to the best advantage. If these matters remain a mystery, either because the student has little experience with essay testing or because the question is unclear, writing will be muddled, error-ridden, inappropriate, or just plain bad in any of a dozen other ways. Furthermore, the test is likely to be invalid, since it will not necessarily measure writing ability.

If the essay test is not in a writing course, the student's job is likely to be even more difficult. If the teacher has not made scoring criteria clear, the student may not even know whether writing ability "counts" or not; sometimes all the teacher wants is a minimally readable accumulation of information, showing understanding of the material. If the purpose of the essay test is to elicit memorized information, as is often the case, a well-focused opening, for example, might actually lower the student's grade; the teacher may perceive the opening as filler and a waste of time. A colleague of mine in the art department thinks he is giving an essay test when he asks his students to "write an essay in which you list the ten most important modern artists." (He awards one point for each artist listed, for a total of ten points.) Susan McLeod at Washington State University has written me about unpublished research she has done, which showed that students who had received instruction in how to take essay tests actually got lower grades on essay tests in the disciplines than those who did not have that instruction. Her interviews with the teachers showed that "whether or not the answer was well written counted for little." What is a student to do under such conditions?

Many students write less effectively under test conditions than they otherwise do, for many of these reasons. One additional reason is that they develop writing anxiety because of their uncertainty about the assignment itself and about the grading criteria that will be applied to the test (Rose, 1983; Smith, 1984). According to a recent study, writing anxiety, a special form of test anxiety, is present when students write "to *any* spontaneous prompt, regardless of how carefully it was composed," but interviews with students showed them pleading for clarity: "uniformly, our students cautioned us about using vague or ambiguous terms, idioms, or jargon" (Haviland and Clark, 1992, pp. 53, 58). In short, a carefully designed writing topic will help students write their best, and find that writing more rewarding, whatever the nature of the topic.

Some topics that would never appear on a large-scale writing test may well be appropriate in class. For example, one college-level test development committee on which I served had devised a comparison-contrast test using two statements about the education of women. One of the statements argued that women should receive higher education specifically tailored for them; the other argued that higher education for women should be modeled on that traditionally offered to the best-qualified men. The committee thought the question would provide a valid test of a student's analytical ability, since the two statements were similar in many interesting ways, yet quite different; in addition (and here is where the committee made its mistake), the topic was on an emotional subject about which there had been much talk, and so one could presumably build on a general fund of informed opinion.

Happily, the committee carefully pretested this topic on a wide range of college freshmen and discovered just how invalid it was—before including the topic on the actual test. (It is more usual to make such grim discoveries only after a test has been given, as grading gets under way.) When we read the pretest essays, we were at first stunned to realize how bad many of them were, how they avoided the analytical task and turned instead into generalized and unsupported statements of belief about "women's place" (very often, to our chagrin, in the home). The essays from students known by their teachers to be excellent writers were often just as bad as those from the weakest writers. Since the responses did not correspond to the writing ability of the students, the question was abandoned and replaced by a more valid one for testing purposes.

But, afterward, several of us on the committee decided to use the question on the education of women in our classes. The pretesting had shown that many college freshmen, even very able writers, are unable to write an analytical essay on a subject that excites their emotions. (The assignment on the Jules Henry passage in Chapter Two is designed to help teach this difficult skill.) These students, under testing conditions, ignore analytical demands for passages they disagree with, or simply ignore such passages, and substitute unsupported opinion, even unexamined stock phrases, for developed argument. Whereas testing seeks to evaluate a student's analytical skill fairly, classroom teaching sets out to improve that skill. So we use the assignment as a practice test in class, knowing full well that many students will perform badly on their first drafts; and then we use the results to help students learn how to deal with such topics. After reading and discussing a paper that handled the topic well, good students will see quickly that they went astray, and they will learn from the experience to respond carefully even to questions that excite their emotions. Since a major goal of composition instruction is to help students learn how to write on more complicated and more demanding topics than they are accustomed to handling, we should not allow the validity standards of writing tests to keep us from challenging our students with new tasks in class. But we do need to reassure them that their first drafts are learning exercises, not valid measures of ability—a useful lesson for all writers in any event.

The luxury of using invalid topics does not extend to tests that seek to measure students' writing ability accurately. The committee would have been unprofessional to use the topic on women's education as a college freshman composition placement test, since good freshman writers perform badly on it. The question in fact embodies a very demanding set of test criteria: it measures experience with complex analysis, a high-level ability to synthesize the ideas of others into one's own writing on short notice, and the maturity and sophistication to handle a controversial subject calmly. These are valuable skills and appropriate criteria for advanced students; on the freshman level, however (not to speak of the high school students who are often asked such questions on tests), such criteria are usually unrealistic and hence unfair.

The difference between topics for testing and topics for teaching is a real and important one. But we must guard against using this difference as an excuse for giving students unclear or inappropriate writing topics in class, since our teaching certainly ought to demand as much care as our testing.

We should also be alert to the recent challenges to the validity of all essay tests brought by proponents of portfolio assessment. Many of these people deplore the essay test definition of writing as an impromptu, unrevised, timed exercise to someone else's assignment. This objection is true only in part. Validity is not a static concept; scores do not exist out of context but must be valid for a particular purpose. Thus, essay test scores may be valid for the placement of freshmen into composition courses but may not be valid as an assessment of what they have learned at the end of such courses.

Structured Versus Open Essay Test Topics

In Chapter Two I set out the arguments for and against structured assignments, as opposed to open ones, in the writing class. The same arguments apply to essay tests, though in this case the argument against open assignments is even stronger. Although I have some limited sympathy for the classroom teacher who wants students to select what they will write about and who is willing to devote time to helping the students discover their topics, this approach has no place at all in test design.

Some teachers, particularly those without much experience in test design, argue that writing topics are a bad idea to begin with: to set a topic is to limit the students' imagination and restrict their freedom to write on whatever is of most importance to them. The best writing, these advocates of liberty insist, is produced from internal motivation, not external demand; therefore, a single set topic cannot possibly meet the internal needs of all those who are writing. Besides, choosing a topic is itself so important a task for a writer that that very choice should be part of the test.

I think these arguments are quite mistaken. The supposed freedom of such assignments turns out to be the freedom for the student to guess what is really required. As every student knows, there is always a hidden assignment behind the free one, and a concealed set of grading criteria behind the hidden assignment. Writing is an unnatural act; and few of us, even professional writers, work for the unrewarded pleasure of it. The demand to write, in school no less than on the job, is almost always an external demand, and an exacting one; few of us find our poetic impulses stirred by difficult required tasks, no matter how we might relish them under other circumstances.

The urge to avoid designing a clear writing topic for a test usually stems from much less elevated motives than a passion for liberty and poetry. At best, it reveals an unrealistic attempt to remove school testing from the reality of a world where writing is a regular unromantic tool of thought and action, a world where performance is demanded on time and evaluated rigorously. At worst, it shows an unprofessional lack of attention to the purpose of the writing test, the distinctions among different kinds of writing, or the appropriate sequence of tasks designed to evaluate a difficult skill.

Freedom is an equivocal virtue. We want freedom to travel, but not freedom from train and airline schedules that make travel convenient and manageable. Certain limitations make freedom possible, as Robert Frost suggested when he, in conversation, said that writing poetry without rhyme is like playing tennis without a net. We do not liberate beginning chess players by allowing them to move the pieces any which way, nor does an editor support the creative journalist who files a sonnet on spring when the assigned political speech turns out to be uninspired. The student who is set free from a clear writing assignment must proceed to construct one before beginning to write the test. The energy used in that construction, usually requiring considerable guesswork about the teacher's implicit demands and concealed criteria, is a great waste of effort that would more profitably be spent in writing well on a clear topic. We liberate our students to write well by constructing for them appropriate and unambiguous tasks, with clear and understandable goals. Such assignments free students from the enervating, distracting, and often futile labor of guessing what we want, why we want it, and how we will respond.

A less obvious version of this longing for liberty has to do with giving students a choice of topics on a test, in the mistaken belief that students will be more free to write well on the topic they choose. This practice is very common on classroom tests, where teachers genuinely imagine that students will benefit from choosing among several possible questions. However, almost no large-scale testing programs any longer offer this kind of choice, because it is much more fair to the students to offer choice within the format of a single topic.

The difference between offering a choice of questions and offering choice with a single question is important. The common practice of asking students to choose one question from *a*, *b*, or *c* usually leads to an invalid test. Question *a* is harder than *b*, which is, in turn, harder than *c*; different questions are never of exactly the same order of difficulty. And often the hardest questions are the most interesting or most challenging, and therefore the most attractive to the best students. So numbers of the best students, who might have performed very well on question *c*, attempt question *a* and do less well than they ought. Many of the weaker students avoid question *a*, gravitate to question *c*, and do better than they ought; other weak students, unaware of the difficulties of *a* or *b*, select them and do even worse than they ought. Normally, the professor grades this three-question test as if it were a one-question test (since every student writes only one question) and grades all responses together according to the same standards. The benefit to the students is hypothetical, not real; there is no evidence to show that students will ordinarily choose the question on which they will do best. The disadvantage, however, is very clear: the results of the examination will not reflect accurately the students' skill or knowlege, since they are responding to different questions testing different aspects of the material.

Large-scale test developers have learned how to offer the advantages of choice to students within the same question. For example, if we ask students to "describe an object you value and say why you value it," all students are responding to the same demand. While some will choose more appropriate "objects" than others, and hence give themselves easier jobs to do, the choice of object is itself part of the test for all students. The question would become worse if expanded: "Describe an object, or objects, or person you value and explain the reasons for that valuation." Since experience has shown that the question becomes much harder to handle when there is more than one subject, the option to choose multiple objects becomes a trap for the unwary. Experience has also shown that people are much more difficult to describe and evaluate than are objects, though they do not appear to be so to most students. Adding the option for students to write about their beloved grandparents, which few will do in other than general or clichéd ways, does those writing the test no favor.

Classroom tests, then, ought to reflect this same concern for giving all students the same question. I used to ask students completing my course in the eighteenth-century English novel to choose from among three questions, each question referring to one of three novels: *Moll Flanders, Tom Jones,* and *Tristram Shandy.* Only recently have I realized how unfair that choice of questions was to my class. The best students often chose to write about *Tristram Shandy,* a quite difficult book, demanding great skill of a writer. I should not have been surprised that my good students often wrote poor examinations. Those selecting the *Moll Flanders* question, however, almost always received a higher grade than those choosing the others. I now ask a single question, on a larger topic (focusing specifically on the relationship of the characters in the novels to their worlds, for example, or on the relationship between the rise of the novel and notions of money), and require frequent references to the novels in the response. The students are just as free to demonstrate what they know—more free, in fact—and the test is much more fair.

Nonetheless, essay questions should not be so binding that they put the validity of the assessment in doubt. One midwestern university has traditionally given its freshmen an essay topic with the first sentence of the response already supplied. This is structured support indeed, but structure that denies the fundamental nature of writing—that the writers should say what *they* have in mind. The Florida test that all college students must pass to advance to junior standing uses a predictable set pattern for its questions, with only key words changing from test to test. According to one disillusioned designer of that test, the drill on previous questions that serves as preparation for this test is "pernicious": "The unfortunate result is that for many students the concept of writing ability has become synonymous with impromptu theme writing on predetermined topics, a condition that mocks our best professional theory and practice" (Brossell, forthcoming).

Notions of freedom in testing, as in life, require considerable thought and experience in order to work in practice as they do in theory. Students taking a test are not free in most senses of the word; they are being required to write and will be evaluated on the relative success they achieve. Under such circumstances, the most meaningful kind of freedom is simple fairness; in testing, that comes down to validity and reliability. When we develop writing topics that lead to clear and valid tests, and when we score these tests responsibly and reliably, we are freeing our students from the arbitrary and whimsical testing and grading that now diminish education at all levels. By so doing, we are striking a great blow for our students' right to learn in a free environment.

A Model for Topic Development

By now, the model for essay test development for large-scale examinations has become well established. This model is worth describing in some detail for several reasons: those undertaking direction of such a test should be aware of current practice; those adapting the model for less exacting testing programs will want to be alert to potential problems from stages they need to omit or compress; and classroom teachers will find that they can (over time) include many of these procedures as part of their usual course and test planning.

Selection and Preliminary Tasks of the Test Committee. The test development committee need not be made up of test specialists, but it must be composed of teachers who know about writing and who are familiar with the kind of students to be tested. This committee has a heavy responsibility: if it does not come up with good questions, no amount of work in scoring or follow-up administration can salvage the test. Good questions are absolutely crucial; and the committee requires the people, conditions, and time to do the job.

As its first task, the committee must create or review a statement that embodies what the test is attempting to discover. If, instead, the committee members begin to consider writing topics before they agree on the purpose of the test, agreement on topics becomes impossible. At the outset, then, the committee members must decide what aspects of writing are to be measured and what kinds of questions are most likely to elicit that information.

Sometimes, particularly in the public schools, a test committee is put in the awkward position of developing a test to criteria that are not well informed. An assistant superintendent, say, or a committee of citizens might have listed matters they regard as important (usually scribal or mechanical), whereas the committee of teachers may well be more concerned with invention, organization, creativity, or other thinking skills. Test questions cannot be developed until these issues are resolved. Numbers of such committees have shown high political skill in working with outside pressure groups, convincing them that mechanical skills can be included as part of a set of criteria that supports rather than undermines the writing curriculum.

When these matters of criteria and purpose have been settled, and not before, the committee can turn its attention to particular writing topics.

Characteristics of a Good Writing Topic. Test development committees have learned to require these characteristics of questions they approve:

Clarity. Students will not waste time trying to figure out what is called for but will be able to get right down to work.

Validity. Good students will receive high scores, and weak students will receive low scores. There will be a good range of scores, without too large a concentration in the middle.

Reliability. Scoring of pretest papers shows considerable agreement by readers, and a scoring guide can be readily constructed to describe score differences.

Interest. The question offers sufficient intrinsic interest so that students will write with some genuine concern and those scoring will not go mad with boredom (and hence become inaccurate).

Each of these four characteristics contains many possible problems. The concept of clarity, for example, often (but not always) includes brevity: time wasted in reading the question cannot be used in responding to the question; long questions tend to contain ambiguous directions and distracting side alleys. But students do need the essential directions. It might well be worth the extra space to replace "Compare and contrast" with "In what ways are the following passages alike? In what ways are they different?" If generally good students are producing personal narratives instead of an expected analytical essay (a common enough result of an unclear question), the directions need to be revised. Questions based on a text, usually excerpted, often pose problems of clarity, since the test committee knows a context that the students do not; isolated passages from familiar writers turn out to have quite different meanings on a test than they do in their customary locations. Clarity problems appear in new and surprising shapes with every new question; an experienced test committee simply accepts the fact that there will be problems of clarity in its questions and looks to the pretest to discover and correct these problems.

Validity problems become apparent as soon as the test committee begins reading a series of pretests. Some questions seem to produce responses that all sound alike; almost all scores wind up in the middle range. These are sometimes questions that elicit clichés ("Should the drinking age be the same as the draft registration age?" "What is the value of a good education?") or simple narratives ("Tell about your summer vacation"). But sometimes even clear and original questions, if they are too hard or too easy for the test group, do not produce a valid spread of scores. Some questions give an unfair advantage to students with a particular kind of knowledge or experience; urban test committees, for example, sometimes have a hard time imagining rural contexts ("Describe what you see when you walk around your block"). The ideal question will allow the weak students to write comfortably enough at their level while it challenges the best students to produce their best work. One sure sign of a good writing topic is that it produces a good range of scores.

If students whose first language is not English are in the test population, other validity problems enter—most obviously, idiom.

Insufficient pretesting allowed one large-scale test to ask students to describe their "pet peeves." The question was easy enough for native speakers; but numbers of international students, assuming that the question referred to some unknown domestic animal, wrote about the care and feeding of the peeve. Again, readers of one essay test asking about truth and justice were astonished to find strained examples drawn from bridges and highways in the responses of nonnative speakers. When they looked back at the question, they discovered why: the students were urged to supply "concrete examples" (J. White, 1988).

Reliability problems are usually the result of vagueness in the question, but they can also come about when the question (intentionally or not) invites the students to take political, religious, or social positions. How can readers grade fairly a frankly racist or sexist essay, or one that seems to argue for idiotic solutions to the problems of the country or the universe? Clarification of the directions to the students may avoid such problems; sometimes, to help keep students on the track, a question will suggest a structure for the response ("Describe . . . use examples . . . then discuss"). If numbers of on-topic papers are ungradable or if the test committee remains unable to reach agreement on the scores of pretest papers, and hence on the characteristics of such papers for a scoring guide, it is time to move to a different question.

An interesting writing topic that works well is a rare find. Most test committees for large testing programs, knowing that no reader will find the four hundredth essay on *anything* interesting, will happily settle for a tolerable topic, as long as it is clear and yields reliable and valid results. Some questions that seem very interesting to the committee will evoke stultifying responses, in practice, and some apparently dull questions seem to tap into the creativity that students are often afraid to display on tests. As in other areas, it is the pretest process that reveals the success of the proposed topic.

Pretesting. With these principles in mind, the test development committee will consider the test specifications, the goals of the testing program, and the students to be tested, and come up with a series of questions for pretesting. This initial step needs to occur several months before the actual test questions are chosen, so that the committee will have ample time to revise its selections or to abandon them and start over.

The pretesting population need not be large (fifty to one hundred students will often suffice), but it must be carefully chosen. Those taking the pretest cannot be students who will take the real test, but should be representative of them, with the same background, ethnic and cultural diversity, and range of abilities. Students at neighboring colleges or school districts will usually serve nicely, and neighboring faculty will normally pretest questions for colleagues as a routine professional courtesy.

Careful reading of the pretests usually reveals that most of the proposed questions do not work, according to the principles I have just listed: the test does not distinguish the best writers from the average ones, most students find little to say or produce only clichés, most scores group in the middle, clear scoring criteria do not emerge, and so on. But one or two of the questions probably will stand out from the rest, often to the wonder of the committee which reluctantly included them. These are the questions to be revised and clarified for further pretesting, and eventually to be used in the test itself.

The fact that test questions must themselves be tested is not well understood, and that lack of understanding leads to many problems in testing. Many years ago, I designed a comprehensive examination for graduating English majors at a selective private college; as a new faculty member, I had a particular stake in producing an inventive, interesting, and responsible four-hour examination. The English department approved the test, for it was indeed inventive and interesting; it never occurred to me that it should be pretested. Grading of the test was most careful, with teams of faculty spending days reading and discussing the anonymous papers produced by generally excellent students. The results were astonishing. Five students from the graduating class failed the test (a high number for this institution); and these students, as we found when we uncovered the names on the tests, were the top five students in the department, including the editors of the literary magazine and the college paper, and all five had already been accepted into first-rate graduate schools. We huddled all of them through graduation, somehow, and went off wondering how such good students could do so badly on their comprehensive examinations. The better question, however, was, what was wrong with the test, whose invalidity had been so thoroughly demonstrated. We had not been trained to ask that question, and it did not occur to me until years had gone by.

One type of question often favored by English teachers usually will turn out to be wholly invalid in a large-scale test, and the committee will want to keep a sharp eye out for such questions during initial development and pretesting. I am speaking here of questions on topics that dominate the news and gossip columns, to which a great fund of stock responses are at hand. George Orwell, in his familiar essay "Politics and the English Language," speaks of the tendency among writers to accept concepts and phrases floating in the air, instead of choosing words that express their particular meaning: "As soon as certain topics are raised, the concrete melts into the abstract and no one seems able to think of turns of speech that are not hackneyed: prose consists less and less of *words* chosen for the sake of their meaning, and more and more of *phrases* tacked together like the sections of a prefabricated hen-house" ([1950] 1968, p. 87). Questions about education or other subjects that elicit emotional reactions invariably call forth stock responses; in such instances, substantial prewriting exercises in class are required before students (particulary the best students) will move beyond the recitation of clichés. Experienced test development committees avoid such questions as systematically as they do those allowing the pious to record their religious experiences; hardened and irreverent committee members will take care to "Jesus-proof" their questions. The experience of test developers is too extensive to be denied: on such topics, few good students will write essays that reflect their actual writing ability.

Large-scale test committees are rarely satisfied after the first pretest. Of a dozen or so questions, perhaps two will have emerged as good possibilities, and these two will have been rewritten, sometimes extensively. A second pretest is necessary, to be followed by a second evaluation of the results for clarity, validity, reliability, and interest. If the test questions emerge from that evaluation with only minor revisions, the committee should prepare a draft of a scoring guide for these questions. If even these questions will not work, the committee will have two choices: begin the process again, if there is enough time, or, with a sense of impending doom, choose the least faulty questions and try to salvage them. Wise test administrators allow time for the first choice.

Classroom Implications. At first glance, this model of essay test development seems too rigorous and time-consuming to be adopted by classroom teachers. Few of us can convene committees to work on our tests, and we do not have the resources or the time to conduct extensive pretesting. But we do have one resource that no test committee can command: we have years to develop and refine our assignments—indeed, an entire teaching career. We have, in addition, an enviable control over our test criteria, since we know (or should know) what we expect our students to accomplish. Furthermore, we can and do pretest an assignment every time we give one, and most of our students are not reticent about problems they perceive in clarity or validity or interest. If we listen to them and revise our writing assignments and tests in the light of their comments and our own evaluation of results, we ought, over time, to develop these teaching tools to a perfection that any test committee should envy. Indeed, on closer examination, teaching faculty have better conditions for test development than any professionally supported test committee could ever obtain.

Why, then, are our tests often unclear, invalid, unreliable, even uninteresting? Why are many of our classroom assignments so lacking in precision that unscrupulous vendors can furnish standard responses to them at so much a page? As long as assessment remains a peripheral concern to us, an afterthought to our curricula, we will neglect the opportunities for test development that we so richly possess. As long as term papers and other writing assignments are seen principally as ritual products for the student to bring to us as offerings for grading, we will fail to use and develop this major tool for learning. Happily, the recent widespread concern for writing in all disciplines is coinciding with increasing participation and interest in large-scale writing assessment. Thus, the knowledge of test development that this chapter summarizes is slowly spreading through the academic community, and it is suggesting by its very presence that we should attend to our writing assignments with renewed care.

Unfortunately, inattention to test development is not solely to be found in classrooms. Many testing, evaluation, and even research programs still make use of writing tests that have been developed in the most casual way—or even imported from a different environment with a different purpose. A few years ago, I agreed with pleasure to direct a holistic essay reading as part of an immensely expensive and important program evaluation; a prominent figure in evaluation was responsible for the entire project. To my astonishment, I discovered that both essay questions used in the evaluation had sprung fully grown from the head of this particular individual and showed not the slightest signs of systematic development. The unstated criteria were quirky and personal and unsuited either to the students being tested or to the program being evaluated. There was no changing the situation; the questions had already been administered. We scored some thousands of essays as well as we could, which is to say not very consistently, since the questions were as unclear and ambiguous as first-draft topics usually are. The prominent evaluator, of course, found it hard to understand the unsatisfactory results, since he was professionally committed to evaluating other people and other programs and had little interest or practice in evaluating his own assumptions about testing.

Topic Types

We know surprisingly little about the differences in performance that are caused by different kinds of writing topics. We can say with some assurance, however, that some kinds of topics are more appropriate than others for some purposes and groups, and that the choice of topic type will have an important influence over the score distribution obtained.

In his description of the development of topics for the National Assessment of Educational Progress, Richard Lloyd-Jones (1977, pp. 37–41) provides a useful analysis of discourse types for testing. He briefly discusses schemes devised by Aristotle and his successors (with particular attention to the complicated models developed by James Britton (1970) and James Kinneavy (1971)) and presents the following three forms of discourse: explanatory discourse (subject oriented), expressive discourse (discourser oriented), and persuasive discourse (audience oriented). This convenient model focuses on two aspects of discourse, its purpose and its orientation, and is intended to serve as an example rather than an inclusive design. Its very simplicity is its particular virtue, however, since it clearly illustrates the different kinds of mental activity involved in different kinds of writing. Since individual styles of learning vary widely and since the various stages of cognitive and moral development have been well documented (Piaget, [1926] 1955; Bruner, 1960; Perry, 1968; Kohlberg, 1981; Haswell, 1991), we should not be surprised to learn that an individual student's writing ability varies considerably, according to the mental operation demanded by a particular writing topic.

Some convincing evidence for such a conclusion has been accumulated by the California State University English Equivalency Examination. From 1973 to 1981, that program tested over 31,000 students, on nine different tests, requiring two different kinds of writing from each student at the same sitting. Essay 1 tended to be a form of what Lloyd-Jones calls "expressive writing," while essay 2 was a comparison-contrast question, an analytical mode close to what he calls "explanatory discourse." During the first years of the test, essay 1 had very little analytical demand; as years went by, more and more analysis was added to that question. In 1973, the correlation of essay 1 scores with essay 2 scores was a surprisingly low .37. By 1981, even with a substantial reading passage added to essay 1, the correlation had only reached .57 (White, 1973–1981). These low correlations suggest strongly that the two different kinds of writing topics used for the two different essays each year produced quite different score distributions. Students who score in the high (or low) ranges on one kind of writing test will not necessarily receive high (or low) scores on a different one with a different kind of question.

But although different kinds of writing may elicit different levels of performance from individuals, it does not necessarily follow that certain modes of discourse are inherently easier than others. If we make a connection between Piagetian cognitive theory and writing mode, we might say that persuasive discourse, for example, requires much more of a "formal operation" than expressive discourse (which is more "egocentric"). On the other hand, we can use the same theory to demonstrate that any writing on any topic is such a complex and advanced skill that it requires formal operations in order to exist at all. And we can draw upon the experience of any writing teacher to show that, although many students have an easier time writing about themselves than about abstractions, some students find it much easier to write about abstract topics than about their own experience. For a full exploration of these issues, with many examples of different kinds of topics, consult Ruth and Murphy (1988).

Until we know more than we now do about the connections among writing topic types, modes of discourse, and cognitive theory, we need to observe certain cautions in the development of writing topics. In the first place, we should attempt to measure anything we call "writing ability" by more than one writing sample, in more than one writing mode. If we use only one kind of topic, we will be disadvantaging those students who perform better in another mode and favoring those who do best in the one mode we test. If financial or time limitations make it impossible to test in more than one mode, we ought to be particularly alert to the validity problem contained in a single-mode test and to the reliability problems of a single-question test.

Second, we ought to resist making assumptions about "easy" or "elementary" topic types. Typically, faculty tend to associate expressive writing with juvenility and explanatory modes with maturity. While there is some justification for doing so in the light of the badly designed expressive topics most of us experienced in school, the equation is improper. "What did you do on your summer vacation?" is a bad topic not because it is based on personal experience but because it is vague, unfocused, and pointless. A good expressive topic demands that the writer find personal meaning in external objects and communicate internal truth to an outside reader. Such an activity is not necessarily easier or less advanced (or less valuable) than another mode of discourse. When John Milton was assigned to write about his feelings on the death of a friend (not, we must confess, a particularly well developed topic), he produced one of the greatest poems in the English language.

Once we dissociate, as we should, mode of discourse from level of difficulty, we become free to consider a wide range of topic types for any ability or age level. College preparatory students need to learn to demonstrate and take responsibility for their assertions, and hence should receive more than expressive assignments. Complex expressive topics may be quite appropriate for upper-division college students; simple persuasive topics may be just the thing for a particular class in junior high school. The goals of the program should determine the topic type, which, in turn, establishes the framework for the actual questions.

Helping Students Do Well on Essay Tests

Students who do well on essay tests are those who can read essay questions (which often means mentally revising badly designed questions into clear and manageable ones), organize their thoughts quickly, understand the school dialect, and edit their finished work. Students who have never learned those skills do much worse than they should on essay tests.

Many students from weak educational systems have done very little writing, and the little they have done has been more or less the mechanical repeating of information. For most students, writing means retelling something that they have read or that the teacher has said, and such impersonal and unorganized writing may have been rewarded by praise and high grades, particularly outside of English courses. (Sometimes, as we have seen, this destructive pattern continues in college.) But now, in college, they are confronted with essay tests that call for some original thought, organization, and editing, all within a tight time limit. Moreover, for a significant minority, the dialect required is a great distance from that spoken everywhere but in school. No wonder that essay tests provoke fear and hostility from these students, who have had little success in writing and little experience with college writing assignments.

We will be doing our ordinary students a great service if we spend some time helping them learn the requisite test-taking skills. Even those who have picked up these skills will benefit from understanding what they have been doing and how they might do it even better.

Helping Students Understand the Question

Two problems cloud students' understanding of essay questions: teachers often do not make clear what is called for, and, even when they do, students do not attend carefully to the demands of the question.

Understanding Essay Directions. Well-constructed essay questions often use a series of code words that students must understand: *describe, discuss, compare, contrast, explain, comment,* and so on. Some handbooks and manuals give definitions of these terms, making clear distinctions among them. Unfortunately, the teachers who write the questions spend little time reading these handbooks, so students must expect considerable overlap and ambiguity, even when the words seem distinct. The problem is not that teachers or students do not understand the "meaning" of the terms; the fact is that the terms have no fixed meaning and will mean whatever the teacher expects them to mean.

For example, many teachers will use "compare" as a direction to show similarities between two objects or views, and "contrast" as a direction to show differences; most handbooks define the terms in this way. Thus, "compare and contrast" will mean "describe both the similarities and the differences." But other teachers (and handbooks) will take "compare" to *include* "contrast," on the logical grounds that comparing two things means placing them side by side and describing what matters. A diligent student who has learned the narrower definition of "compare" and cites only similarities will not receive full credit. A protest that the teacher should have asked for "contrasts" if differences were to be shown is likely to fall on deaf ears.

Because of the uncertainty of these terms, teachers should either explain them to the class or define the terms on the test itself or create questions with explicit instructions. For instance, as I suggested earlier, instead of directing students to "compare and contrast" two quotations, a question could ask students to "show in what ways these two quotations are saying similar things and in what ways they are saying different things." The longer version is somewhat cumbersome, but it does not depend on students' knowing the hidden definitions of "compare and contrast." But, of course, a student would have to know what "show" means (does it include "use specific detail"?), in order to proceed, so there is no way to avoid using some sort of code.

An even more confusing direction is the overused term *discuss*. Many teachers will use this directive when they mean something as vague as "say something about the subject." For many students, this turns out to be an activity analogous to what in computer talk is called "a file dump": an undifferentiated list of all information available, without organization, coherence, or context. A high grade can be earned for such a file dump—if that was the teacher's intent. But the teacher may well mean—indeed, ought to mean—something much more precise, such as an argument about the strengths and weaknesses of a particular position. If that was the intention, a file dump will elicit a low grade and teacher complaints about inability to focus and organize. In fact, the teacher has gotten what was asked for but not what was really sought. The imprecise question has led the students into confusion and the teacher into frustration.

Reading the Question. Students will benefit by practicing the reading of essay questions with pen in hand. In the first place, they need to see and circle the key directions and consider what the words mean. Many students interpret *all* directive words as "say something about" (which is in fact all that many teachers mean); students need to understand that different directions may actually call for different kinds of responses. "Describe" usually requires specific detail; "explain" is likely to call for definitions and analysis; "analyze" suggests taking something apart to see what it is made of; and so on.

The students also should recognize and circle the different *parts* of the question, so that they can remember to answer the entire question. Many students urge teachers to number the separate sections on the question itself (Haviland and Clark, 1992, p. 52), but such numbering can be misleading if the question asks for a single coherent essay in which several different topics are addressed. Many students will answer the subquestions in a series of paragraphs, sometimes numbering them diligently, but will fail to connect these parts into the coherent essay required.

Finally, students need to be aware of the mode of discourse that the question is calling for. Questions that require expository writing can present a special problem for our freshman students today. Although researchers in the London schools two decades ago (Britton and others, 1975) found very little personal writing and a great deal of rote expository writing, many of our beginning students can only write personal narratives. They will write personal essays on college placement tests, regardless of what the question may be or how far from it the narrative may wander. One sure way for a student to fail an expository essay question is to answer it with a personal experience narrative.

Some questions may intentionally mix modes: "Analyze the quotation and then illustrate it by some personal experience." Students need to see that such a question expects the narrative to be subordinate to the discussion of the quotation and connected to it. Sometimes the emphasis seems to be reversed: "Describe an occasion in which you . . . , and say what you learned from it." This last question normally elicits a personal narrative with a perfunctory moral tag on the end. Perhaps such a narrative and tag are what the question really seeks, but often what is really required is very much like the preceding question. If there are good reasons to believe that the question is in fact basically looking for exposition, the student should decide on the concept first and use the description to illustrate the concept; that is, the student should write an expository paper, with its evidence drawn from personal experience.

Not every question will be expository or complex or demanding. Sometimes, particularly on short placement tests, a narrative or description is all that the question calls for. While not all students find personal or descriptive writing easier than expository writing, most do; such writing poses few organizational or interpretive problems, since a simple chronology will usually serve quite well and the student is the final expert on the meaning of his or her own experiences. Such a test will examine a student's ability to marshal memories in reasonably error-free prose.

The basic point is to train students to read the question carefully and to help them gain experience at writing in different modes, so that they can make a rapid, accurate judgment of the kind of writing that may be required on an essay test. In recent years, as more and more teachers are learning about ways to ask precise questions, students are more and more likely to encounter clear directives. They may not know why the clear test struck them as a good one, or why they felt more capable and successful as they answered it, but they will naturally enough be pleased with teaching and testing that clarifies rather than confuses.

Responding to Unclear Questions. Unfortunately, most essay questions are not designed with care or precision, and students have come to expect vague questions on essay tests. Even well-trained and experienced students may be surprised to receive low grades on a precise essay question because they have not responded to the question asked; these students have become so accustomed to unclear questions that they habitually ignore them and write whatever they choose on the general topic. We need to prepare our students for the unclear questions they will receive from most of their professors, and we need to help them see the difference between different kinds of unclear questions. Most of all, they need to know when a question makes precise demands that they must follow and when in fact it really requires them to construct their own question. Needless to say, under tight time limits, a question that sets out a clear task is much more manageable than one that does not.

When the question is not clear, it becomes the student's responsibility to construct a clear question and then answer it. This way of handling the question is never evident, and many students will respond to unclear questions as they do to the ubiquitous "discuss"—that is, by simply jotting down everything they know about the topic, in the hope that they will somehow hit upon whatever the teacher is looking for. Sometimes that works, since a vague question suggests that the teacher has no clear response in mind. But a much more productive tactic for students is to try to turn a vague question into a precise one that can be answered clearly.

For example, a music class is faced with the following question on the final exam in a course dealing with nineteenth-century European symphonies: "Beethoven and Brahms. 30 minutes."

Many possibilities open up. Some students in the class begin writing immediately, telling everything they know about Beethoven (mostly his biography, with dates of the nine well-known symphonies), followed by whatever they can list about Brahms, with dates; at the end, when time is up, they stop in mid-sentence and scrawl, "Out of time." Wiser—or test-wiser—students do not start writing without thinking. They take five minutes of the thirty to list on scratch paper a few connections between the two composers, recognizing that the question must represent some kind of comparison and contrast. They know that they can write only three or four paragraphs, so they decide that one paragraph will deal with similarities, a second with differences; a final paragraph will speak to the importance of the two composers in the history of music; an opening paragraph will—well, they're not sure, so they leave space for an opening paragraph to be added at the end, stating the question that they (as it turns out) have answered. These successful students might produce an opening paragraph stating that Beethoven and Brahms are both German Romantic composers who displayed different forms of romanticism; two paragraphs might follow, comparing and contrasting a few aspects of their romanticism; and a closing paragraph could suggest that later composers, such as Anton Bruckner and Gustav Mahler, drew on both forms of romanticism. Concluding with a few minutes to spare, they reread their essays, fix up the spelling and insert a missing word or two, and move to the next question.

The excellent students I have just described may or may not happen to know more about nineteenth-century music than the mediocre students, writing as fast as they can without a plan, but they will probably get higher grades. They will also find essay tests more rewarding and less exasperating than the others will.

Sometimes the questions are even less clear than "Beethoven and Brahms." A typical one will give a quotation with no directive at all, or the quotation may be followed by the direction: "Discuss." But what is the student to discuss? Again, most students will proceed with a file dump—disgorging as much information as possible on the page. But the careful, well-prepared student will pause to construct a question before responding, so that the essay can follow some kind of organization. What is the quotation saying, and how does it relate to the material of the course? (Most essays written in response to texts fail to examine the text in much detail.)

These students will mark up the quotation, and sketch out meanings and connections, as they decide on the central idea of their response. If time is short, they may begin by leaving space for an opening paragraph and proceeding to write an analysis paragraph, expecting their own point to become clear as they write. Soon they realize that the quotation illustrates a particular point of view, perhaps a common mistake or a particular insight, in the field; the task then becomes to show how the quotation achieves its goal: an analysis question. Or perhaps the quotation needs to be proved, or disproved, by an ordered citation of evidence: the question calls for an argument. Whatever the students decide, it is impossible for them to write out an answer until they have a good sense of the question.

For example, consider the question that asked students to "discuss" the following quotation from Mark Twain:

> The best swordsman in the world doesn't need to fear the second best swordsman in the world; no, the person for him to be afraid of is some ignorant antagonist who has never had a sword in his hand before; he doesn't do the thing he ought to do, and so the expert isn't prepared for him; he does the thing he ought not to do; and often it catches the expert out and ends him on the spot.

Because the quotation was accompanied by only a vague directive, many students had a great deal of trouble with it. Some were convinced that they should devote themselves to a discussion of dueling; others decided to call up whatever they knew about Mark Twain and so related the quotation to *Tom Sawyer* and *Huckleberry Finn*. Many students began writing about dueling as an example of something, only gradually coming to realize the essence of the quotation; by then it was too late to revise and reorganize the essay. The most astute and test-wise students marked up the quotation carefully, usually by underlining the three characters whose actions are being described: the best swordsman, the second best swordsman, and the ignorant antagonist. These students listed descriptors and examples for the three character types. A typical example looked like this:

Best swordsman: expert, like the Redcoats in 1776.
Second best swordsman: good, plays by the rules, the French.
Ignorant antagonist: makes his own rules, like the Revolutionary Americans.

As the experienced students marked up the quotation and reflected on it, they became aware that the best way to "discuss" it would be to explain the three character types and then relate them to some area they knew (here, the American Revolution). Those of us on the test development committee decided that we would even the field for the test takers and devise a precise directive that pointed out the most effective way to handle the question:

Write an essay that explains what Mark Twain means by his description of the "best swordsman" and the "ignorant antagonist." Relate his concept to an area about which you are well informed.

By giving these directions, we changed the examination so that it no longer tested students' experience with handling unclear essay questions, but, instead tested their ability to write an essay handling complex concepts. The results still showed a great range of abilities, but the more precise question allowed the examination to elicit the information about students that we really wanted.

Teachers helping students do their best on essay tests will use their knowledge about directives in two ways: to revise their own questions so that they are clearer, more answerable, more precise in their demands; and to give students practice in responding to essay questions that are none of these, and hence require the student to construct a question before answering it.

Understanding the Role of Memory

Most essay tests contain a hidden demand: to call up material for the essay from memory. Many students have a rich and full memory

store, stocked with personal experiences, reading, history, arguments, and much more. Such students are never at a loss for a topic,
though they often need help in organizing, focusing, and developing the material they have at the ready. Most essay questions simply
assume ready access to a rich store of material.

But many students do not have that access, nor do they have
the background in remembered reading, intellectual conversation,
and reflective introspection that the typical essay question draws on.
Essay testing is particularly frustrating and difficult for these students until they have learned how to call up from memory the
events, details, and examples that are needed for most essay questions. Furthermore, they will be expected to take an analytical and
evaluative stance toward these memories, a stance that may seem
unnatural to some who are not used to the academic culture. We
ought to help such students understand and practice the kinds of
memory exercises that most essay questions take for granted.

One effective way to practice memory exercises is through
group discussion of responses to typical essay questions. The Mark
Twain question is a good example. What historical examples besides the American Revolution would illustrate (or argue against)
the quotation? What special activities might be called up for the
essay? (One student used his knowledge of chess to show that the
quotation was dead wrong where only skill mattered. "Ignorant
antagonists" do not last more than ten moves against an expert
chess player.)

Working Within Time Constraints

The usual time constraints of essay tests encourage students to produce first-draft writing that is faulty, disorganized, unclear, and
unfocused; the constraints also limit the memory search that is often
a hidden requirement of the question. The secret to helping students do well on timed essay tests is to suggest ways, even under
severe time limits, to hand in second or third drafts *without writing
earlier drafts*. (The single greatest waste of time during an essay test
comes from recopying drafts.) That is, the good test taker will find
a way to do a first or discovery draft in the head or on scratch notes
and then to write a more finished draft in the time allowed.

In addition, time must always be saved for rereading and editing during the last few minutes. Experienced test takers will normally write on only one side of the page and will write on every other line, so that there will be plenty of room for neat revisions; they will also leave space at the start for a new opening to be written after the essay is finished. Any writing process that leaves out time for revision usually produces weak work. As any writer with a deadline knows, planning is usually crucial for success. Most students will appreciate help in planning for successful essay test writing, and experience with revision in the testing situation will carry over to more leisurely writing plans.

How long should an essay test take? Sometimes the institution establishes an exam schedule, and the instructor must simply fit into the schedule. But often the teacher or test committee can design a time span that is appropriate for the purpose of the test. A test is, in one sense, a means of gathering information, and the time required for the test should depend on the complexity of the information sought. Essay tests usually follow one of four patterns.

The Twenty-Minute Essay

Twenty-minute essay tests are designed to produce two or three paragraphs that show mechanical competence and fluency. If the question is well constructed, it will allow the students to begin writing almost immediately—perhaps a personal experience essay or a descriptive essay with a simple chronological structure. If the question is not clear, if it poses organizational problems, if it asks for much reflection, or if it makes other impossible demands for the time allowed, the student will have to rewrite the question so that it can be answered in two or three paragraphs of hasty writing. Some students will explain in an opening sentence, "I can't possibly write about the three most impressive teachers I have had, so let me tell you about my Advanced Placement teacher, who is the main reason I am now in college. . . ." Such a procedure may seem risky, but the people grading the test will recognize the good sense of accomplishing the possible, particularly if they are reading many essays that show the despair and confusion of attempting the impossible.

The Thirty-Minute Essay

Many large-scale testing programs have begun to use the thirty-minute essay in recent years, often at the college graduation level. The best-known programs are the California Basic Educational Skills Test (CBEST) for teacher candidates and the Medical College Admissions Test (MCAT). The time frame is administratively convenient, since two essays will fit neatly in one hour—the same reason that essays of this length often appear on final examinations.

In contrast to the twenty-minute test, the thirty-minute test allows for an organized and coherent essay of limited complexity. But successful students will need to manage their time with great care: five minutes or so for close reading of the question and brainstorming (on paper), another five minutes to arrange and focus the ideas (deciding on the one central idea the essay will demonstrate), fifteen minutes to write three or four focused paragraphs, five minutes to edit and revise. Even with this comparatively short time span, students should be encouraged to write on every other line, so that corrections and additions can be inserted neatly at the end.

The Forty-Five-Minute Essay

Forty-five minutes remains the standard essay time span, and it allows for thoughtful, organized, and somewhat creative responses. In this time span, the first ten minutes or so can be spent analyzing the question and outlining a response, almost half an hour can be spent writing, and time still remains for careful editing before the end of the test. Students should resist the impulse to recopy their drafts, since they need all the time allowed for organizing, writing, and editing. There is now time to do extensive editing or even revision in the space between lines, on blank left-hand pages, and on the blank opening page. An opening paragraph that relates to the closing paragraph and that points to the best ideas of the essay should be written last.

Some teachers give their students a formula for writing the forty-five minute essay. For instance, the "five-paragraph theme" is a widely used strategy that can lead to limited success. This formula requires the student to have exactly three things to say about any topic. The first and last paragraphs list the three; the three middle paragraphs assert each idea and give a bit of evidence for each. The formula persists because it provides an easy, all-purpose organizational scheme; however forced or mechanical, it does help students who cannot come up with an organization that reflects what they have to say. Those who dislike the formula complain that it provides an organizational scheme as a substitute for having something to say. When students use the formula mechanically, they are likely to turn out essays that stick out during essay readings like a manikin on the cheerleader squad. Most students will have more or less than three things to say; some students will have nothing to say, and dividing nothing by five (paragraphs) still leaves nothing, even if it has the appearance of an essay. The strategy is particularly weak on development and coherence and is clearly inappropriate for some kinds of essay questions. But many instructors continue to teach it, on the grounds that some organizational scheme is preferable to none.

Instead of providing such formulas, teachers would do better to offer their students a range of organizational possibilities, since different students will learn and write in different ways. Some students will do best using formal outlines; others will be most productive using clustering (jotting down ideas any which way on the page and later connecting them with circles); still others will profit from structured problem-solving mechanisms (heuristics). Some may even need to learn a few stress-reducing techniques before they can begin to write well under time pressure. But every essay reading turns up some writing of astonishing quality, evidence that some students can be creative under the pressures of time. Indeed, forty-five-minute essay questions have produced some of the most memorable student writing I have read. One cynical reader, hearing me make this remark, offered one possible explanation: "They write better on the test because they spend more time on it than they do on their term papers." There is certainly something to be said for the intense concentration on a single topic that an essay test provides.

I remember an anonymous student Advanced Placement essay I read twenty years ago on Tolkien, still the best piece I've ever read on *The Lord of the Rings*; I am still moved to tears at the memory of the placement essay on failure by the Vietnamese boat

person (she had failed twice at suicide); I remain stunned at the
medical school clinician who wrote about Loren Eiseley's *Star-
thrower* that the futile but necessary gesture of returning one star-
fish to the water was like his nights in the emergency room,
patching up those who would return even more wounded the next
night. In our passion for the writing process and in our quest for
revision, we should not forget that some students can turn out fine
work in an intense but short period of time. We need to be careful
about defining "the writing process" as if there were only one or
two right ways to proceed, and we need to remember that revision
sometimes make writing worse—particularly personal experience
writing, whose power and voice sometimes disappear as students fix
up their drafts to meet what they take to be teacher expectations.

One-, Two-, or Three-Hour Essays

As the time span increases, questions can become more complicated.
A typical two-hour test, for example, may be an open-book question
on essays read in advance; it may call for detailed analysis of several
of these essays, comparison and contrast, and connections to the
student's experience. Curiously, the writing quality does not seem
to improve much beyond that of the forty-five-minute exam; the
essays will simply be longer. Much of the additional time seems to
be spent on worry, rereading, and recopying of drafts.

Students taking long essay tests should spend the extra time
thinking the question through and organizing their responses so
that the draft they write will seem to be a second rather than a first
draft: it will be focused on a single controlling idea, organized
around a sequence of connected assertions, and developed by use of
examples and detail. In addition, students should save a substantial
amount of time at the end for writing the first paragraph, revising
the response, and editing it so that the essay they hand in is really
a third draft, even though it has been written and edited only once.
The best preparation for such tests is extensive practice in organizing and revising complex papers.

The Craftsmanship of Essay Test Writing

Despite all the good advice about organizing writing on essay tests,
very few students actually do organize their writing. Most students

offer implacable resistance to a practice that would surely improve their test writing and their grades. There are, I think, both theoretical and practical reasons for this resistance.

Some students have so little experience in reading, discussing, and writing about ideas (as opposed to experience) that a discussion of organization is premature; such students need help with invention and development strategies before they have much to organize. But most of our college students have plenty to say, some experience with exposition and argument, and a reasonable background of information to draw upon; yet they still have not learned how to organize their writing.

Many of these students have picked up a half-baked theory of writing, based on the muse theory of poetry: either the muse will inspire you with a terrific piece of first-draft writing, or the muse is absent and no amount of work will produce anything worth reading. In either case, there is no point in organizing or revising; in fact, such activities are an outrage to the muse, an attempt to impose reason on a mystical process. As evidence, there is the occasional brilliant first draft that can only be damaged by revision.

Even without this dimly perceived romantic theory, many fluent college students see no point in organizing their work, since fluent first drafts (really discovery drafts) have often won them praise and high grades in the past. Too often, what has really mattered about writing has been correctness in mechanics and a certain amount of repetition of key ideas from the text or from lecture notes. When we speak of organizing thoughts and going through a series of drafts, we are changing the rules of a game that some students have learned to play successfully. "You can make me write," one student wrote on an essay test, "but you can't make me think!" We need to make clear that we are intentionally changing the rules that have allowed fluent students to avoid thinking about and revising their work. That may have been good enough in the past, but writing and thinking must now go together; organization and revision are necessary for almost all successful writing, whatever the patterns of performance may have been.

One good way to combat these destructive attitudes toward writing, I am convinced, is by way of assessment. Not until students have become able to distinguish good from weak responses will they realize that their work both needs improvement and can be improved with planning. They need to work with scoring guides and other student papers, gradually internalizing critical standards that they can then begin to apply to their own work. And they need enough practice with revision to see that they are capable of recognizing their own best ideas, organizing them, providing evidence and connections for them, and rearranging them in improved order. In short, organization as a concept assumes that we are looking at writing as craftsmanship in critical thinking, not inspiration or mechanics. Not until students have made that conceptual leap will advice on and practice in organization have much effect.

Some teachers have found that regular practice in writing and writing assessment in class are the best means of helping students conceive of writing in this new way. If we value writing as a discovery process, which need not be organized or edited in preliminary form, we help students understand the difference between discovery drafts and finished drafts. A writing journal—ungraded but collected and checked—in which students summarize and react to reading assignments is a powerful tool for reshaping attitudes about writing; "five-minute writes," during which the pen must keep moving, can open class periods and launch students directly into discussion. Such activities accustom students to writing as part of their regular thinking, talking, and reading activities and can help them understand the necessarily unshaped nature of draft writing. Such materials must be shaped before they become products submitted for grading. Peer grading and peer response sessions conducted in class when papers or drafts are due can open students' eyes to the possibilities of organized writing as critical thinking. Practice in writing timed tests and peer grading of those tests will reinforce the need for planning, organization, and revision.

The world is now filled with organizational schemes, and for good reason: people seem to have a wide variety of ways of proceeding, depending to a great extent on their learning styles. Outlining works well for those who proceed in a linear fashion and are comfortable with categories and subcategories. But outlining feels like a straitjacket for other kinds of students, who need a more open and holistic way of coming up with and arranging ideas.

We can help our students learn the most effective way to

organize their essays by giving them a series of options and by recognizing that our own way of organizing will not work for everyone. Besides outlining, we should be able to illustrate nonlinear procedures, such as clustering, cognitive mapping, simple listing of assertions, and other useful schemes for grouping and ordering ideas. Above all, we should demonstrate that only organization before writing will allow students to write second drafts on essay tests, because there is never time to write a first draft.

Editing and Revising

It is important to distinguish editing from revising, a much more elaborate activity. During revision, we move paragraphs about, insert new pages, discard whole chunks of prose, reorganize, come up with new ideas, and so on. Editing is a humble cousin of revision, though it may sometimes lead to revision: sentence structure sometimes is awry because the concept is half-formed; a paragraph requires more than a few transitional words to restore coherence and, instead, must be developed into two or more new paragraphs. But, in general, editing is the last phase of writing, a matter of tidying up the mechanics so that readers will not be distracted by errors.

Not until we get to the forty-five-minute essay can we reasonably talk about revision; almost all essay tests allow insufficient time for that activity. (This limitation of essay tests, which makes it difficult for writers to use an extended writing process to produce good drafts, has led to the recent emphasis on portfolio assessment. See Chapter 6.) So the final few minutes of every essay test should be spent on rereading and editing what has been written. Good writers will be able to make some revisions, usually additions and deletions of sentences, as they edit, but most students should probably use this time for polishing and cleaning: inserting the words that are almost always omitted during a hasty draft, correcting the inevitable spelling errors, replacing faulty commas with semicolons, checking subject-verb agreement, and so on. No matter how much the grader of the essay tries to allow for hasty errors on exams, a cleaned-up paper will almost always receive a higher grade; some teachers find it extremely hard to respect the views of writers of error-filled prose, however intelligent the writing may be.

Some students want to bring dictionaries or thesauruses to tests, so that they can look up troublesome words. Though we must respect the impulse to use reference materials, they usually do more harm than good on timed essay tests. The dictionary may help on spelling problems, but the time lost is usually not worth the improvement; in most cases, the presence of the dictionary suggests that the student should do editing while composing, instead of as a clean-up operation afterward, and the constant interruption while writing destroys the essay. The thesaurus is even worse; it encourages the students to use longer and odder words rather than the clear ones they have in mind. There is so much to do during the usual timed essay test that reference books become distractions rather than supports. Some students feel so insecure without their references that it would be unsettling to forbid them, even on brief tests, but we might suggest that the students merely stroke the books from time to time, for the comfort of their presence. They are more helpful if left unopened during the limited time allowed for most essay tests. Not until we get into two-hour or longer tests will they be of much use.

During the last few years, the decreasing price and increasing power of laptop computers have made them more available for students taking essay tests; in particular, students with various handicaps are using them to great purpose. These portable machines will surely become more and more common as the millennium approaches. With their increasingly sophisticated word-processing capabilities (including dictionaries, thesauruses, spelling checkers, and grammar checkers), they may soon make efficient editing such a routine part of essay test writing that it will no longer affect grading. Then we will be able to focus, as we should, on what the student has to say and how it is organized, developed and expressed.

Computers have the potential for changing writing assessment in many additional ways. Although I am skeptical that they will alter writing itself substantially, computers can alter the way we read and respond to writing. Some writing classes in well-equipped schools are using bulletin boards and e-mail systems as part of the writing process, with provision for almost constant and wide-ranging response. New assessment devices might emerge from such practices, and computer writing might even lead to some kind of computer scoring. I have not yet seen much evidence, however, for the usefulness of these innovations for assessment—or even for teaching—though they do have their enthusiastic supporters. We must wait and see.

Essay Testing and the Wider Curriculum

Some writing teachers complain about essay tests and do not consider them "real writing," but many teachers outside the English class have come to regard these tests as a creative and active alternative to the multiple-choice tests that are customary in their fields. Essay tests can enable writing teachers to make direct connections between the instruction and assignments they give their students and the tests these students normally take outside of the writing class. Furthermore, a student who has learned to write well under the particular pressures and time constraints of an essay test has learned a series of skills that apply to all kinds of writing. No one would argue that all writing is test writing, but most students will be writing essay tests—and performance on essay tests will have large consequences for students. For this reason, writing courses ought to help students learn how to do well on essay tests. And those who teach writing courses ought to take the lead in helping their colleagues design essay tests that will support their educational goals and allow students to do their best.

CHAPTER 4

How Theories
of Reading Affect
Responses to Writing

The way that we conceive of reading has a profound effect on the way we understand and respond to what we read. For example, if we believe that meaning resides essentially in the text we have before us, as do most of those trained in traditional ways to teach literature, we will believe that our job as readers is to gain access to that (largely external) meaning. If, however, we believe that meaning is a function of our own (basically internal) creativity in relation to black marks on a white page, we will regard readers more as producers than as recipients of meaning. This distinction, which may not seem to be a difference to some readers and which may seem artificially exaggerated to others, has loomed very large among those concerned with critical theory in recent years. My concern in this chapter is to connect these two prominent theories of reading to recent concepts about responding to student writing and, eventually, to writing assessment.

The Formalistic Theory of Reading

Much of the formal criticism developed in the 1930s and 1940s rested on the supposition that the reader's task is essentially to submit himself or herself to the text, in order to discern the meaning that resides there quite independently of either the reader or the author (who, after producing the text, becomes just one more reader). A good expression of that idea appears in Mark Schorer's influential essay "Technique as Discovery," first published in the *Hudson Review* in 1948:

> Modern criticism has shown us that to speak of content as such is not to speak of art at all, but of experience; and that it is only when we speak of the *achieved* content, the form of the work of art, that we speak as critics. The difference between content, or experience, and achieved content, or art, is technique.
>
> When we speak of technique, then, we speak of nearly everything. For technique is the means by which the writer's experience, which is his subject matter, compels him to attend to it; technique is the only means he has of discovering, exploring, developing his subject, of conveying its meaning, and, finally, of evaluating it. And surely it follows that certain techniques are sharper tools than others, and will discover more; that the writer capable of the most exacting technical scrutiny of his subject matter will produce works with thickness and resonance, works which reverberate with maximum meaning [p. 67].

Schorer is arguing for strict attention to the form of a piece of writing as the way to understand its meaning. Although he is writing about literature, the same approach would hold for any sort of reading: Every writer—including every student—shapes experience or knowledge by technique. That technique gives the work meaning and is so embedded into the very construction of the writing that it virtually constitutes the writing. In practice, this theory leads to an intense concentration on the text, which "reverberates" with its meaning on its own; the work *itself* has content—thickness and resonance—independent of author and reader. Our task as readers is to understand so much about technique that we can obtain entry into the achieved content of the work and hence come to understand the "maximum meaning" it has to offer.

English teachers will recognize this approach to reading as

what was called the New Criticism during its period of greatest influence, from the early 1930s to the late 1950s. It seized the imagination of two generations of teachers and critics, revolutionized the study of literature, and led to an extraordinary production of articles, books, and editions illuminating literature. It still seems to be the dominant theory of reading followed in the high schools, where its relatively antiseptic and often mechanical application to literature has sometimes turned students away from reading for pleasure.

Although much has been written about the implications of this theory of reading for the study of literature, few have considered its profound and far-reaching effects on the teaching and measurement of writing. On the positive side, it urged readers of student writing to attend to the texts that the student produced, rather than to the student's social class, appearance, or moral predisposition. Since the theory argued that language and thought are in fact the same thing, the teacher could face with a certain valuable skepticism the student who claimed, "I know what I mean but I just don't know how to say it": "If you don't know how to say it," one could self-righteously reply, "then you don't know what you mean!" Most important, the theory called attention to the craftsmanship of prose, what Schorer calls "technique," and to the way that such craftsmanship conveys meaning. In so doing, this theory provided a useful if limited framework for the teaching of writing, since craftsmanship is always teachable, if not always learnable, in a way that inspiration, say, is not.

However, the belief that meaning resides in the text itself caused a series of theoretical and practical problems for writing teachers, particularly in relation to responding and assessment. Even though every sensible teacher knew that we must respond differently to a student text than to a finished piece of literature, the theory gave no good basis for such a different response—much needed by our best students—and suggested few practical ways of coping with the weakest of our students. Most damaging of all, the theory urged us to consider student writing as a product to be analyzed, as if every student composition were a failed Shakespeare sonnet.

This concern with writing as a product supported a preoccupation with editing and the appearance of the student text. The very weakest of our students, whose products were particularly un-sightly, were declared "remedial"—that is, verbally diseased—and sent to do therapeutic exercises in grammatical workbooks (which kept them busy and gave us the illusion that they were learning something). Our expectations (that is, our reading theory) had to change before we could understand how to teach such students, as Mina Shaughnessy has convincingly demonstrated (1977).

Some of the more extreme partisans of recent theories argue too loudly that "writing is a process, not a product," and hence confuse the issue. Writing is, as everyone with common sense knows, a product (in most cases) as well as a process. Every student turning in a paper to be graded, every scholar producing a paper for delivery or publication or promotion, every employee sending off a memo knows perfectly well that writing is an important and measurable product. We make ourselves foolish if we ignore that aspect of writing. Our students rightly expect us to evaluate their writing products, and they need such evaluation in order to im-prove. But the theory of reading, and hence of writing, that defines writing as *only* or even *principally* a product distorts the teaching of writing. It turns the writing teacher into only a judge of texts and limits teacher intervention (and hence value) to the end of the writ-ing process, where such intervention is not likely to do much good for the essay at hand. It also provides some justification for multiple-choice usage testing of writing ability and for overconfi-dence in the results of essay tests. Furthermore, when writing is defined as a product, the contents and the evaluation of writing portfolios will reflect that definition. Many portfolios do not in-clude evidence of the writing process; and even when they do, many teachers do not trust the revised form of writing as much as the first draft for portfolio assessment purposes (Hamp-Lyons and Condon, 1993).

It thus strikes me as no accident that three movements in the teaching of reading and writing began to take place at about the same time: (1) Proponents of writing as process began articulating their views and pursuing their research. (2) Measurement of writing by holistic evaluation of actual writing began to gain prominence and acceptance. (3) Poststructural theorists began arguing that read-ing is a process, a creative interaction between reader and text. Although the three movements were quite independent, operating in entirely different circles, each in its own way represented a rebellion against formalism and against the traditional ways of thinking about reading and writing. The formalistic focus on the text as product, to the virtual exclusion of all else, had come to be as constricting for the teaching and measurement of writing as it was for the reading of literature.

Poststructural Theories of Reading

An early sign of this change appeared when a group of scholars began to reassert the claims of rhetoric, the ancient discipline concerned with much more than form—most particularly, with invention and audience response. Edward P. J. Corbett's *Classical Rhetoric for the Modern Student* came out in 1965, the same year that Ross Winterowd published *Rhetoric and Writing*; five years later, Young, Becker, and Pike published their influential *Rhetoric: Discovery and Change* (1970). During this period, Richard Young, Janet Emig, and many others began to focus the attention of composition teachers on the writing process and on the many possible areas of useful teacher intervention. Research into the writing process, including the ways in which children learn to write, has been flourishing on many fronts (see, for instance, Flower, 1979; Flower and Hayes, 1980, 1981; Perl, 1979; Britton, 1970; Britton and others, 1975; Krashen, Scarcella, and Long, 1982).

At the same time that this burst of activity in the field of composition was going on, poststructural literary theory was taking root in many of the graduate schools; for example, Jacques Derrida's *Of Grammatology* appeared in 1967. In addition, Wolfgang Iser's *The Implied Reader* appeared in 1974; Stanley Fish's *Is There a Text in This Class?* (1980) collected his major articles from the 1970s; and there were outpourings of books and articles from reader-response and deconstructionist critics, and a covey of new journals such as *Diacritics* and *New Literary Criticism*.

In many ways, the differences among poststructural critics are large, and arguments about those differences have created a lively, if minor, new industry: David Bleich and Norman Holland argue about varieties of subjectivism, and Iser and Fish by no means speak with the same voice as they debate the ways in which readers interact with texts. Indeed, Fish himself speaks with different voices, arguing at length with himself (1980), as is typical of critics for whom texts have lost their traditional moorings, and even debating in public with conservative opponents to the politics of deconstruction. We speak of Derrida at our peril, and we must be sure which manifestation of Roland Barthes or Hillis Miller (early or late) we are quoting if we are to be true to the context of their evolving thought.

Nonetheless, it remains possible to speak of these theorists as a group in certain restricted contexts. They unite in their opposition to the old New Criticism and its belief that meaning can be independent of social contexts and reader response. As we approach the end of the century, much of the force of poststructural criticism seems to be dissipating; its distance from moral, social, and political concerns as well as its arcane language and extreme complexity now appear to be a bit old-fashioned. Like all critical movements, however, it has left behind an essential insight that remains a permanent part of reading theory: opposition to the belief that meaning resides entirely in a text. It is this opposition in particular that has substantial implications for the teaching and evaluation of writing.

Like most traditionally trained readers, I initially found this position hard to understand; I was incredulous that serious critics could allow meaning to escape the control of either the text or the critics. I recall posing a question to Norman Holland during a session on psychological criticism at a Modern Language Association convention (I ventured that I had told a student she had "misread" a play), only to be told by this normally gentle man that I was "unforgivably arrogant." Although Holland is more extreme than most reader-response critics, he was emphasizing his belief that every reader creates a text; his *Five Readers Reading* (1975) comes perilously close to presenting a text as a Rorschach blot, open to whatever the reader may discern. Another school of theorists, the "deconstructionists," have their roots (and language, unfortunately) in French philosophy rather than in psychology; they disavow psychological subjectivism, but nonetheless argue that, at best, the text offers only a guide to the reader, as if it were a musical score that must be performed or (to use a favorite term) "played" in order to become meaningful.

A convenient and inclusive summary of many of the attitudes expressed in these poststructural theories was published in the Fall 1982 issue of *Critical Texts*. In this article, Vincent Leitch captures the destabilization of the text, the peculiar language of the writers, and the relocation of the reader from the outside of the reading process (where the job was to discern the meaning in the text) to the center of the process (where we join with or even replace the author as creator of meaning):

> In the era of post-structuralism, literature becomes textuality and tradition turns into intertextuality. Authors die so that readers may come into prominence. Selves, whether of critic, poet or reader, appear as language constructions—texts. What are texts? Strings of differential traces. Sequences of floating signifiers. Sets of infiltrated signs, dragging along numerous intertextual elements. Sites for the free play of grammar, rhetoric and illusory reference, as Paul de Man puts it. What about the "meaning" or "truth" of the text? The random flights of signifiers across the textual surface, the dissemination of meaning, offers [sic] "truth" under one condition: that the chaotic processes of textuality be willfully regulated, controlled or stopped. Truth comes forth in the reifications of reading. It is not an entity or property of the text. No text utters its truth; the truth lies elsewhere—in a reading. Constitutionally, reading is misreading. Post-structuralism wishes to deregulate controlled dissemination and celebrate misreading [p. 3].

The theory of reading elaborated by Leitch—despite the peculiar use of language and the extremism of the literary criticism—has important implications for the teaching and assessment of writing. There is an undoubted faddism in this year's—or is it last year's?—jargon. As I write, the language in fashion is derived from feminist theory and social constructivism. A little while ago, Saussurian linguistics and French philosophy were all the rage; before that, a combination of Lévi-Strauss anthropology and Jungian mythology shaped a daunting vocabulary, and, not long before that, Freudian and Marxist terminology were absolutely required. We might say that new insights require a new language, or, if we are wicked or jealous, that in literary criticism as in clothing new name brands create an artificial demand for a standard product. But we ought not to let the shifting fashions in terminology disguise from us the radically new conception of reading that is contained in virtually all critical theory emerging over the last three decades.

Thus, we need to regard poststructural criticism and the passage I have just cited as part of a resistance movement to the narrow formalistic reading theory of the "new" critics of the past. The text loses its privileged status as an object of study or reverence and becomes "strings of differential traces" with which the reader can play. The reader has to "misread," because there is no meaning or truth in the text itself—which is a process, not a product. The process of reading itself becomes an object of study, and the examination of the reader's movement through the text in part substitutes for what used to be considered the meaning of the text. The author's intentions, the reader's individual associations with words, the reading situation, and all kinds of other matters outlawed by formal criticism can now be considered as part of the total meaning a reader creates from the text.

In short, these theories of reading have brought a new liberation—some would call it anarchy—into the reading process and placed a much heavier reponsibility on the reader to create meanings that may or may not be present on the page for other readers. The writer is not relieved of responsibility by this process, but now must assume a new responsibility: to create the kind of reader he or she needs for the text being produced. The teacher is also not free to abandon texts to naive readers, though we are forbidden to declare that some misreadings are wrong. Our obligation is to help our students see what other, highly sophisticated readers have made of the text, so that they can enrich the text with various readings.

When we return to the task of reading and evaluating student writing in this new context, we find that this revolution in the concept of reading has an eerily familiar air to it. Where have we

been accustomed to seeing writing that is, to adopt Leitch's terminology, a "chaotic process of textuality"—writing that makes sense
only to a peculiarly sensitive reader, one who must "misread" in
order to understand? Where, as teachers of writing, do we regularly
see texts that can be called "sequences of floating signifiers"? Whatever one can say about literary texts in this regard (and I do not
mean to trivialize the elaborate concepts Leitch alludes to), we can
surely agree that this is a most apt description of the first- draft work
our students hand to us for response and assessment. I do not say
this in mockery. The simple fact is that recent theories of reading—
their definition of textuality and the reader's role in developing the
meaning of a text—happen to describe much of our experience as
we respond to our students' writing. That is, we know that we need
to consider the process of writing as well as the product before us,
and that much of what the student is trying to say is not clearly
conveyed by the words on the page.

The kind of "misreading" that Leitch describes is different
from the misreading inherent in the New Criticism, where all meaning was assumed to lie in the text. When we limit ourselves to what
the student has put down on paper, we function as literalists, ignoring our intuitions of what the student *meant* to say or our predictions of what the student *could* say if he or she followed the best
insights now buried in the present text. This formalistic misreading
of student writing, which pretends to be objective, demands that the
student believe that *our* concept of what was written is what is
"really" there. By comparing the student text with what Nancy
Sommers (whose work I will discuss shortly) calls our "ideal text,"
we appropriate the student's writing, deny the creative impulse that
must drive writing, and turn revision into editing to please the
teacher's concept of the paper. This supposed objectivity makes us
not only less effective teachers but less insightful evaluators, since
we are likely to be content with the equivalent objectivity claimed
by usage testing or simple product measures.

Once we accept the necessity of "misreading" as the post-
structuralists use the term, we tend to be less sure of the objectivity
of our reading and more ready to grant to the student possible
intentions or insights not yet entirely present on the page. Even
more important for our teaching, we can respond to early drafts

with questions rather than with judgment (or invective!), since our aim is to urge the student back into "the chaotic process of textuality" (that is, the flux of ideas behind the writing), where revision occurs. As evaluators, we will tend to read holistically, looking for what is done well, even if it is implicit, rather than analytically, looking for what our model tells us is error.

The recent theories of reading differ most sharply from the old New Criticism in their underlying assumption that meaning is not necessarily identical with expression. This assumption allows us to spend time, as we should in our writing classes, on both invention and revision. We know from our practice as teachers and as writers that the act of invention, the discovery of what we have to say, goes on throughout the writing process; we learn as we write, and successive drafts bring us closer and closer to an understanding of the previously unknown, not to some predetermined coding of the known. As teachers of writing, we seek in the texts our students produce that sense of original vision, that unique perception of new combinations of experiences and ideas that Derrida punningly calls *différance*. Our creative misreading of the drafts we receive, our perception of possibilities as well as product, and our awareness that we see on the page only a "trace" of a mind in action then allow us to ask our students to pursue and refine these traces in revision.

This theory of reading brings reading and writing together as parallel acts, both of them consisting of the making of meaning: the writer seeks to make meaning out of experience, while the reader seeks to make meaning out of a text. Writers, as several critics have reminded us (Iser, 1974; Ong, 1975, Meyers, 1982), create readers as well as texts; the writer needs to keep in mind the "implied reader" designed by the text, and to see this reader as an active partner in creation. Bad prose or ineffective writing often asks us to be people—or readers—that we refuse to accept. Thus, the best composition teachers help their students improve their writing by making them conscious of readers and of the ways that readers interact with their texts.

It is for these reasons, I think, that the most effective teachers of writing are traditionally those who are the most human and the most demanding of their students. Whatever their curriculum, they establish themselves or other defined audiences as live and sympathetic readers willing to participate in the quest for meaning that is writing. The research that Nancy Sommers (1982), Sarah War-shauer Freedman (1987), Peter Elbow and Pat Belanoff (1989), and others have published on teacher response to writing tends to confirm these impressions. They point out that the effective writing class decenters authority, recognizing that every writer is an authority on what he or she is writing. Readers can grant that authority to the writer without necessarily granting it to the text at hand, and therefore they can urge revision without taking ownership of the paper from the writer. (Surely, the most irritating question a writing teacher can hear from students about their revisions is "Is that what you wanted?" Revisions should take them closer to what *they* want.)

Sommers caustically deplores the confusion she has found in the routine paper markings of college writing teachers. These markings almost universally treat the student text as simultaneously a finished product with editing faults and as an unfinished part of the writing and thinking process. It is as if our confusion about evaluation is somehow bound up with a confusion about the nature of the student text, an odd form of literature created for the sole purpose of being criticized. Sommers finds that writing teachers tend to say the same things about student writing, even though the texts in front of them change, as do the writers. "There seems to be among teachers an accepted, albeit unwritten canon for commenting on student texts. This uniform code of commands, requests, and pleadings demonstrates that the teacher holds a licence for vagueness while the student is commanded to be specific" (Sommers, 1982, pp. 152-153).

Sommers has demonstrated that there is a widespread problem in responding to student writing, and her findings are not disputed by more recent scholars. I earlier alluded to this problem as a measurement issue, which it surely is, and suggested that an understanding of the process and materials of systematic measurement of writing would help to remedy the problem. But we need also to see the problem as a reading issue. As teachers of writing begin to apply process theories of reading, they will become much more useful and constructive commentators on student papers. They will see their endless hours of work on these papers as part of the writing process, rather than simply "grading" products, and they will be more ready to invite other readers and different judgments (perhaps from other students) to become part of this process. And when they must function as more or less simple evaluators, as in the grading of a test, they will be more ready to join in a community of readers to share judgment, as is the case in the typical holistic essay or portfolio reading (discussed in Chapter Ten).

Holistic Scoring and the Interpretive Community

The theories of reading posed by poststructuralism, despite their elaborate jargon, tend to support what many of us have been doing intuitively. We have been reading student papers creatively, coaching the writing process, and considering ourselves more than simple graders of products in our classrooms. Sheer humanity and good sense have kept us responsive to much more about our students than just the texts they produce. And we have found ways, such as holistic scoring, to express that fuller vision of our students and their writing.

Those who have been developing process theories of reading have also had to face the pedagogical implications of their theories. Just as holistic methods of assessment allow us to consider writing as more than just the sum of its parts, so Stanley Fish's concept of "the interpretive community" rescues his theory of reading from the anarchy of pure subjectivism and the severe limitations of naive readers. I am linking these two concepts here not merely because a holistic essay or portfolio reading exemplifies Fish's idea in a number of interesting ways but because together they show how some poststructuralist theories and the best composition practice support each other.

Fish's interpretive community is made up of those whose common agreement about how to read texts becomes an agreement about how they will "write" those texts for themselves:

> Interpretive communities are made up of those who share interpretive strategies not for reading (in the conventional sense) but for writing texts, for constitut-

ing their properties and assigning their intentions. In other words, these strategies exist prior to the act of reading and therefore determine the shape of what is read rather than, as is usually assumed, the other way around. . . . This, then, is the explanation both for the stability of interpretation among different readers (they belong to the same community) and for the regularity with which a single reader will employ different interpretive stategies and thus make different texts (he belongs to different communities) [Fish, 1980, p. 171].

This useful concept enables us to return to the problem posed by Nancy Sommers's research. Most composition instructors seem to have a coherent set of powerful assumptions and strategies for approaching (Fish would say writing) student texts. We not only get what we look for, according to this theory, but we actually create what we look for when we read student papers. The grim sameness in much of the teacher commentary collected by Sommers and her fellow researchers suggests that many of us are caught in a pattern of response of our own making, which we then blame on our students. Process-oriented programs for writing teachers are trying to shake up an out-of-date interpretive community. They are suggesting that we should revise what we ask for—and thus what we get— from student writing.

Part of the value of a holistic scoring session stems from exactly this effect on the participants. Such a reading depends on the establishment of a temporary, artificial interpretive community, a group of teachers who agree to agree on scoring standards for that particular test or set of portfolios. The various techniques detailed in Chapter Ten are designed to create such a community, so that the readers will agree on group standards, internalize them, and achieve high rates of scoring reliability. These ad hoc and temporary communities of readers determine the meaning and value of the texts they grade and, in their workaday way, demonstrate the validity of Fish's idea.

Some faculty members object to what they regard as the coercive nature of the interpretive community of readers scoring an essay test. Readers in the world often do not agree, they will argue; so the consistent standards of an essay reading falsify the nature of reader response. Furthermore, the pressure to agree for the sake of reliable scoring reduces the rich variability of reader response and makes some readers use criteria they may not believe in. The forced agreement for the sake of fairness to the students grates on some teachers, who feel compromised or even violated when they must listen to the opinions of others and adjust their grades to those of their colleagues. Other faculty, among whom I count myself, argue that forcing faculty to test their grading standards by comparing them with those of their colleagues is a reasonable and healthy exercise. Besides, agreeing on standards for a particular essay question and student group, for a specific assessment purpose, is not the same as agreeing on more global concepts of writing, which no experienced academic would imagine faculty to be able to achieve with cordiality. There is no question that the interpretive community established for an essay reading does some violence to the fierce independence and total privacy, particularly in grading, that some faculty members treasure and pretend is good for students.

Nonetheless, many readers leave a well-conducted holistic reading buoyed by the professional and human communications that have taken place, and some are able to shift into a new interpretive community for student papers as a result. As they see high levels of agreement among their colleagues, looking for what is well done in writing conceived as an expressive whole, they gain confidence in their own abilities to respond fairly to student writing (and to students) and to discuss openly the evaluation procedures they use. This confidence, in turn, can lead to more open evaluation techniques in their classroooms, with strong implications for the encouragement of revision. Participation in the test- or portfolio-scoring interpretive community thus can radiate into participation in the wider community of professional teachers of writing; this enhanced sense of community, in a lonely and solitary profession, tends for many readers to be one of the most beneficial by-products of holistic readings.

The nature of the community in a holistic scoring session is thus more important than cost-cutting administrators realize. If an unpleasant environment, tyrannical leaders of the reading, or insufficient time inhibit the development of a true community of assent to both the process and the scoring criteria guide, the reading simply breaks down—because the needed community breaks down. This is yet another reason that scoring guides need to be developed by teams of experienced and sensitive readers only after reading through a large sample of student writing to the question in hand; such guides are devices for developing an interpretive community and hence ought never to be imported from other groups. Furthermore, this concept of community helps us see why the most effective chief readers never simply impose standards on a group, or, if they must make decisions about standards, do so only after full and substantial discussion. The readers must "own" scoring standards before they can work together as a reliable team by bringing similar expectations to the papers or portfolios they grade.

An interpretive community of readers drawn together for a holistic scoring has obvious differences from an interpretive community of sophisticated readers of Shakespeare, in Fish's construct. Fish is concerned wholly with the reading of literary texts, while we are looking at the evaluation of student texts. But it is a nice irony that reading theories developed among theoretical literary critics should have a strong objective correlative among practical writing teachers trying to assess writing. The concept of the interpretive community allows us to integrate poststructural reading theory into our teaching and assessment practice. The principal benefit accrues to the students of writing teachers who understand that reading, no less than writing, is a process of the creative imagination, not a mere product to be analyzed.

CHAPTER 5

Responding to
Student Writing

Though there is much debate these days about the most effective methods of responding to student writing, there is a clear consensus about the *least* effective ways to handle student papers. Far too much of what teachers do with student writing is picky, crabby, arbitrary, unclear, and generally unhelpful. Unfortunately, most of us model our teaching behavior on the teachers we had in school and college, and most of us have much more experience with negative or useless responding than with effective patterns. Because of this modeling experience, we need to make conscious decisions about how we will respond to student papers; these conscious decisions will help us avoid merely repeating what some of our teachers did to us.

Purposes and Effects of Responding

The educational purpose of responding to and evaluating student writing ought to be the same as the purpose of the writing class: to improve student writing. (There is another administrative purpose we must serve, to screen out those who do not write well enough, but I will return to that gatekeeper function later.) We seek to improve student writing in many ways, but in responding to writing we have one overriding goal: the student needs to see what works and what does not work in the draft, so that revision can take place. Thus, it does little good for the teacher to judge writing, or to grade writing, without making the kind of response that allows the writer to understand and respect the reasons for that judgment. If the student can simply dismiss the teacher's views as mere personal opinion, the writing will not improve. Writers (like all learners) improve when they can internalize evaluation—that is, when they can themselves see what needs to be changed and how to make those changes. Conversely, if the draft is truly finished (and very few are), the writer needs to see just where its excellence lies, so that it can be repeated.

Clearly, a grade on a paper, with no comment or only a cryptic phrase or two, will not add much to student learning. Sarcastic or harsh comments will allow the student to displace dissatisfaction with the paper (the teacher's intention) with dislike of the teacher, and thus will short-circuit learning. Steady red-marking of all possible errors will bewilder and frustrate students, who cannot profit from an overload of correction; such papers tend to receive a cursory glance from the student before being thrown away. Puzzling abbreviations (k, d, fs) are useless to the student, though they may mean "awkward," "diction," and "fused sentence" to the teacher. Even the generalized positive comments made by well-meaning softies ("nice work," "I enjoyed reading this") frustrate students who want to know what the teacher found "nice" and what made reading enjoyable.

For many of us, in our student days, the writing and submitting of papers was part of the general antagonism inherent in education, the war between student and teacher. We did our best to figure out what the teacher really wanted, often puzzling for hours over obscure directions, or no directions, and using much creativity in what we called "psyching out" the professor. Then we would hand in our papers and hold our collective breaths while we waited for more or less mysterious judgments to appear when the papers were returned. If we made mechanical errors, we could expect offended snarls, but we often received those snarls anyway, for unpredictable reasons. However, we didn't complain much, because in our heart of hearts we knew we were guilty of unknown sins. We didn't pretend to know "grammar," which was an impenetrable puzzle of arbitrary rules of linguistic conduct, and we thought that the teacher did, and would punish us for our unintentional and inevitable violations. It was all part of the war, and, like Marine recruits, we expected random humiliation. The grade was all that really counted, since revision was rarely required or rewarded, so we developed various ways of ignoring the comments a few teachers sometimes provided.

Two recent books have looked closely from different perspectives at these patterns of responding. In *Response to Student Writing* (1987), Sarah W. Freedman reports on an ethnographic study of two successful ninth-grade teachers in the San Francisco Bay Area and on a national survey of two groups, 715 secondary school students (grades 7-12) and 560 successful K-12 writing teachers. College faculty have much to learn from this compact descriptive study of successful school practice, rare though it is. Freedman's consistent optimism about her study sample breaks down when she considers general practice: "The statistics remain dismal about any large-scale change in writing classrooms in this country" (p. 163). Opposed to Freedman's intense practicality is the highly theoretical *Encountering Student Texts* (Lawson, Ryan, and Winterowd, 1989), in which the various contributors attempt to place the reading of student texts in the context of poststructural literary theory— as I did in the previous chapter. Unfortunately, neither of these approaches provides much hope that the destructive patterns of responding that are common in American schools and colleges are likely to improve. My hope in this book is that the power of assessment will induce some of the needed changes.

Since many of these patterns do remain, it is interesting to consider what purposes they served and continue to serve. Unclear assignment, harsh commentary, lack of expected revision, emphasis on grades—all add up to an exclusionary design, with concern only for product. That is, this pattern is one that rewards the academically canny and privileged, who can be depended upon to know already what is being taught. The purpose of the grade and comment is to reward virtue and punish vice, and the moral overtones of the conflict lead naturally to harshness. Students who do not show evidence of good writing are considered socially and morally offensive, wasting the time of the university and the professor. The teacher's red pen symbolizes the scarlet letter, which, on English papers, is rarely an A. It demonstrates the moral offense of the "errors" it excoriates and the pain of the teacher who is forced to mark them. Some teachers maintain this metaphor in their conversation; they will talk of taking a batch of papers home for the weekend and "bleeding all over them."

What this pattern most obviously lacks is a concern for writing as learning, for the teaching of writing as supportive of learning. What it unconsciously enforces is the gatekeeper function of schooling, rewarding the privileged and excluding almost all of those whose parents are of the wrong class, income, or national origin. Teachers who unrepentantly continue this pattern claim that they are upholding "standards," as if it were somehow wrong to help students learn.

The concern for standards is real and important, but it should not serve as an excuse to indulge in negative responding patterns or mere social selection. An essential part of the writing teacher's job is to teach and enforce standards of performance that will allow the student to succeed in college and beyond. This is the gatekeeper function of writing courses, the socializing function of writing instruction, as I called it in Chapter One, an institutional (rather than educational) matter that makes many teachers uncomfortable. Some large state universities make freshman composition virtually a wing of the admissions office, expecting the staff to winnow out the unqualified, so that university resources will not be expended on teaching them. The moral dilemma such a situation poses is difficult indeed, and every teacher will resolve the conflict between teaching and selecting in his or her own way; but this conflict should not lead to the use of assessment and responding only as an administrative selecting tool. Nor should it lead to a narrow definition of writing as a mere test of certain skills that the institution may define as necessary.

The uses of writing are so large—as a tool for learning new material, as a means of power in a verbal world, as a way to understand complex ideas, as a route to understanding the self, and so on—that we do not want to narrow our purpose as writing teachers merely to judging and enforcing group standards. We must accept some responsibility for standards, for the sake of the institution and for the students who will be moving through it and required to fulfill its demands. But if we accept the profound value of writing and its many uses, responding to writing becomes extraordinarily complex, calling for some special thoughtfulness on the teacher's part.

The pressures of time and the force of tradition often keep us from thinking through the purposes and effects of responding to a particular set of student papers. Most teachers proceed to "mark" a set of papers without much consideration of options. They read each paper through, red pen in hand, marking mechanical errors as they go, writing comments of one sort or another in the margins, and concluding with a grade and a comment justifying the grade at the end. Such a procedure can give sensitive and supportive help to students, since it demonstrates a careful reader's responses, but it does not make sense to respond to every assignment in the same way.

Must every assignment be graded, or be graded on the same scale? Must the teacher read and mark every word of every piece of writing done in a writing class? What is the point of marking careless mechanical errors on drafts that will be revised or that are not designed for a demanding audience? Are we taking ownership of the papers away from the students by our markings and asking the students to say what we want instead of what they want? Are we sufficiently aware of what recent literary theory has taught us about the problematics of reading texts, including student texts? What are some useful ways of involving students themselves in the evaluation and response that every writer needs? How can we structure our comments, and student peer comments, so that students will want to revise their texts for their own sake, rather than for ours? Questions such as these ought to arise before the red ink begins to flow. The answers to such questions should make the immense amount of time spent with student papers more productive, more interesting, and (perhaps) less time-consuming.

Responding to Drafts

Responding to writing does not begin when the teacher starts to read the students' essays; it starts much earlier, at the point when the assignment is made; a careful assignment makes the task of responding to the papers it elicits easier for the instructor and more useful for the student. The teacher may discuss the assignment and ask the students to go through some prewriting exercises; examples of previous papers on the assignment may be distributed and analyzed. Surely this is a valuable response. But more valuable still is the presentation by the student (to the class or to a small peer group) of early ideas for writing.

The advantages of making such presentations are obvious: the student must gain ownership of the ideas presented, must get to work early on the task, and must come up with ways of demonstrating the major concept of the paper and making it interesting to others. The response to these presentations must be a delicate combination of support, encouragement, and rigor. If the topic is not going to work, or is unworkable in the form presented, this is the time to help the student see the problem, when there is enough time to change. If the evidence is not convincing or is lacking, the student needs to hear that from the teacher or from the peer group. But responses at this early stage need not be harsh, since their only function is to help the student do good work. No grades and no penalties for mechanical errors (the twin nightmares of many students) are imposed at this stage. Good responding practice will begin with class discussion of the assignment, continue with class or group discussion of individual plans for the assignment, and then move into a consideration of steps for revision.

We may talk about writing as discovery and revision and even schedule due dates for work in progress; but unless we build respect for revision into our evaluation of writing, our students will not believe us. If we continue to give a single grade for the finished (or not-so-finished) writing product, we are in fact saying that the product is the only thing we value. Therefore, the logic for rewarding the work in progress is compelling, and not only for the reasons I have been stating. Term papers, and student essays in general, are among the least valuable products in a world of waste paper; only a tiny percentage of them are saved, and only a minuscule percentage are published. They do serve as products to be graded, but the only real reason for their production is as testimony to student learning. In many cases, that learning is better measured through the steps of production than through the final formal product alone.

This is a delicate balance, for too much grading simplifies responding and irritates everyone. Some teachers give grades on one kind of scale for drafts, bibliographies, and the like—say, a numerical scale similar to that used in many holistic scoring sessions (typically, 6 high to 1 low); the final draft then can be graded on the usual A to F scale. Other teachers, concerned about the imposition of authority and ownership implied by constant grading, use peer group responses and a simple check-off system to note the completion of parts of the task. It all depends on the goals of the course and the assignment. But the central point remains: any composition instruction that attempts to inculcate good writing habits should both require and respond to stages of the discovery and revision process.

Whatever the grading or responding system, the comments on drafts should focus principally on the conception and organization of the paper. There is no point in spending much time on mechanical errors, aside, perhaps, from a note reminding the student that the final copy needs to be edited: "Make sure to clean up the copy after you revise, so that readers will be able to attend to and respect what you have to say." Premature editing is the enemy of revision; some writers pay so much attention to spelling and punctuation that they neglect to attend to what they are saying. The basic job of draft writing is to discover and develop the subject, not to worry about mechanics.

Experienced teachers have developed various schemes for reading early drafts and concentrating on their ideas, development, and structure. Some teachers skim the work before commenting, attending particularly to the opening and closing paragraphs; sometimes the first sentence of each paragraph will give a clue to the structure, or lack of structure, of the paper. It is always useful to identify the central or controlling idea, circle it, and comment on its interest and possibilities. At this stage, questions are more useful to students than are assertions. Instead of writing "coherence" or "coh" in the margin, we might say, "I have underlined the two separate ideas you are pursuing in this paragraph; can you connect them? If not, which one do you want to focus on?" Or "Your point in this paragraph makes good sense, but it seems to conflict with what you said in your opening. How do the two ideas relate?"

Finally, if we want students to attend to and profit from our reading, we will apply two commonsense rules: we will not overburden the students with more commentary than they can handle, and we will find positive and encouraging ways to suggest improvements.

Authority, Responsibility, and Control

One major difference between the teaching of writing and the teaching of other subjects has to do with the role of the teacher. In most college courses, the teacher demonstrates authority (through expertness in the field), is responsible for the substance of what students are to learn, and maintains control over the course. However, each of these concepts operates differently in the writing course.

The teacher, of course, continues to exercise the authority that derives from knowledge and experience. The teacher knows more about writing than the students do and has, of course, done more of it. The teacher is certainly a more practiced and skillful reader and is able to apply that skill to the reading of student texts. Therefore, the teacher has the authority to structure the syllabus, make assignments, and evaluate student writing. But the students will not learn much about writing if they are merely passive recipients of the teacher's knowledge. Many studies support the need for active participation by students in the writing class if effective learning is to take place. Since the students must think their own thoughts, invent, discover, write, and revise, they must themselves develop some kind of authority.

Thus, the teacher must be willing to share some of the authority that comes inevitably with the instructor's role. If they are to write with a real voice, students must believe that they have, or can gain, authority over their subjects. When they write about personal experiences, that authority usually comes naturally enough: they are the only ones who really know what happened, and they have the right to speculate on what it means. But that tenuous sense of authority tends to disappear in the face of analytical assignments or printed sources. Frequently, students will merely describe what the assignment asks them to evaluate; or they will summarize or quote someone's argument, even though the assignment asks them to relate it to their own or someone else's ideas. Adolescent assertiveness about everything turns, in college, to a trained unwillingness to take a stand or to claim authority before the "expert" professor or the printed source. Therefore, the writing teacher must find ways to help students understand the kind of authority all writers can claim (or earn). Some students simply cannot write for professors who assert, or seem to claim, too much authority over too many aspects of the material. I remember well a diligent student's hesitant question after I gave the class an assignment to write about a Renaissance poet: "Are we supposed to like Skelton?" Like many passive students, she had given all authorial authority (note the relation of the two words) to the teacher, or, more likely, I had unwittingly laid claim to so much authority that she saw no space to assert any of her own. Until I was able to convince her that her response to the poem was important and could not come from outside, she was voiceless.

Many conscientious writing teachers not only deprive their students of the authority all writers need but also unintentionally assume responsibility for the papers their students produce. The most obvious sign of this shifting of responsibility from the student to the teacher occurs when the student tries to revise an early draft in the light of the teacher's comments. Almost invariably, the student will not change anything that the teacher left alone; all revisions focus on the corrections suggested by the teacher. The result is often very odd, sometimes considerably worse than the original. The revised portions of the paper are often much better, particularly if the teacher's comments led the student to rethink and reorganize the best ideas (as comments should). But the paper as a whole is now out of balance, with the original untouched portions, which seemed all right in the draft, now in need of work. When we say this, the student is often outraged: "You saw nothing wrong with it before!" In the student's eyes, and perhaps in our own, we have become responsible for some, or all, of the paper. "Is this what you wanted?" we may hear, as if it were now *our* paper.

The attitude we take in our comments is crucial here. We must convey to student writers that responsibility and ownership remain with them and that they need to do more than merely respond to our comments. We ought not to assume the role of editor for the student (marking every error is a common mistake, leading to student frustration or apathy in the face of too much red ink), nor ought we to tell the student what the paper should do. We should rather express any problems we have with the paper, point out the questions that the paper raises in our minds, and ask the writer to attempt to resolve these problems. We should always be friendly, even when we are feeling overburdened and crabby, and we should always find something to praise and encourage. At most, we might suggest some options or alternatives, but we must refrain from taking over the paper, even if we are convinced that we know just what it ought to be doing. As I suggested earlier, pointed questions are often more effective than assertions: "This seems to be your central idea; why does it first appear here, in the next-to-last paragraph?" "The second half of this paper seems to be on a different topic than the first half; which topic do you want to focus on?" "This original idea opens up exciting possibilities; can you find a way to examine them?"

A sensible posture to take toward drafts is to comment only on a few central matters: the ideas, the structure, the author's perspective or voice, for example. Certainly, sound pedagogy suggests that all comments contain something positive. Perhaps a comment about mechanics at the end ("The paper has sentence errors that ought not to appear in the final draft") might be useful in some cases. But good teaching is clear about goals; therefore, if we assume that substantial rewriting of the current draft will take place, we ought not to fuss about the spelling of words that may well disappear. We need to encourage risk taking in drafts, the trying on of ideas and arguments that may not work out or that may turn out to be very exciting.

Finally, we need to have a healthy portion of humility in the face of student texts, even of student texts we have trouble respecting. After two decades of poststructural theory, we can no longer imagine that the text is a simple object or that our reading of it is somehow objective or neutral. We must be aware that the value of a text is negotiated, culture-bound, located in social structures. We come to student texts as we come to any other texts, out of our own positions as people of a particular class, color, gender, age, and background. We respond as sensitively as we can, and we must finally record our evaluations on grade sheets; but the arrogance, arbitrariness, and ethnocentricity of some teachers of the past might well be left behind along with their lessons in elocution and penmanship.

Collaborative Writing

In one sense, all writing is collaborative: every writer needs some kind of audience, some conversation, some reading, some responding. The peer groups that are now part of many writing classes serve as sounding boards for initial ideas, responders to drafts, even editors for presentation copies of final drafts. The picture of the writer as a solitary genius, holed up in an attic, emerging on occasions waving a manuscript that expresses his or her inner self, has not been a useful one for writing instruction. In fact, much of the writing done outside the university (and, increasingly, in the university) is now actually accomplished by teams. Collaboration in the writing of reports and papers has become a more and more common method of producing texts.

Collaboration offers special challenges and possibilities to the writing class. Some teachers will regularly establish teams to produce papers: the teams will allot portions of the tasks involved to their members, compile the drafts, and submit a single paper for evaluation as written by the team. The teachers who espouse this procedure claim that student involvement is much higher than in more traditional writing classes and that the results are much more satisfactory. Classes using the computer as a normal means of text production slip naturally into the collaborative mode, as an extension of networking and regular commenting on electronic texts. In some fields, such as business or science, collaborative writing is becoming so much the standard that writing courses that ignore team production seem quaint and old-fashioned. But establishing a curriculum and writing assignments for collaborative groups requires a complete rethinking of the writing course.

Responding to collaborative writing offers challenges that have not yet been well resolved. Is the writing workshop approach, with teams going about their writing and responding to the work of other teams, too unstructured for college writing courses? Will students leaving such a class be well prepared for the individual production of term papers, theses, or other college work? Is it fair to give a high grade to each member of a team if only some of its members actually did the writing, however excellent? Is it fair to give a low grade to each member of a team if some excellent writers have been insufficiently influential to determine the quality of the team paper? Can the team members themselves give different grades to their own members?

Like other innovations in writing instruction (such as portfolios), collaborative writing offers unusual opportunities to inventive teachers. In the course of the next decade, accumulated experience with this mode of teaching will help us find ways to meet the challenges of a shifting emphasis from individual to group writing, challenges now only dimly emerging. With the increasing use of computers for writing, we are likely to see more and more collaborative writing in all composition classes as time goes on.

Using Student Response Groups

Whether or not we choose to allow or require collaborative writing in class, we might well consider using student response groups as a way of expanding the audience for student work beyond the teacher's desk. When the teacher is the only audience, the students inevitably personalize the response; instead of working to improve their writing, they will work to please the teacher, which is a much less valuable goal. And instead of internalizing writing standards, they will wait for the teacher's judgment before assessing their own drafts.

Although the basic reason for establishing student response groups is to provide this additional audience, these groups are valuable for other reasons as well. Most students feel comfortable working in small groups and getting to know each other; they also learn more from each other than we suspect. Students may be used to hearing, and ignoring, teacher complaints about mechanics, but they have to attend when some of their friends say, "This is really a mess; I just can't read it." As they explain their ideas and their evidence to a small group, they often find themselves changing their preliminary views; as they tell each other why they like or don't like drafts, they are forced to use the vocabulary of writing assessment in an active way. Even large lecture classes profit from some small-group work, which enforces the importance of active rather than passive understanding.

Since some students may find group work initially uncomfortable, we need to establish the goals and procedures of student response groups in advance. And we cannot assume that students from all cultures will respond to group evaluation as positively as most American students do; students from some cultures find group work very threatening, even bewildering, if their culture forbids verbal criticism because of the need to save face. Simply asking groups to read and respond to each other's work may lead to useless ("I really like this") or destructive comments. Unless they are instructed otherwise, most students will follow the patterns they have learned in school and will focus on mechanics or other real or perceived mistakes. They need to be instructed to focus on positive and useful responses (for example, "What is most successful?"), and they cannot do too many things at once ("Attend to these three questions").

Different teachers, and different teaching styles, will use small groups in different ways. For teachers using collaborative writing, small-group work begins with the assignment itself, as the group members parcel out different tasks among themselves. The group is itself at the core of the writing process and must meet regularly to assess progress and quality of its own work. When the assignment is completed, the group itself receives the grade.

Other teachers will use student response groups as part of a force for what literary theorists call "reader-response criticism." This theory assumes that readers create as well as respond to a text. Thus, it is essential for writers to hear what a variety of readers perceive as they make their way through the text. The writer must not be defensive or argue for his or her intentions; the writer's job is to be silent and take notes as members of the group detail their movement through the piece of writing and their reactions. If the writer would like to produce a different set of reactions, revision is called for.

Still other teachers ask student groups to function descriptively: to describe to the author what they see as the controlling idea of the piece of writing, what its assumptions and arguments are, and how they understand it to be organized. Others focus on evaluation, with the group emphasizing suggestions for revision. And some teachers use the group simply as a means of socializing students into the college community of writers.

Anne Ruggles Gere, in her illuminating discussion of the theory behind writing groups, argues that "learning to write means learning to use the language of a given community, and writing groups provide a form in which individuals can practice and internalize this language" (1987, p. 96), since "literacy does not function in isolation" (p. 123). The forty pages of bibliography appended to the small volume are testimony to the continuing depth of interest at all levels in writing groups.

Here is an example of the use of groups for a limited purpose: to give a response to the writers of a personal experience essay. The first assignment in Chapter Two—which asked students to describe a character from childhood, using detail that will convey an emotion—is ideal for group discussion. In each group, which should not exceed five students (four is better), the students can be instructed to read the other students' papers and to write down the emotion that each writer evokes; each student should specify one word or phrase in each paper that evokes the emotion most clearly. After everyone has read the papers, each writer calls for discussion of his or her paper, writing down the responses of the group without being defensive. The group should not spend much time hearing what the writer "really meant to say"; the writer needs to hear what the group has heard the paper say. The inevitable comparisons and dissonance in the group give the writer a clear sense of the relative success of the paper and of possible revisions.

Each assignment and each draft lead to different possibilities for group work. Sometimes, instead of a group of four, pairs of students can be used. Teachers may want to reshuffle the groups, so that patterns of response do not become fixed or too personalized. And they may well want to develop a sensible mix of group work with class work, just as they will probably rely on groups more heavily for drafts than for presentation copies of student writing.

Teachers with a heavy student load may want to use group responses for early drafts and to devote their own reading time to more finished work. If the campus is computerized, teachers may use computer groups as well as class groups, and may be able to insist that drafts be sent through spelling checkers or subjected to group editing before they are submitted to the teacher.

Teachers unaccustomed to writing groups sometimes imagine that students will be unwilling to share their work with others or that they will value only the teacher's comments. Rare is the American student who cannot work in groups because of personality difficulties, and though students from other cultures may present special problems, faculty who have begun to use groups find that most students are more ready to revise and to meet deadlines if they know that other students will read their work. Student responses may not be professional, but under professional guidance they can be helpful and less threatening than teacher responses. And students are less tolerant of inflated or pretentious language than many teachers are; a student comment of "cut the bull" can serve as a healthy check on the usual student perception of what "English teachers like to read." Most important of all, the student response group offers a range of responses to the student paper, making it seem more important and more worthy of attention. Despite my own skill at reading and responding to student papers (which I, at least, value highly), my own students invariably report at the end of the term that the most valuable activity in class is the group work they regularly undertake.

The Presentation Copy

We need not ask that every paper students write be revised and edited to a high level of polish. Some students, of course, will have little trouble editing their final drafts to near perfection, but most students find this an onerous and frustrating task, particularly if they did not grow up in homes where the school dialect is spoken. If we have many students for whom the preparation of final drafts is a major burden, we may want to specify the level of polish necessary for each assignment. After all, most of us are content with less than top performance in many aspects of our lives, even though we might be able to do a first-rate job when it is absolutely necessary. Some teachers feel that every paper should demonstrate the highest level of polish and that such a demand shows high standards, even though few students will meet the demand. But I think it is equally demanding, and more sound pedagogically, to specify that certain papers will require high polish, and then to really insist upon it; meanwhile, other papers, particularly drafts, can exist and succeed in less perfect form.

If we can be content with some work from each student that never enters final draft, which we could grade for stated criteria that do not stress high polish, we can be particularly demanding of the work that will reach presentation level. Our students need to know what is involved in presentation-level work, including standard citation form and clean mechanics, and they need enough practice in producing work at this level so that they—and we—know they can turn it out when needed. But they also need to know that writing is much more than editing and that clean copy is not equivalent to good writing. When the paper is to reach presentation level of polish, we can use all of our editing skill to work with the students; our responses will be detailed in every way. And we will ask students to keep producing drafts until the writing has achieved the required high level of polish.

As the student paper moves through prewriting and drafts, the teacher must keep responsibility with the writer, even as student groups and the teacher respond to the sequence of drafts. Editing for high polish and grading of final products may occur; but responding to student writing includes the entire range of support that teachers, acting as coaches more than as judges, can give their students. The result of such teaching will be students more ready to revise, more willing to see writing as a form of critical thinking, more aware of internalized assessment criteria, and more ready to be responsible for their own learning.

CHAPTER 6

Using Portfolios

A portfolio is a folder or binder containing examples of student work. For generations, faculties in the fine arts have used portfolios for assessment and grading; the final examination in a class in drawing, or painting, or architectural design, for example, will often require students to submit a portfolio of their work, which will be displayed, critiqued, and graded. More recently, writing teachers and writing programs have used portfolios for assessment; and many schools and colleges have begun using them for various purposes: screening students for advancement, assessing the outcomes of general education programs, evaluating teachers, providing students with employment dossiers, and so forth. This chapter summarizes the strengths and weaknesses of portfolios and looks at a number of possible uses of them in writing programs.

When used for assessing a student's writing, portfolios can include numerous examples of that writing, produced over time, under a variety of conditions. Unlike multiple-choice tests, they can show the student's actual writing performance; unlike essay tests, they can provide several different kinds of writing and rewriting, without time constraints and without test anxiety. Whereas most evaluation instruments provide a snapshot of student performance, the portfolio can give a motion picture, a metaphor made popular by Patricia Hutchings of the American Association for Higher

Education. Some programs allow (or require) revised drafts to be included with the first draft, so that students can appear at their best and can demonstrate to themselves and their readers what they have learned to do. And if the portfolio also must include a self-assessment essay, students wind up taking responsibility for their own learning. (In Resource B, that essay is called a reflective letter.)

Portfolios are still relatively untried for writing assessment, but early reports from experiments are very positive: students usually find the portfolios inherently meaningful and worthwhile—a record of work they have done and want to keep. They do not feel this way about tests. At the end of the term, only a few students will come around to pick up their final exams (if they are made available), but virtually all will make an appointment to retrieve a writing portfolio. Why? Exams are by their nature external, usually a mere testing device for the benefit of the teacher and the institution. But students *own* their portfolios, particularly if they have revised and tended them for months or even years.

Portfolios pose problems for assessment because of their sheer bulk and the uncontrolled conditions under which they are produced. The mass of portfolios can be daunting. Even twenty or twenty-five portfolios at the end of one writing class form an intimidating pile of papers, over 100,000 words to read. Several classes or an entire freshman composition program multiplies the quantity, of course. And when, as at some institutions, each graduating student is required to submit a portfolio compiled throughout the college years, the job of reading and evaluating these portfolios is a truly massive undertaking.

The uncontrolled conditions for portfolios pose another set of problems. Since the production of the portfolio contents cannot be closely supervised, validity problems are inevitable: a weak student with no outside responsibilities may produce a more substantial portfolio than a better writer who happens to be single parent supporting a family; or students may get help of various sorts (from consultations in the writing center to purchased papers from unscrupulous commercial firms), so it may be hard to know just what we are assessing. If the portfolios include responses to assignments from other teachers, we may not understand the context of some classes or the assumptions behind the particular work (although we might ask students to provide this information); we may also be evaluating the assignments as well as the responses, since better assignments tend to elicit better writing.

Teachers who use portfolios, then, must maximize the advantages of this method of assessment while minimizing the disadvantages. Those who can perform this balancing act will find that portfolios are the most valuable means available for combining assessment with teaching.

The Teacher-Graded Class Portfolio

When portfolios are used in a single writing class, each student is expected to keep all drafts, revisions, and presentation copies in a folder, as a record of the term's work. The student brings the portfolio to conferences or to the writing center, and for the final "exam" is asked to revise the most interesting papers in the portfolio and to write a self-assessment as a foreword to it.

Such a portfolio has important advantages for the student in a writing course. In the first place, the portfolio exemplifies the teacher's definition that writing is a process, not merely a product. Although the portfolio contains a series of products, as a whole it is evidence of the student's writing process. In a good portfolio, some papers may be revised three or four times, and even the least talented writer will notice the changes from early drafts to presentation copies. The portfolio also demonstrates that the students are really writing for themselves, not just for the teacher or for the grade; almost all students take pride in the portfolio, want to preserve it at the end of the term, and are impressed at the quantity (if not the quality) of the work produced. Furthermore, if the portfolio includes, as it should, some in-class writing, revisions, and a self-assessment, it also protects students from the temptations of plagiarism; because the portfolio contains so much work that must be genuine, anything that is not genuine is usually obvious to both student and teacher.

Teachers have many options for assessing the portfolio. They might, for example, pay particular attention to one or two papers with multiple revisions, to give a "process grade" on the student's ability to improve from draft to draft; such a grade rewards "effort"

by students who have not yet learned how to produce excellent final products. Perhaps that process grade can be combined with grades on the products, to give a fairer term grade than one based wholly on final drafts. Again, teachers might allow the students to restrict the portfolio to a few papers they like best, or to several essential papers, along with their notes and drafts. The point is to promote student ownership of the portfolio, even though the teacher must finally grade the work, and to demonstrate that the writing grade depends on more than a finely edited product. Some experienced teachers even refuse to grade the portfolio at all, though that strikes me as an unfortunate loss of a powerful assessment tool.

Since the portfolio will probably include papers in the process of revision, the terminology for student drafts calls for some thought. Many teachers will ask for a "first draft" and a "final draft" without clarifying what those terms mean. The student usually thinks of the first draft as a rough set of notes, whereas the teacher usually wants the first draft to be what the student thinks of as the final draft—that is, an unedited but coherent piece of writing. Because of these problems with terminology, I suggest using more precise terms. For example, the term *zero draft* might be used for the prose that emerges from the student's rough notes; after revision, this draft then becomes a *discovery draft*, which usually requires reorganization, focus, and development. Typically, for instance, the discovery draft will not state its principal concept until the next-to-last paragraph; the student has discovered the real topic by writing about it. An experienced writer will realize this, throw away everything preceding that paragraph, and produce a new draft with that paragraph as the opening. But students hate to throw away anything and need the help and encouragement of a professional to see that the function of the discovery draft has been fulfilled if the writer has come to discover what he or she really wants to say.

The draft that revises the discovery draft will normally display the development and organization that a college paper needs, but this *final draft* is often much in need of editing. Some teachers will delay editing comments to this stage and, for a few selected papers, require a *presentation copy*, with careful editing and a high degree of polish, as a revision of the final draft.

But we do need to allow for different writing processes. Not every student—or every professional, for that matter—will follow this typical pattern. Some writers seem able to compose a series of initial drafts in their heads, and these writers turn out first drafts that need little revision; other writers may find that editing is not the tedious last clean-up stage of writing but instead is the spur that leads to revision. Such exceptions—and they are rare—may not be able to meet a portfolio requirement for all stages of a particular writing task. The "writing process" is a concept, not a formula, and different writers, or the same writer on different occasions, may find a variety of routes to the finished paper.

The portfolio allows a teacher to review several different essays that have gone through a series of stages, each of which calls for different grading criteria. The zero draft requires the student to collect thoughts, references, and experiences that stake out the area for the paper. The discovery draft revises the zero draft with the goal of finding out what is really interesting and worth saying about the area. The final draft focuses and develops that idea as fully as time and talent allow. The presentation copy revises the final draft for a demanding audience that expects the developed, interesting idea to be expressed with standard sentence structure, spelling, punctuation, and footnote form, and that will appreciate control of tone, metaphor, and diction.

Although not every paper in the portfolio needs to include these stages (or other possible stages in a variety of writing processes), the portfolio is the only assessment device that can evaluate a student's ability to understand revision processes. We may talk about revision (we usually do), but portfolios enable us to support that talk by collecting and evaluating several papers in multiple drafts. If the portfolio were to include only a collection of final drafts, we would lose this opportunity to document the revisions that show what the students have learned about the writing process.

Course portfolios do leave teachers with a great heap of folders to get through at the end of the term. But no one demands that they reread every word of every draft of every paper in every portfolio. They must read selectively, and since they have come to know the students pretty well, they can decide where to invest their limited time. This is not cheating: the portfolios are part of the course, prepared so that the student will have a record of work to be proud of. "Did I really write all this?" a typical student will ask, with some bemusement. "You sure did," the teacher and the portfolio will reply. "And some of it is really good, better than anything you have done before. Take it home and be proud of it."

The Team-Graded Course Portfolio

Because of the value of portfolio assessment, some colleges use it for assessment outside the individual classroom. In these colleges, the student prepares a portfolio for evaluation and presents the portfolio to an assessment team that includes faculty members who have not taught the student's writing class. The team might be as simple as the course instructor and one other member of the composition staff or as elaborate as a course review board that includes the composition director and several experienced teachers. This team then evaluates the portfolio, and that evaluation will play an important (perhaps even predominant) part in determining the student's grades in class or even advancement to upper class standing.

This procedure has several clear advantages. Most important, the class teacher is relieved of full responsibilty for grading and thus becomes more a coach than a judge, helping the student prepare the best portfolio possible for the assessment that is to come. The student comes to see the teacher as a supporter rather than as an adversary. The teacher's comments and grades show the student how other people will probably grade the portfolio. Rather than giving a failing grade, the teacher can merely indicate that a portfolio with papers of this quality probably will not pass. Any system that turns the teacher into a valued coach is likely to assist in student learning and, incidentally, make the teacher's life much more pleasant.

Students will sometimes find the unknown portfolio team even more threatening than the (partly) known course instructor and will resist team grading; everyone is likely to be suspicious of outside evaluators, naturally enough. And some teachers may initially be uneasy about losing some of their power of assessment. If the assessment team works in secret and if the results are handed down as law without appeal, these concerns will grow and eventually undermine the entire portfolio plan. But if the members of the composition staff work together to define the portfolios and the grading standards, the classroom teachers should find the operation supportive rather than threatening. And once they see the portfolio assessment team as "us" rather than "them," they can allay student concerns by their confidence in and support of the grading standards. Those responsible for the portfolio team need to consider how to maintain the genuine collegiality of the program.

Furthermore, the imposition of a team grade for portfolios can establish standards that reflect the institution rather than the individual teacher. Although most writing programs make attempts to normalize standards, they usually have only a slight influence on how teachers grade. Every student knows that some teachers are hard, others easy, the rest in-between. But with team grading, those harmful differences are evened out, since everyone works to achieve fair and consistent grading of the portfolios, whoever the class teacher may be. To be sure, some teachers will be more effective than others, thus advantaging their students. But the enforcement of reliable standards for grading will help less effective teachers and their students improve, since all students will be subject to the same consistent and appropriate criteria.

Of course, that impersonalization of standards is a disadvantage of staff grading, for it may also work some injustice in particular cases. Many teachers feel uncomfortable with grades given to their students by others, particularly by others who do not know the students they are grading. Perhaps the excellent student whose work dropped sharply in quality because of a divorce or a parent's death ought to be given special consideration. And perhaps the good work of the talented writer should not receive as high a grade as it appears to deserve, since the teacher knows that even a little revision from that student would have produced truly superior work. Every department contemplating team assessment of portfolios will need to decide how the team grade will be related to the course grade. Perhaps the portfolio grade could be made a set percentage of the term grade, which would remain the responsibility of the class teacher. Or the portfolio assessment team could give a pass-fail grade to the portfolio and leave the letter grade for the course to the teacher.

Decisions also will have to be made about procedures for scoring. The most prominent procedural issues are (1) content of the

portfolio, (2) treatment of the original grades and comments on portfolio contents (whether to retain or remove them), (3) scoring
procedures, (4) criteria for scoring reliably, and (5) appeals
procedures.

Content of the Portfolio

When an assessment team is evaluating portfolios, the number of
items in the portfolios must be limited, so that they can be read in
a reasonable amount of time; but the papers must represent what
matters for the course, as defined by the composition staff. What is
to be included and why? Before that question can be answered, some
decisions must be made about the purpose of the evaluation.

One such purpose might be to determine or strongly influence the student's grade in the course; the teacher might not be
permitted to vary more than, say, one grade from the assessment
team's portfolio grade. For this purpose, the composition staff's
consensus about what determines a student's grade for the course
will shape the decision about the required content of the portfolio.
Perhaps the portfolio should contain the first paper in several
drafts, the last paper in several drafts, two examples of in-class
writing, and a self-assessment. Perhaps the portfolio should contain
only the three best papers the student has written. Perhaps all that
is needed is the research paper, including all notes and drafts. Or
the team members may want to see specific kinds of writing and to
apply particular standards to that writing, so that specific papers
may be needed. The grading and selection criteria must be written
out well in advance and distributed to all students and faculty. A
few sample or composite portfolios, exemplifying a variety of
grades, should be available in the library to anyone interested (with
suitable care for privacy issues).

Another purpose might be to evaluate the freshman course,
or an entire curriculum, rather than individual students. How
much writing is in fact being required, how is it being responded
to, and what are the standards? For this purpose, the porfolios
should be as complete as possible, but only a sample of them need
be evaluated. Every student will file a full portfolio of all work done
in the course, and an administrative assistant will randomly select

a few from each class, concealing the instructors' names (unless everyone agrees otherwise), and the assessment team will read without preconceptions to find out what these portfolios indicate is going on in the course as a whole.

Still other purposes will require different definitions of what the portfolio must contain. The essential principles to keep in mind are the need to match purposes of the assessment to the curriculum—what is actually being taught—and then to portfolios and to be clear about just what is being measured. Remember, a portfolio is not a test; it is only a collection of materials. Those materials must be specified, and an evaluation procedure must then follow, if the operation is to make sense.

Treatment of Grades and Comments

If the portfolio is to be used for the generation of a new grade, it seems fair to remove all the comments and grades of the teacher (or to include a copy of the original before the teacher responded to it). Otherwise, the new grade will surely be influenced by the original grade and by the comments written on the paper. However, the removal of grades and comments entails an enormous amount of clerical work, either in collecting unmarked originals or in erasing or obliterating what the original teacher wrote; moreover, the assessment team will lose the expertness of the original comments, which reflect the class context and the details of the assignment. (The actual assignment as handed out is, of course, a necessary attachment to each paper, but it is often only a skeleton of the task in context.) For essays based on reading material, this expertness may be crucial, unless the members of the assessment team read all the material assigned. If the course allows a wide range of reading materials, it may be impossible for the assessment team to know every piece of reading, and instructor's comments may then be necessary.

Scoring procedures

Experience with essay tests has shown that reliable readings can take place only at controlled sessions, with all evaluators reading at the same time and place, under direction of a chief reader. This experience may not hold true for portfolios (they are still relatively untried for assessment in writing), but it probably will, since the scoring of portfolios seems in every way even more difficult than the scoring of essays. Thus, if the evaluation is to be consistent and therefore meaningful, careful planning of a scoring session will be necessary.

Such planning involves many details, including facilities, time management, funding, and personnel. Sample portfolios, illustrating different levels of performance, and scoring guides will need to be prepared in advance. Each portfolio should be read twice, with discrepant scores given a resolution reading. The size of the portfolios and the complexity of the scoring will determine how fast the reading can go. A small sample scored in advance will give a reasonable estimate of the pace. For example, if each reader can score five portfolios an hour, forty readers will require (after a training period) two hours to score two-hundred portfolios twice.

Informal procedures, such as parceling out the portfolios to faculty to take home and treat as they wish, may seem less burdensome, but such procedures merely disguise the nature of the work and make it unreliable. Sometimes it seems too much trouble to work for consistency in scoring, particularly when the results may be as crude as a pass-fail score. But unreliable results are unfair and unprofessional. Assessment worth doing is worth doing well—that is, in a fair way that gives dependable results.

Criteria for Scoring Reliably

Again, the experience of essay testing suggests that considerable effort will be required to get all readers to use the same scoring criteria. Besides developing a scoring guide and compiling sample portfolios, the composition staff must decide how the various components of the portfolio will be weighted. Are the same criteria to be applied to first-draft, in-class writing as to a research paper that has gone through multiple drafts? If not, and good sense suggests not, how are the criteria to be applied? Though these are difficult problems, they tend to be manageable in particular cases, as long as they are dealt with in advance. The research on portfolio grading conducted at the University of Michigan suggests that such matters as distrust of the authenticity of revision or premature decision making by raters—sometimes as early as the first page of the portfolio—must be discussed and monitored (Hamp-Lyons and Condon, 1993). But such difficult labor pays off for the staff and the curriculum as well as for the assessment. Members of a composition staff working together to decide the purpose, then the content, then the scoring criteria for portfolios are really determining the meaning and standards for the composition course, a most worthwhile activity.

Appeals Procedures

If the portfolio assessment will determine a student's grade, advancement to another class, or graduation, some appeals procedure will be necessary. As with any other kind of assessment, portfolio assessment is not perfect, and some mistakes will be made. If the assessment team renders a grade that a student, perhaps backed by his or her teacher, feels to be wrong, the case must be heard. However, if the assessment team has developed a demonstrably careful and reliable method of scoring, appeals should be kept to a minimum. A simple description of the complex and expensive scoring mechanism will sometimes make the student realize that the scoring decision was made with care. To discourage frivolous requests, the appeals board can require students to submit a written statement of appeal and to provide specific evidence of procedural or other error. If the appeals board then decides to review the portfolio, it needs to reestablish the context of the original scoring, using the same scoring guide and sample portfolios at the different score levels. But too many appeals will simply choke the system and should be taken as a sign that insufficient care and groundwork have gone into the assessment program.

Portfolios for Barrier Assessments

Barrier assessments serve as hurdles that students must get over if they are to continue progressing toward the degree. Some institutions will not allow a student to advance or to graduate without passing some kind of writing assessment. Many institutions now use essay tests, sometimes in addition to multiple-choice editing tests, for this purpose. Increasingly, however, portfolios are replacing these barrier tests, since they give a more accurate picture of a student's writing ability.

Barrier assessments are different from other kinds of evaluation primarily because of the extremely high stakes involved. A student who does not pass the barrier may not proceed, no matter what other abilities, course grades, or teacher recommendations he or she may have. The nature of the barrier puts great pressure on the assessment: since it essentially deprives some students of their property rights in their education, it must meet the highest standards of validity and reliability. For these reasons, the passing score on barrier assessments tends to be very low; if only the grossest kind of incompetence fails, there is less likelihood of court action. Nonetheless, the logic of the barrier assessment is reasonable enough: if the student cannot read or write at a minimum level, upper-division work is sure to lead to failure, and graduation from a college would be farcical. The student's progress to the degree should be held up until reading and writing are adequate.

But as this ideal enters practice, many problems develop. For example, shouldn't minimum proficiency be a matter of entrance requirements, not midstream barrier tests? And what do we say of students with many high grades, even in upper-division courses, who fail the barrier assessment? What about talented students in some fields, such as mathematics or music, who may be very weak at verbal skills? And what do we do about students from non-English-speaking homes or from homes with variant dialects of English, who, nonetheless, are succeeding in their course work? Portfolios solve many of these problems, since, by their very nature, they demonstrate writing and thinking in a school and course context, rather than in isolation, as with a test. Many students who cannot pass a timed writing test can still turn in written work that, after due revision, will meet reasonable standards.

Chapter Ten will discuss large-scale portfolio assessment in more detail. But we should note that, as the scope and stakes of the assessment expand, its implementation difficulties do also. As we went from the relative ease of the single-class portfolio assessment to the much greater complexity of the course assessment team, the problems expanded greatly. As we move to school, university, or statewide assessments, the problems increase again, geometrically. For example, how do faculty assessment teams score papers written in a discourse community they may know nothing about, or may even dislike? How can they grade analyses of books they have not read, written for contexts they do not share? Essay tests used for barrier assessment are subject to the same questions, but the tests are normally written to a single text or question, so an assessment team can develop special expertness for the scoring. Portfolio assessments lack those controls; indeed, their particular virtue is that they are free of such limitations. But that very freedom makes their use for barrier testing more risky, even though they represent new possibilities for context-sensitive and increasingly valid writing assessment.

Portfolios in the Future

The advantages of portfolios, great as they are, seem at present to be balanced by a series of problems that may or may not be manageable. Of all the problems described in this chapter, none is more resistant than the time burden that portfolio reading places on teachers already overburdened with too many classes with too many students. Nonetheless, portfolios may well be the wave of the future in writing assessment.

As we approach the year 2000, scores of campuses and hundreds of faculty are engaged in portfolio experimentation. Granting agencies are funding portfolio projects for freshman placement, for general education outcomes, and for numbers of other purposes. The energy and resources furthering portfolio assessment remind me of the surge in interest in essay testing that occurred twenty years ago, an outpouring of creativity that handled (though it did not solve) the problems of reliability and validity that seemed insurmountable at the time.

One of these portfolio experimenters, alluding to literary theory, told me that she favored portfolio assessment because it was "a deconstruction of assessment itself." That is, when we use portfolios, we cannot reduce assessment to tests and then to test scores for the sorting of students; similarly, we cannot reduce all writing to first-draft exposition, since many different kinds of writing are included and regarded as valuable. Just as portfolios cannot be reduced to tests, the deep humanity of students' writing, reflecting, and thinking cannot be removed from portfolios; that creative unmanageability is both their strength and their weakness. But we must be careful in deconstructing assessment; for if we lose validity and reliability in the process, we lose assessment itself, and portfolios then become another version of individual teacher response. If portfolios do become the standard method of evaluating writing, we will be able to rest assured that writing itself remains valued, taught, and always somewhat unpredictable. We will also know that education remains a matter of thinking and creativity, despite all the forces that drive colleges toward mass measures of information processing. But before all this can occur, we will have to learn how to handle this new assessment device with care, fairness, economy, and responsibility.

Part Two

Writing Assessment
Beyond
the Classroom

The first part of this book focused, for the most part, on *formative* assessment—that is, assessment whose purpose is to improve student writing. Thus, much of our concern was with classroom assignments and ways to help students move through the process of successfully writing on them. As we move away from the classroom in this part, we will be attending more to *summative* assessment, designed to produce information about the writing ability of students in groups.

This aspect of assessment makes many teachers uncomfortable, since they necessarily see students as individuals, developing as writers and as people. But summative information about the writing ability of students is vitally important for policy decisions, and those who make such decisions must have that information. Many of those decisions directly affect teaching, since budgets allocate sparse resources to programs that can show success and increased funds reward institutions demonstrating their effectiveness. Placement testing helps students enter the curriculum at a place where they can succeed; equivalency testing helps students move ahead rapidly by demonstrating they already know what some college courses are designed to teach. Barrier tests determine standards for advancement, degrees, entry into and exit from professional programs. Researchers too must have summative measures if they are to reach conclusions, and those conclusions sometimes lead directly to curriculum change and new teaching materials. Whenever such questions as "How good is it? Does it work? How many succeed? Are we getting our money's worth?" are asked, summative assessment seeks to provide answers. However much teachers may suspect the motives and results of summative assessments, no sensible person can dispute their importance.

Just as politics is too important to be left to politicians, so summative writing assessment is too important to be left to assessors, who have in the past largely defined goals and procedures. The chapters in this part urge writing teachers to take part in summative as well as formative assessment, and describe recent advances in large-scale writing assessment.

Chapter Seven looks at the interplay of language and theory of assessment, showing how different kinds of summative writing assessments emerge from the different worldviews of different disciplines. Chapter Eight focuses on the particular ways in which universities assess writing for such purposes as placement or graduation certification. Chapter Nine turns to the measures customarily used to assess writing ability, with particular attention to the differences between multiple-choice and essay testing.

Chapter Ten is addressed to the teacher or administrator charged with scoring large quantities of essay tests or writing portfolios; it gives practical details about the most effective procedures now in use. Chapter Eleven summarizes much of the previous four chapters, discussing the pitfalls that await the unwary conducting large-scale writing assessments.

Chapter Twelve turns to program evaluation, the difficult attempt to document the effectiveness of such writing programs as freshman composition, writing across the curriculum, and writing-intensive courses.

The concluding chapter looks back at twenty years of writing assessment, with an eye to the political and academic issues that have emerged, and then forward to an uncertain future.

CHAPTER 7

Language and Reality
in Writing Assessment

Many college faculty members (particularly in the humanities) think of assessment as something that is used for classroom activities such as grading individual student papers or examinations. Unfamiliar with the pervasiveness of assessment beyond the classroom, they rarely understand or respect assessments of programs and institutions, particularly when these assessments use measuring devices derived from educational or social science research. Often, they regard these activities as the "threat" I described in Chapter One and simply withdraw into indifference or opposition.

But such assessment is too important and its implications too far-reaching to be left to assessors and other specialists in measurement. Writing instructors must recognize the legitimacy of the questions behind large-scale assessment (such as "How well does this program work?") and must contribute to the theory and practice of writing-assessment programs. In an era of tight budgets and increasing competition for diminishing educational dollars, we can no longer depend on an undemonstrated belief that our work with students is worth the enormous cost to our institutions. As we are accustomed to telling our students, simple assertion and reassertion of statements of value do not constitute convincing proof; evidence is required, evidence credible to an audience that may not share the writer's beliefs.

135

One major problem those of us in the humanities must deal with when we work with assessment beyond our classrooms is the language we encounter. Like divorcing couples in law courts, we find our most intimate experiences subject to a technical vocabulary that somehow distances and changes what we know from experience. This disconnection between what we know and what we hear from others is not simply a matter of vocabulary, though it may seem so at first, but actually a matter of a worldview derived from a wholly different discourse community. If we are to participate in legal or assessment matters, we must learn what these outsiders mean. Not until we understand the reality they inhabit and express in their language can we seek to alter that reality. But it is extraordinarily difficult to break through our own patterns of language and thought in order to reach that understanding. I offer my own experience as an example.

Some years ago I attended for the first time a conference unknown to me or to most college English faculty: the Assessment Forum of the American Association for Higher Education (AAHE). I was there to give a paper on the measurement of writing ability and on the evaluation of writing programs. The experience of that conference ought to have been routine; after all, I have directed a variety of large-scale writing programs, and I have been speaking and publishing on writing assessment for over twenty years—to English faculty. But the experience of hearing papers and discussions at that conference was not at all routine; it was both troubling and enlightening, as well as quite new in unexpected ways.

My first reaction to the sessions on writing measurement at AAHE was that I had entered a new world. The papers not only made different assumptions about writing than I, as a writing teacher, writer, and researcher, normally make, but came out of a wholly different scholarly community of discourse, one that calls itself "the assessment movement." The references were entirely unfamiliar, the procedures were different, and the approach to the subject struck me as insensitive to what writing is all about. All these differences seemed to center on the way people spoke (and hence thought) about measurement: I was in a foreign country, the language was different, and that difference changed everything. I had entered a new discourse community in a field in which I was a well-published specialist, and none of my knowledge or experience seemed to matter. And yet the discourse was about measuring writing ability and evaluating writing programs; that is, it was about something that has (however accidentally) become my specialty. I felt disoriented.

When I returned home from AAHE, I found a flier from the publisher of the first edition of this book. Since this pamphlet featured the publisher's special list on assessment, I anticipated a little extra publicity. But my book was not included in the list of books written by the measurement community, because (my editor later told me) it had been written by a writer and an English professor rather than a professional assessor.

I then remembered an even odder experience along these same lines, from my days as a testing-program administrator for the huge California State University system. Since one of our testing programs happened to accumulate a large amount of information about student performance on both a multiple-choice usage test and an essay test, and since we also had a declaration from each student about his or her race, it seemed interesting to compare the relative performance of racial groupings on the two kinds of tests. The charts we came up with revealed that students who called themselves "white" performed in roughly similar patterns on the essay and on the multiple-choice test, whereas those who called themselves by one of three minority racial group labels had sharply different patterns of scores. For example, over 11 percent of the black students whose writing sample scores formed a bell curve were clustered at the bottom of the score distribution by the usage test. (See Chapter Nine for these charts and a full discussion of them.) When I showed these results to English faculty, we all drew the same conclusion: the performance of the minority students on the essay test (which did not vary from that of the whites in pattern, though the mean score shifted down) showed that something was wrong with the multiple-choice test (which placed large numbers of *all* minority students at the lowest possible score). What, we asked, was wrong with the supposedly "objective" writing test that gave such low scores to minority students whose actual writing received a good range of scores from trained writing evaluators?

But I was stunned to receive a quite different interpretation of the results when I presented them to a group of admissions deans and specialists in educational measurement. The results, they agreed, showed a difference between the two score distributions, but there was another possible interpretation of the meaning of the difference. This group argued that the problem test for the minorities was not the multiple-choice one, which grouped them at the bottom, but the essay, which distributed them normally along a bell curve. "Who scored these essays?" one dean asked. When I said that trained composition faculty scored them, reliably, I saw knowing smiles exchanged. They knew that lily-livered English teachers cannot be trusted to grade minority students' writing with the severity it deserves. What, they asked, was wrong with the essay test that allowed too many minority students to get high scores?

We could simply call these differences in ways of looking at writing measurement one more example of different disciplinary attitudes toward multiple-choice testing. Or we could smile sadly at the barely covered racism that "knows" that minority students must receive low scores on any test. But I want to press beyond those generalizations. I think it is useful to see the issue (and the others I have mentioned) as a conflict between discourse communities, between ways not only of *reading* the world but also of *writing* the world, of seeing and then making sense out of what we see. For this second group of observers, *minority* is a group term so associated with such concepts as "inferior" or "impoverished" or "remedial" that the only data that can make sense to them will confirm this linguistic and conceptual view of the world. Some administrators, such as the deans of admissions at large institutions, necessarily deal with categories, and their language experience disallows data that conflict with their verbal categories. The faculty, on the other hand, accustomed to dealing with individual minority students, of varying ability, have less trouble accepting data confirming that varying ability; teachers must see individuals.

Reality and Language: The Sapir-Whorf Hypothesis

Lawyers say that no one is as untrustworthy as an eye witness. That is a nicely practical statement of the problem with simple radical positivism, the belief that an obvious reality is "out there" to be observed. Poststructural theorists in various fields, including literature, argue that supposedly fixed texts or objects are really creations of individual observing minds. But how do our minds construct the special reality we think we are merely observing? Some linguists and some philosophers will argue that we tend to see what our language culture *makes* us see and that we ignore or find irrelevant those things or ideas that lie outside of our language community. Winston Churchill is supposed to have said that England and America were two countries divided by the same language. I believe that our disciplinary and professional divisions, with their own languages, form distinct ways of seeing that divide us from each other in destructive ways. The particular gulf between writers, writing teachers, and writing researchers (who are usually, though not always, in English departments) and the measurement specialists in the assessment movement (who are usually in psychology or education departments) is particularly unfortunate for writing programs, since many of these programs are evaluated by members of the other discourse community. The choice of an evaluator often means the selection of a unique set of assumptions and definitions that emerge out of the language of the evaluator's world; the implications of such a choice, particularly when made without much attention to this issue, can be profound, affecting the funding or even the survival of the program.

This problem of the relation of language to perceived reality is familiar to linguists and philosophers of language, who have long debated the concepts developed (out of Platonic and Germanic idealism) in the 1920s and 1930s by Edward Sapir and Benjamin Whorf. (Sapir died in 1939 and Whorf in 1941.) The Sapir-Whorf hypothesis asserts that our words strongly affect or even determine our world, that our language may determine what we see and what we understand. For example, Whorf (who worked as an insurance adjuster) was intrigued by the high accident rate at one location where large cans of liquid petroleum were used. He discovered that the cans were marked "empty" when the liquid was used up, despite the fumes that remained; workmen would toss cigarette butts into the "empty" cans, causing explosions. Despite experience, the accidents continued, for how could an "empty" can be dangerous?

With a change in sign came a change in perception, and the accidents stopped (Whorf, [1940] 1956, p. 135).

For Sapir, people who speak in different languages perceive the world in different ways, but the world is there to be observed:

> Language is a guide to "social reality." . . . Human beings do not live in the objective world alone, nor alone in the world of social activity as ordinarily understood, but are very much at the mercy of the particular language which has become the medium of expression for their society. . . . The fact of the matter is that the "real world" is to a large extent unconsciously built up on the language habits of the group. No two languages are ever sufficiently similar to be considered as representing the same social reality. The worlds in which different societies live are distinct worlds, not merely the same world with different labels attached [(1928) 1963, p. 162].

This "weak theory" suggests that we can affect people's perceptions by changing their language, as happened with the "empty" but dangerous gas cans. If the theory holds, as I think it does, then conscious awareness of the way language shapes perception can keep us from being bound by our language. By becoming aware of that language and changing it, we can overcome the hold that language has on the way we see the world.

Whorf extends Sapir's concept into what is known as the "strong theory" by arguing further that the world itself is a social construction made by language out of the random flux of experience:

> We dissect nature along lines laid down by our native languages. The categories and types that we isolate from the world of phenomena we do not find there because they stare every observer in the face; on the contrary, the world is presented in a kaleidoscopic flux of impressions which has to be organized by our minds—and this means largely by the linguistic sys-

tems in our minds. We cut nature up, organize it into concepts, and ascribe significances as we do, largely because we are parties to an agreement to organize it in this way—an agreement that holds throughout our speech community and is codified in the patterns of our language. The agreement is, of course, an implicit and unstated one, *but its terms are absolutely obligatory*; we cannot talk at all except by subscribing to the organization and classification of data which the agreement decrees. . . . We are thus introduced to a new theory of relativity, which holds that all observers are not led by the same physical evidence to the same picture of the universe, unless their linguistic backgrounds are similar, or can in some way be calibrated [(1940) 1956, pp. 213–214].

Whorf does hold out some hope of community when he suggests that a linguist with command of a great many languages would be "most free" from linguistic restraints to perception, but he is unable to find an example of so liberated an individual: "As yet no linguist is in any such position" (p. 214).

The strong theory of the Sapir-Whorf hypothesis is now rather out of fashion in linguistics, although the echoes of that theory in reader-response and poststructural literary theories (as we saw in Chapter Four) continue to resound: "In the realm of knowledge, everything is constituted during a certain time by one or more people. Some 'things' are included, some are excluded, some are marginalized. Boundaries are set up" (Leitch, 1985, pp. 22–23). We might also note that new theories of "chaos" in the physical sciences have placed the observer at the center of the observed "reality." But I do not want to pursue the strong theory further here. I do, however, want to extend the weak hypothesis to the professional discourse level, where our language communities have a profound effect on all aspects of our lives. In particular, the language specializations that largely define our disciplines and allow us to work as "professionals" also cut us off from important other communities. We do not see or read or value these other communities, and so we cut ourselves off from important dimensions of perception and knowledge. The other discipline seems to us "soft" or "education-ist" or "unprofessional" or, perhaps, merely incomprehensible. I myself fight this perception all the time, since I often work professionally with those in other disciplines; but I confess that my Ph.D. in English literature has so confirmed a particular discourse community that I routinely find it hard to respect the scholarship of nonliterary communities. So do all of us with the same humanistic language training. And we have good as well as bad reasons for doing so.

My earlier reference to varying interpretations of minority test results is one example of this problem. Here are two others, each illustrating another facet of the ways in which our language communities affect our vision of the assessment world. My hope is that increased awareness of the issue will lead to increased attempts to overcome the limitation of perception we all experience because of our specialized languages.

Truth and the "True Score"

The first example is a bit technical. It has to do with the different definitions of what we are trying to learn about students from a test (or any other measurement device), an important conceptual difference between the measurement community and the writing community. At the root of this issue is the concept of a "true score" for a test. In classical test theory, a student taking a test is presumed to have a "true score," which represents the accurate measurement of the construct being evaluated. Since no test is perfect and conditions are never ideal, the observed score a student achieves on a test will normally be at some distance from the true score, a distance whose probability is expressed mathematically by the Standard Error of Measurement for the test. Thus, a student's observed score is made up of the "true score" modified by an error score; the best test will reduce that error score as much as possible.

For many kinds of measurement, such a concept and such a language work reasonably well. We need to be aware, however, that to speak of a "true score" suggests a purity and objectivity of measurement, a value-free and meaningful reality associated with other kinds of truth: true love, perhaps, or true religion. Such language authorizes a profound belief in the value of tests and test scores, and allows even heavily subjective multiple-choice tests to be called "objective," as if they had been created by the same computers that score them. Those who use the language of true scores and objective tests, and subscribe to the entire statistical view of measurement, are driven by their language to envision tests as a way of achieving a vision of truth, ideally free from social values or subjective judgment or disagreement; any such matters are called "error," the serpent to be stamped out of the garden. Measurement becomes a reality of numbers and charts, equations and computers, scorecards for the nation's schools, and percentile ratings that rank skills to several decimal places. Most of all, like all truth, it is to be believed.

But when we evaluate student writing (not to speak of writing programs or high schools), we sometimes find differences of opinion that cannot be resolved and where the concept of the true score makes no sense. Using controlled holistic scoring, we can achieve high inter-rater reliability, but some papers resist agreement. Despite the scoring guides, sample papers, and other methods of increasing reliability detailed in Chapter Ten, you grade Kelly's paper a 4 while I grade it a 3; there are so many aspects to writing that you are focusing on some while I attend more to others. In practice, we simply add the two adjacent scores, call the paper a 7, and move on. Is our difference of opinion to be called error? Not at all. In fact, historically, such differences about value in most areas of experience tend to be more valuable than absolute agreement; they combine to bring us nearer to accurate evaluation than would simple agreement. The same is true in measurement of writing ability, where some disagreement (within limits) should not be called error, since, as with the arts, we do not really have a true score, even in theory. Yet if we imagine that we are seeking to approximate a true score, we exaggerate the negative effects of disagreement and distort the meaning of the scores we do achieve. Sophisticated statisticians have been aware of this problem for some time. Some decades ago, a team headed by the distinguished statistician L. J. Cronbach developed a "generalizability theory," based on a "consensus score" rather than a true score (Cronbach, Rajaratnam, and Gleser, 1963). A consensus score can yield useful measurement, reflecting the social process of judgment, and offers sound statistical data. But the language of measurement resists so human a matter as consensus, with its acceptance of the value of differing opinions.

The concept and language of the "true score" are so powerful for the assessment community, the definition of error in measurement so narrow, that generalizability theory seems to rest in an odd byway, reserved for the poets of statistics, who rarely sing. Instead, the harsh language of classical statistics, with its agricultural and phrenological roots, still governs (Whorf would say creates) the world of academic measurement. That is to say, the world of assessment, despite the realities offered by other discourse communities, remains largely a universe of true scores, measurement errors, pretests, posttests, and, in general, numerical positivism. Some leaders of this community, aware, as Cronbach was, of the need to liberate it from its narrowness, have tried to promote larger concepts, such as "performance measures" instead of product measures, or multiple measures instead of single tests (see Adelman, 1988; Shale, forthcoming). The AAHE Assessment Forum shows a good bit of unsuccessful verbal thrashing about, as sophisticated assessors try to transcend their language and reach out to the rest of us. Complaints from the floor about language and assumptions miss their target, since the assessors simply repeat their terminology or puzzle over what they see as ignorance. The result seems to be a sense of frustration on all sides. Why can't you, we say to each other, simply see what we mean? But the differences between the realities of divergent language communities undermine even the best-intentioned discussions.

Values and "Value-Free" Assessment

My next example is more personal. I mentioned in Chapter Three that some years ago I worked as a writing-test director as part of a large and well-funded program evaluation project for a major foundation. The project director, a prominent figure in the field, was noted for what he called "value-free assessment"; that is, the evaluation must not concern itself with the intentions of those running the program to be evaluated. The evaluation should not, his argument went, depend on the perceptions of the insiders; the evaluator should be "free" of such distortion, assessing not what the program intended to do but only what it "really" was doing. There is a double naiveté in such a theory, it seems to me. The first is the belief that the outside evaluator will be more professional if he or she is unaware of the values, assumptions, and language of those being evaluated; the second is the belief that by being so unaware the evaluator is in fact free of values and thus a neutral observer of reality. A retreat within the barricade of one's own language community reverses the road to freedom suggested by Whorf, who said that only familiarity with many languages could set us free of the structures that bind our perceptions. But this well-paid assessment specialist, with many publications, regarded his own value system as "value-free," thereby confusing freedom from the values of a project with freedom from all values.

This naiveté about his own value scheme shortly showed up in some equally naive practice. The essay questions for students, whose scoring I directed, were not developed in the usual way by the scoring team—that is, by devising test criteria, creating a series of questions that met the criteria, pretesting the questions to see whether they worked and were scorable, and so on. The evaluator believed that such a process would express the values of the program, and so—he simply made up the questions himself. In his view, his questions were value-free because he had constructed them and he was, by his own definition, value-free. His questions struck me as amateurish, filled with another discipline's jargon, expressing ambiguities and untested assumptions. In his discourse community, my objections to the questions were trivial and unsympathetic to the assumed definition of good writing that prevailed in his field: writing, to his community, is a matter of retelling information in a particularly passive version of the school dialect. But we were unable to discuss the matter, since he did not perceive our conflict as one between two value systems. His language led him to see our difference as a conflict between the values of English teachers and a neutral, value-free objectivity.

There was a particularly ironic aspect to our differences over the meaning of the word *value* in this assessment. He brought at least two contexts and a developed worldview to the word: first, the measurable context of the assessor looking for true scores (which would represent the value of the students' improvement) for statistical analysis; and, second, the behaviorist context with its suspicion of abstract values, from which an assessor should be "free." I, on the other hand, brought an entirely different set of meanings and contexts to the word, and, hence, to the measurement. For me, values emerge from a philosophical, moral, literary, and religious background; to be free of values is, for me, impossible or, if it were possible, disastrous. Furthermore, the values added to students through writing and reading are so profound and far-reaching that anyone who wants to measure them should seek substantial consultation and have a full awareness of the many problems involved. The definition of value bereft of value (in my terms) is as dangerous for my worldview as the "empty" gas cans Whorf observed were for the smokers on the job.

Living with Language Worlds in Conflict

Most of us in the field of writing have problems with the assumptions, language, and methodology of the assessment movement. The language of the assessment community too often defines writing as a skill, made up of component and teachable parts, expressed in measurable products. But the community of writing teachers rejects almost every part of that definition. We see writing as a complex mental process, intimately related to critical thinking and development of the self, as much an art as a skill. As with art, the products matter and can be evaluated, but they are fleeting and changeable expressions of a developing mental activity, the underlying structure we are really working with and seeking to improve. And we have become increasingly vocal about measurement devices that diminish the importance of our work.

The writing teachers' usual hostility to multiple-choice or value-added assessment has in the past been dismissed by the assessment community as a comic eccentricity by naive subjectivists who do not much know what they are doing. And, I must admit, the willful resistance on the part of writers, writing teachers, and artists to numerical language and knowledge has its disagreeable side. I have been in the unfortunate position of attempting to present correlations and even an occasional chart to groups of English department chairs, who directly became a glassy-eyed crew unwilling to move an inch from their own language community even to consider data that were necessary for their own survival. But this resistance is not merely to data and to methods of calculation but, rather, to the whole view of the world that statistical measurement represents.

Like the word *value, measurement* is a chameleon term whose meaning depends on the language community that uses it. Measurement that reflects the complex nature of our work, such as holistic evaluation of essays or portfolio assessment, has been embraced by writing teachers, since it appears in a language that can take account of what we do. When we can adopt statistical terms and numerical values without diminishing the meaning of what we are about, we should use them. But we must be careful. Numerical language and the worldview it brings can be dangerous and even comic where it does not apply. For example, when the Archduke in the film *Amadeus* complains to Mozart that his music has "too many notes," we laugh at the comments. Too many soldiers, a ruler might say, or too few taxes; that is the world of counting by numbers. But too many notes in an opera? This is the comedy of a clash of discourse communities, of applying the worldview of a specialized numerical language where it does not fit.

Recently, some prominent members of the assessment movement have begun to speak of the need for new assessment models: "authentic assessment" and "performance assessment" have taken on new respectablity, and the simple multiple-choice tests have lost some of their credibility—at least in theory. Some writing teachers have even begun to appear at assessment conferences and to publish in some of the assessment journals. A little dialogue and a few attempts to bridge the gaps between communities are taking place. At this point it is hard to say whether this willingness to hear each other represents a genuine rapprochement or simply worlds in conflict. But I hope these efforts continue, since we have much to gain from each other. The assessment community needs the more complex measures of complex tasks that the writing community has been working with for two decades; the writing community, as it moves more and more into portfolio assessment, must find ways of gaining statistical credibility for its measurement efforts.

We should not expect a blending of different languages and perspectives to come easily. We *are* caught in the languages we speak and in the discourse communities of our disciplines. But there are several courses of action we can take. In the first place, we should recognize the limits of the world that our languages allow us to see, and we should not automatically assume that those who do not share our views are unprofessional and wrong. That is, we ought to be aware that we are necessarily limited by what we know and by the language that lets us know it. This chapter illustrates the difficulty of such a large view; I try hard to respect the assessment movement, but I clearly think that its proponents are wrong-headed when it comes to writing. At the same time, I sometimes find myself arguing strongly against the unwillingness of my English department colleagues to understand what the assessment movement is all about—not to speak of the different language communities *within* English, with their different assumptions about teaching composition, reading literature, welcoming minorities into the academy, and so on. A tiny community of like souls, bi-linguists in measurement and writing, is starting to emerge, and those who are members of it are much in demand as interpreters. We need to keep reminding ourselves that others do not necessarily share our views, our language.

Beyond that, we ought to strive to learn other languages, to become linguists of other disciplines, to enter into the perceptions that our colleagues possess because they speak "foreign" tongues. Most crucially, when we evaluate programs, we need to recognize that language differences are crucial and necessary; they express different value systems, different understandings of education, different views of the world. Therefore, we should try to understand and value knowledge from communities outside our own—even reading books on our own fields by outsiders and attending conferences such as the AAHE Assessment Forum as well as the Conference on College Composition and Communication or the Modern Language Association. Some of us might be able to forge links between these discourse communities, but most of us can only recognize the chains that bind us. Certainly, and most practically, evaluation of writing programs ought always to be the responsibility of a *team* that represents different discourse communities, and, just as certainly, any such evaluation should require multiple measures.

Finally, all those who get involved in program assessment need to listen much more than they speak when they try to evaluate the work of those who speak and think in tongues they do not really understand. The gulf between language and reality is not merely a theoretical one; we live in different worlds, often in conflict, and in educational measurement we need always to keep the warning flags flying.

CHAPTER 8

Assessing
Writing Proficiency

Writing proficiency is one of those slippery terms that hide an even more slippery concept. Consider the variety of performance measures now in use. Some overachieving tots pass proficiency tests on alphabet blocks to win certificates at kindergarten graduation ceremonies; second-graders in my home town must be able to identify punctuation marks and write their names to make it into third grade; high school graduates must be able to fill in a job application and write a paragraph with three complete sentences before the school board gives them a diploma; college students seeking to demonstrate that they need not take the required upper-division writing course at my university must write a three-hour documented comparison-contrast essay based on readings assigned in advance; prospective teachers in California must complete two impromptu essays to set topics in an hour before they may begin their teaching careers. Although it is hard to imagine a single description that would apply to these various tests, they are all comfortably known as "proficiencies," and everyone seems to accept them in both theory and practice as authenticating writing ability.

In many instances, the term *proficiency* seems merely to replace the workaday term *skill*—on the well-established bureaucratic principle that long words for simple concepts are more dignified than short words. But an additional sense of adequacy, sufficiency for a particular purpose, is conveyed by the word *proficiency*: if someone is *proficient*, he or she is demonstrably capable. The fact that some of those who pass their "proficiencies" are *not* particularly capable—in fact, are at best minimally functional at a few skills—sometimes makes the terminology of proficiency testing seem pretentious.

A limited notion of writing proficiency, articulated in a set of definitions of skills and guides for teaching, can become a means of defining writing as merely a set of socializing skills. But such skills—accurate spelling or clear footnotes or any set of subskills unrelated to thinking—do not constitute writing proficiency itself. Since teachers will teach to their understanding of what proficiency tests measure, such measures must be worth teaching to. The pressures to perform well by seeing one's students perform well on such tests are simply too great to resist. Thus, those who define the proficiencies, both through documents and through tests, have a heavy obligation to ensure that the definitions support the teaching of writing. Such definitions need particularly to guard against the tendency of tests to trivialize writing, sometimes despite the best of intentions.

Even assessments that call for student writing will often emphasize form over substance or deny the importance of revision, and hence do not support writing instruction. For example, I mentioned a school proficiency test that asked for a complete paragraph but then defined a paragraph as consisting of three complete sentences. The deeper concept of paragraph cohesion—that sentences ought to relate to each other and to a central idea—did not enter into the definition. The even more substantial concept that the paragraph ought to have something to say to an audience, something of some significance to somebody, also was not present. As a result, the teachers did not teach paragraph development or writing but, rather, the identification of sentence elements; instead of leading teachers to abandon a mechanically oriented workbook and to replace it with real writing instruction, the new proficiency requirement confirmed the importance of the workbook and returned teachers to it.

A similar substitution of form for substance in proficiency requirements has led to the apparent immortality of the five-paragraph theme, which I discussed in Chapter Three. Defining writing proficiency as the ability to produce a short, grammatically correct essay to a set topic invites such patterned responses, and some holistic scorings weigh mechanics and other formal matters more heavily than many writing teachers prefer for first-draft work. As writing programs seek to accommodate the concept of the writing process, they are beginning to substitute longer essays, including revision time, or portfolios for the short timed essay, with its inevitable emphasis on form and fluency.

Since colleges and schools vary widely in their curricula, students, and faculty, it is not possible to suggest here the kinds of proficiencies appropriate at various levels. Indeed, the sensible law requiring proficiency testing for high school graduation in California specifically demands that each school district develop, define, and administer its own proficiency tests. In all instances, however, if proficiency tests are to be useful to the students and teachers who must cope with them, they must be carefully developed and must support writing instruction.

Purposes of Proficiency Assessment at the University Level

The extension of writing-proficiency testing to the university level represents a relatively new phenomenon on the American educational scene. Subject matter comprehensive examinations are, of course, both traditional and common at the graduate and undergraduate levels, and placement testing has been common since Harvard began examining entering students in 1874. But only within the last twenty-five years has a special writing-proficiency certification begun to be added to course requirements for the college degree—no doubt as a reflection of general discomfort with university educational standards. Sometimes these certifications take place as an added exit examination for freshman composition; sometimes they occur at the point of entry to upper-division standing ("rising-junior exams"); and sometimes they are graduation or degree requirements, to be completed after achievement of upper-division standing or even classified graduate status.

To those outside the university community, it might seem odd that the bachelor's degree should need the support of additional certification in writing skill; if a college degree does not in itself certify a high level of literacy, one might well wonder if it means anything at all. Nonetheless, in recent years, such solid members of the university community as the City University of New York, the Georgia State University system, and the California State University have felt it necessary to protect the quality of their degrees by a writing-certification requirement. A moment's speculation about the meaning of this requirement will illustrate just how pervasive these matters have become. Two particular aspects of university admissions procedures have a great deal to do with this new requirement: (1) the expansion of college opportunities to previously excluded groups and (2) the expansion of community college programs that satisfy university requirements for the first two years of study leading to the bachelor's degree.

The advent of open admissions to the City University of New York in 1970 was only the most prominent example of the expansion of college opportunity over the last three decades (Lederman, Ryzewic, and Ribaudo, 1983). The social forces behind this development are too well known to be repeated here, although the degree or permanence of institutional change these forces have brought about is by no means clear. (As we move through the 1990s, an odd and informal alliance between conservative politicians—seeking to reduce expenditures on education—and liberal faculty—seeking to protect educational quality under financial pressure—has begun to restrict access to higher education once again.) A substantial number of students who had either not experienced or not accepted English as a socializing discipline began to appear in college classrooms in the 1970s, even at the most selective institutions. Faculties were faced with increased numbers of students for whom the conventions of academic written prose were a mystery and for whom the traditional freshman English course seemed inappropriate.

Responses varied. Some institutions, well aware that inexperience with the conventions of prose did not necessarily mean inability to learn, made few changes in curriculum; they simply expected new students to make rapid adjustments, sometimes with minimal counseling support. Other institutions, well aware that the same inexperience presented a serious handicap to students who would have to write papers for a traditional faculty, instituted a wide range of remedial courses (with placement testing) and support services. Meanwhile, a general decline in student verbal ability, suggested most dramatically by a precipitous decline in Scholastic Aptitude Test scores, added a considerable group of traditional students without skill at academic writing to the new populations. For these reasons and many others, it became much more difficult to enforce high academic standards in freshman English courses.

At the same time, more and more students were beginning their university work at community colleges; after graduating from the colleges, and receiving certifications that they had completed all general education requirements, including writing proficiency, the students transferred to four-year colleges. Although the two-year colleges tended to take seriously their responsibilities for writing instruction and general education certification, many of their composition classes were occupied by large numbers of students who were not likely to proceed to four-year institutions. It became difficult for these community colleges to maintain standards, and the four-year institutions receiving their transfer students with writing requirements fulfilled became increasingly uncomfortable with such certification.

While these forces and others were diminishing the actual standards and the credibility of freshman-level writing certification, the universities were experiencing an increasing fragmentation of their curricula. Fewer students were majoring in the humanities and other liberal arts disciplines, and increasing numbers were pursuing majors they felt would lead more directly to jobs in business and technology. Except at a few highly selective institutions, the traditional faculty consensus that writing well was important in all fields became less and less dependable. Teachers who assigned term papers or essay exams found increasing numbers of advanced students for whom such work was new and surprising. And employers began to complain more loudly than ever that degree recipients could not write as needed on the job.

Thus, the new writing-proficiency requirements at the university level represent a widespread belief that a student may complete course requirements for a bachelor's degree and still be unable to write at an acceptable level. The new certification requirements also assume, with somewhat less justification, that college can and should define a level of writing proficiency appropriate for all graduates and that such an achievement can be certified.

Types of Proficiency Assessment in Use

Various institutions have been implementing policy on the writing-proficiency requirement in recent years, and it is instructive to review the procedures that are in use. As always, the assessment problems have turned out to be much greater than they were imagined to be, and every method of implementation has shown both strengths and weaknesses.

Multicampus Testing

The principal advantage of a large-scale proficiency test is its overall efficiency. Substantial resources can be brought to test development, administration, scoring, and analysis; participating campuses can realize the benefits of the test without incurring much cost. Such long-standing programs as the New York State Regents Examinations for high school subjects have demonstrated the advantages of establishing statewide standards of proficiency in various fields. Yet large-scale proficiency testing in writing is fraught with special problems. The statewide examinations in Georgia and Texas, for example, have aroused substantial faculty opposition from those who find them insensitive and inappropriate for their particular campus or students. Since any definition of writing proficiency must be developed through discussion and consensus, and since the writing standards of a campus are a major component of the educational quality offered by that campus proficiency testing in writing perhaps should not be conducted on too large a scale.

The twenty-campus California State University established a systemwide *placement* test for entering freshmen in 1977 but did not do the same for the graduation proficiency requirement established in the same year. The economies of scale that were obviously beneficial for the placement test seemed much less sure for the proficiency requirement. Those responsible for establishing such a test had to ponder several questions: Is a test the best device for certifying writing proficiency? What kind of test would certify writing proficiency over a wide range of campuses, majors, and professional programs? Can a single writing-proficiency standard be established for English majors at San Francisco State, accounting majors at Northridge, animal science majors at Pomona, and forestry majors at Humboldt?

Of all writing tests, the proficiency test is the most political, the hardest to agree on, the most dependent on instructional agreement. While the large-scale test gains uniformity of standards and certain economies, it loses the nearness to instruction that alone gives the concept of college writing proficiency a meaningful context. Probably the best method of demonstrating writing proficiency is through the completion of a demanding course requiring a substantial amount of writing and rewriting, with some sort of coordination and assessment beyond the classroom to confirm consistency of standards. If such an instructional program cannot be instituted, a second-best option is a portfolio assessment with wide participation by faculty from a range of disciplines. A writing-proficiency program ought to encourage such methods of certification, since a series of writing samples will provide more reliable measurement than any one test can, and careful response and instruction during the course or after the portfolio review will lead to improved writing overall. A test is often a weak link in assessment and is generally an unsatisfactory alternative to instruction. The further a test moves from instruction, the more problems it accumulates, and large-scale writing-proficiency testing is no exception.

These pedagogical and psychometric principles developed into a compelling argument against a large-scale proficiency test in California. If writing proficiency (that is, the thing itself rather than the test) is the goal of the program, responsibility for certifying that proficiency should be placed within the college curriculum, not outside it. That is, the test cannot in itself improve student writing; it can only at best lead to a strengthened writing-instruction program. (I am frequently astonished at the view that an assessment will, all by itself, improve education—as if a good fever thermometer could replace physicians and pharmacists.) If the test is entirely separated from the curriculum, it might not even do that, since such separation seems to turn the test into a hurdle to be gotten over rather than an important part of learning. For these reasons, the

California decision was to resist statewide certification and remand the requirement to the individual campuses in the state university system. As these campuses have wrestled with the problem, they have provided laboratory cases of the variety of ways to implement such a requirement on a single campus.

Campus Testing Programs

An individual campus faced with implementing a writing-certification requirement is likely to turn first of all to a single test. Particularly when the campus is large and complex, a test offers many advantages: a single standard, sometimes imagined to be "objective"; an addition to the quality control of the campus without the effort of reviewing or changing the curriculum; and a simple funding apparatus—a test fee. The test provides the answers, so there is no need even to raise the questions; everything looks deceptively simple. But the test is the beginning of problems, not the end of them. Even if all the cautions in this book (particularly in Chapter Eleven) are followed, the test becomes a major enterprise in itself. Special attention must be given to continuous test development, to student advisement both before and after testing, and to test security and cheating. Fly-by-night outfits are likely to appear in town the weekend before the test with expensive materials and cram courses in test taking. Students who have failed the test several times become increasingly desperate and, with only the test between them and their degrees, may tend toward increasingly desperate measures. Meanwhile, pressures to lower the standards of the test or to provide exemptions for an increasing number of special cases become almost irresistible, and the test starts to look more like an entrance-level minimum competence exam than an exit-level test of writing proficiency.

At the same time, those students who do not pass the test after one or two attempts and who seriously want to improve their writing will make continued requests for the establishment of a course to teach them the skills they lack. The result of such requests has been a new and appalling course: the *upper-division* remedial English course. These courses are never called "remedial" in their title, since no one is willing to admit that the institution enrolls juniors and seniors without writing proficiency; hence, they are given a wonderful variety of pseudonyms: intensive English, grammar review, proficiency test preparation, and the like. With the exception of a few heroic and responsible faculty, the teachers of these difficult and unpleasant courses are generally those with the least experience, status, and knowledge.

Some faculty claim that a single proficiency test, despite its problems, is still the most effective way to raise literacy standards on their campuses. As large numbers of students with particular majors fail the test, the faculty in those fields must recognize their responsibility to teach writing in their courses, and only the test can convey that message. But it is extremely difficult to include substantive matters on such a proficiency test, and the standards for scoring tend to become very low; after all, the test is an absolute barrier to the degree for a wide variety of students, and it is politically impossible to fail too large a percentage of graduating seniors. In addition, some inept students, unwilling or unable to take additional writing courses, may wind up taking the test repeatedly, hoping that some miraculous event will allow them to pass. Students for whom school English is a second language or a second dialect pose special problems, not easily dealt with, and students with these difficulties often cannot pass a timed essay test without special consideration. When one is involved in scoring such examinations, numbers of essays turn up written by students taking the test for the ninth or tenth time. Not only is there an air of desperation in the exams of such students, but their recurrent papers serve to lower disproportionately the overall quality of test performance.

I remember well my visit to a campus in the Southwest that prides itself on its rising-junior writing test. The test has become an established bureaucratic operation, with a staff and budget that rival those in any instructional program. Prime concerns are security of the test and statistical purity in the scoring of it. Much talk on campus has to do with the test: for students, somehow passing it; for faculty, defending it as a badge of righteousness; for administrators, maintaining it in the face of increasing pressures, which they interpret as attacks on standards. As for writing—well, nobody talks about writing, or writing instruction, or writing as learning, as thinking, as creativity. Everybody talks about getting the test "out of the way" so that students can graduate. There is no evidence, not even anecdotal evidence, that writing has improved on this campus. To the contrary, writing has come to represent a punishment, as it is for the grade school students whose teacher threatens, "If you kids don't quiet down, you'll have to write a thousand words." I see the assessment program on this campus as a classic case of means replacing ends, of a test actually substituting for the goals it is intended to achieve.

These examinations violate an essential general principle of testing: no single test is sufficiently reliable to be depended on, by itself, for a major decision about students. A second proposition, which this book argues as forcefully as it can, is almost as important: when assessment becomes separated from teaching, both teaching and assessment suffer. And when passing a test begins to seem unrelated to learning, we ask our students to become cynical about learning itself.

Course Certification

The foregoing arguments are so compelling to some faculty committees and administrators that they decide to omit proficiency examinations entirely, and depend wholly on certification by the teachers of courses. Students who pass particular courses will be presumed to be proficient writers, and there is an end to it. But that procedure is no more an end to problems than a test is. Again, new difficulties present themselves. Where is responsibility for the certification course to reside? Some campuses will decide to remand certification of writing proficiency to the department of the student's major. History majors should write well enough to please historians, engineers to satisfy the engineering faculty, and so on. But that decision tends to work out very badly, since many of these instructors know little about the teaching and measurement of writing, and some of them may be less than adequate writers themselves. Thus, results tend to be so uneven as to diminish the requirement: some departments become very demanding, requiring a disciplinary writing course with high standards, while others become cynical and designate a course that may have no more than a single essay examination, if that. On one campus, a course in musical composition (designated by a satirical music department) and a course in computer programming (proposed by a naive math department) were supposed to satisfy writing-proficiency requirements.

In an attempt to make such course designations more consistent and fair to students, some campuses will establish guidelines for writing-proficiency courses and even faculty committees and administrators to enforce the guidelines. (Such procedures sometimes lead to writing-intensive course requirements, a variation I take up next.) Thus, departments may be required to designate courses that call for, say, five separate writing assignments adding up to five thousand words and include some attention to revision. The most effective of such programs require a common assessment of some kind, a midterm or final exam or even a portfolio, in order to bring the faculty together to agree on a consistent set of standards.

When such common requirements are in fact enforced, and they seem to work only on relatively small campuses, the certification program can both ensure standards and support teaching. However, the coordination effort called for is strenuous and even extraordinary, involving as it does agreement among a wide variety of faculty on matters generally held to be private: course curriculum and grading standards for departmental offerings. But the effort pays off handsomely. Not only does the writing-certification program become an embedded part of the education in each major, but a de facto faculty development program in the teaching and measurement of writing ability is likely to emerge.

Unfortunately, with no common assessment or strong coordinator to hold together such a program, the centrifugal forces usually become too strong to resist. In departments with little or no training or interest in the teaching or assessment of writing, the program will relax into a series of departmental courses that may or may not involve writing and are taught by new faculty members. Therefore, some campuses with experience in this area no longer expect the academic departments to certify writing proficiency. All students must pass an English department writing course or a course administered by the English department. While such a procedure reduces the problems of administration and inconsistency, it tends to confirm the destructive myth that only the English faculty need be concerned about student writing. In addition, it puts an immense strain on English department staffing, which usually must accommodate freshman composition as well, and diminishes the emphasis on the study of literature, which most English departments wish to maintain. The proficiency course becomes a burden to be borne by unwilling literature teachers, the English department alone is responsible for denying degrees to students approved by everyone else, and the rest of the faculty (whose lack of concern for student writing has spurred the demand for proficiency certification) are free to continue business as usual.

Writing-Intensive Courses

A popular variation on the course certification requirement is the establishment of an institutional "writing-intensive course" requirement. Every graduate must complete a certain number (usually two or three) of "W" or "WI" or "M" (for Writing in the Major) courses, so designated in course listings; sometimes one or more of those courses must be taken outside the area of the student's major.

The "W" program usually begins with a strong vote of confidence from the faculty and the administration, since its advantages are many and obvious. Faculty from throughout the university will be teaching the certification course, so responsibility for student writing is disseminated as it should be; faculty teaching the "W" courses will become so attuned to the power of writing as part of learning that they will carry that pedagogical understanding over into all of their teaching, even spreading the word to their colleagues; the writing course helps induct students into the discourse community of the major, an often neglected but important task; students will understand that writing is often required in courses that are taught outside the English department; instead of creating a new testing program or a new curriculum, the institution simply has to adjust its existing courses to fit the "W" requirements. A simple adjustment of general education requirements takes place, and a cadre of enthusiastic faculty from a variety of disciplines volunteer to offer the opening set of "W" courses.

But the "W" program is filled with traps for the unwary and usually leads to an unimagined fiasco. For example, in the mid 1980s a large state university in the East launched itself into writing across the curriculum in a well-publicized attempt to improve the thinking and writing of its graduates. The university senate required "W" courses to be instituted in each department; three "W" courses were required for the degree. The administration promised four kinds of support: a consistent faculty development program, an improved and supported writing center, enrollment caps of twenty for the "W" courses, and a long-term effort to support formative as well as summative assessment of the program.

Five years later, as evaluator of the program, I found the shambles of what remained of the ambitious and laudable design. None of the four administrative promises had materialized. The faculty development program and the writing center had been sacrificed to a budget cut, a new administration had felt no obligation to the assessment program, and the enrollment caps had been made the responsibility of each department chair, whose budgets depended on high enrollments.

At a meeting of those teaching the courses, I heard that so few "W" courses were offered that enrollment pressures caused by the requirement had led to average class size over fifty, that the faculty were angry and frustrated at being asked to teach writing with no support under such conditions, and that very little writing was going on in the (ironic laughter) writing-intensive courses. From the department chairs, I learned that the weakest teachers and the least attractive courses had been designated "W," since the requirement ensured survival for both.

In a devilish twist, faculty teaching non-"W" courses had sharply diminished their writing requirements, since their "W" colleagues were now supposedly teaching and requiring writing, thereby relieving them of that time-consuming responsibility. Even the most dedicated "W" teachers were doing more harm than good, since they had received no training in ways of using writing to assist learning. One physicist took me aside to tell me that he was devoting many class sessions in his "W" course to spelling and punctuation (though he himself had only the dimmest understanding of them), despite the demands of the class material and the lack of time to read student writing. I tried hard to praise him for his good will, but when I asked him if he had found a way to teach revision to his students, he looked surprised and puzzled, so I changed the subject.

I was not surprised to find, at a meeting with students, that some of them did not know what the "W" requirement stood for (work in class?). No assessment of the "W" program had been conducted and none was contemplated, and it was just as well. Recently, over a thousand graduating seniors had the requirement waived, since insufficient "W" courses were offered for them. Net result of the new writing program: less writing throughout the curriculum, cynical faculty, mocking students, graduates even less prepared to do critical thinking and writing than before.

But I have also seen a "W" program that is still effective after five years—indeed, becoming more effective as it matures. The University of Missouri in Columbia began modestly, with a single required "W" course, and in 1993 expanded that requirement to a second "W" course. As oppposed to the eastern university, UM saw to it that the necessary support structures for the "W" program were protected and developed. The writing center is well funded, with professional direction, excellent facilities and staff, and budget for tutors. Although UM does not require small classes for the "W" designation, classes that surpass twenty are budgeted for trained teaching assistants to help with the writing instruction. A powerful campus committee oversees the program, reviewing course curricula and insisting that its list of course requirements be included in the actual curriculum of each "W" course; these requirements include a minimum number of words for students to write, a minimum number of revisions, and a paper that debates issues in the field of the course. Most important, the university has continued to sponsor well-reputed seminars in writing, attended not only by the faculty but by various administrators.

Despite the high morale, continued support, and favorable reputation of the University of Missouri's "W" program, it is not free of problems. The program assessment has only begun, and a few skeptics are unconvinced that the large investment in the program is paying off. The faculty teaching the "W" courses murmur about lack of rewards for the extra work their teaching requires, and the program director is concerned about "burnout" as the enthusiasm for a new program settles into routine. As the program expands, it is unclear whether the faculty will continue to volunteer a sufficient number of "W" courses to meet enrollment demand. And the program has not yet encountered an entirely new administration that may have different priorities.

Nonetheless, universities that take writing seriously, as the University of Missouri does, can make a writing-intensive program work successfully. But no one should minimize either the difficulties or the expense involved over the long term.

Test with Course Option

Some campuses have tried to combine the advantages of certification through a test with those of a certification course. For example, those who fail the campus test are not required to keep retaking it until they pass; they might be certified as proficient despite a failing score on the test if they receive a passing grade in, say, English Z, Intensive English.

The advantages of this procedure are clear. Most students will presumably pass the test and receive certification. Only the weakest students will need an upper-division writing course, so the staffing burden and expense for such a course are no longer overwhelming. If the test is responsibly run and the course well staffed, the quality of the college degree is protected without the necessity for every department to review its curriculum and without the elaborate structure of the "W" requirement.

However, this procedure, unlike the one that follows, winds up combining the worst aspects of both test and course certification. Since the test is the primary means of certification, all the pressures on the test will urge a higher passing rate and lower standards; the test will generally be seen as a minimum proficiency test, to be failed only by dumbbells. Thus, all the problems of the single-campus test procedure will remain, with the single important exception that adequate writers who do not test well will now have a more appropriate route to the degree.

Meanwhile, it is hard to exaggerate the negative effects on the course that must be taken by those who fail the test. The resentment felt by the teacher assigned to teach the upper-division remedial class is usually matched or overmatched by the resentment of the students forced to take it. No one expects it to be a substantive class; some simulacrum of minimum competence is bound to be the goal. The (usually young and inexperienced) teacher is solely responsible for upholding university literacy standards, under great pressure from students who have managed to get by until now despite poor writing ability.

Thus, the test with course option tends to be a depressing method of certifying students' writing proficiency. Both the test and the course behind the test tend to be public embarrassments, euphemistically titled and attended with reluctance by everyone involved. One major urban university now lists between sixty and seventy-five sections of an upper-division remedial writing course each term and hires a trained corps of graduate students to teach this pedagogical oddity each year. Those involved argue that the course is well taught and essential, particularly for the large numbers of able students for whom English is a second language. Nonetheless, the test is exceedingly elementary and the course hardly above the high school level despite its upper-division designation. One wonders whether the proficiency program in fact protects university standards or, rather, protects those faculty throughout the university who neglect their own responsibilities toward their students' writing.

Portfolio Assessment

Peter Elbow and Pat Belanoff gave great impetus to portfolio assessment in writing when they began to publicize the proficiency program begun at the State University of New York at Stony Brook. In two articles (Belanoff and Elbow, 1986; Elbow and Belanoff, 1986a) and in two book chapters (Elbow and Belanoff, 1986b; Belanoff and Elbow, 1991), they demonstrated how a portfolio assessment team could replace test scoring for proficiency assessment at a good-sized university. The students were required to prepare a portfolio from their work in the composition class, and the class instructor was involved, but not predominantly so. In evaluating the portfolios, the portfolio assessment team was able to maintain consistency and reasonably high standards, with sensitivity to the differences among students and among faculty. The advantages of portfolios, which I set out in Chapter Six, were made evident, and the enhanced validity of the entire operation seemed clear.

The most convenient and up-to-date description of the program, giving substantial detail and a gloomy projection for the future, appears in the collection of essays edited by Pat Belanoff and Marcia Dickson (1991). The historical review by Belanoff points out that, with the departure of Elbow and the gradual distancing of the assessment team from the instructional staff, the portfolio program is starting to seem more and more like just one more test. Nonetheless, the Stony Brook program demonstrated that relatively large-scale portfolio assessment can be practical and enormously advantageous to the teaching program; it also demonstrated how difficult such an assessment is to maintain. Many other institutions, such as New Mexico State and Alaska Southeast, have developed portfolios for proficiency assessments, adapting the Stony Brook model to their own programs.

We probably will not know until the end of the century whether portfolios will overcome the enormous problems of cost and reliability to survive as a serious large-scale assessment device. We do know that an institution willing to support portfolio assessment and with devoted leadership can develop a powerful and meaningful assessment that supports the teaching of writing. We also know that small campuses, such as Alverno College, can make portfolios the center of the student learning experience: the Alverno student builds the portfolio throughout the college years and uses it in many ways.

I encourage institutions to attempt portfolio assessment if the faculty leadership is willing to give a major effort for some years to the project—and if the resources are available. But I do urge caution, for all the reasons I have outlined in Chapter Six. In addition, assessment by a designated evaluation team has the built-in danger of separating assessment from teaching; the time-consuming reading of portfolios exacerbates that problem by reducing the number of participants in the assessment to a team of specialists willing and able to do the job.

Effective Certification Through General Faculty Involvement

Since student writing proficiency (however it may be defined) is a result of consistent attention by the general faculty to student writing, and since the call for certification outside the curriculum reflects dissatisfaction with faculty standards, any serious certification program must involve the faculty as a whole. I am not speaking here of altering existing departmental offerings to form "W" courses but rather of establishing a separate upper-division writing course—as part of a university's general education requirements— to be taught by faculty in the disciplines.

Most of the other methods of certification avoid the painful and political process of involving the faculty in fundamental curriculum change. Yet a felt need for a certification program—the assumption on which we are proceeding here—ought to be seen as a demand for such change. Testing programs extraneous to the curriculum have problems because they treat symptoms and actively avoid dealing with root issues. Although a certification program that does not involve many faculty is relatively easy to put in place, it is also easy to dismantle when attention or budgets turn elsewhere. Since no real changes are involved, the program tends to be more cosmetic than actual, despite the energy expended by those committed to it. Even the "W" course program is largely extrinsic, since it involves additions to ordinary courses, and these additions can easily be dropped. Furthermore, since the only campus check on a "W" course is a curriculum review, no one can feel sure that students passing the course have demonstrated much writing proficiency.

The best way to certify student writing proficiency at the college level is to require of all students a passing grade in a significant general education writing course at the upper-division level, a course with clear, common, and public standards. If such a course becomes an accepted requirement, no one will consider it to be remedial, and all the pressures on the course will urge substance and quality.

What appears to be the major disadvantage of this procedure turns out to be a substantial advantage: the faculty must be willing to include the certification course as part of the required general education program, at the upper-division level. Woodrow Wilson once complained that it is easier to move a cemetery than a university faculty, yet without such movement a writing-proficiency program is bound to be rather an empty gesture. If the faculty as a whole is willing to assume responsibility for student writing and to demonstrate that responsibility by adding and teaching an upper-division general education requirement, the pressure for proficiency certification outside the curriculum is bound to disappear in time. The greatest success a writing-proficiency program can achieve is to become unnecessary; if most faculty members decide to require writing in their classes and demand high-quality work, so large a proportion of students will pass any certification system that it will wither away. (I administered such a program in the 1960s and presided happily over its abolition. Those were the Good Old Days.)

Once a writing-proficiency course is part of the required curriculum, many of the problems we have been describing become manageable. Staffing demands need not fall only on the English department but can be spread throughout the institution, with all the advantages of widespread concern for student writing. Coordination of the program remains necessary, and difficult, but each institution can draw on its tradition of coordination, common course requirements, and common examinations for multisection general education courses. Most important, those teaching and those taking the course will have no incentive to debase it; it will in fact seem more like a senior honors seminar than a remedial writing course, and students as well as faculty will bring inventiveness and interest to it.

Experience has shown that a common examination or portfolio assessment is absolutely necessary if the centrifugal forces that are always at work on advanced courses are to be resisted. If the staff teaching the proficiency course each term must meet to plan, discuss, select, and grade a common examination or the portfolios of all students taking their classes, there will be a built-in corrective to the tendency to specialize the disciplinary content of the sections or to diminish the importance of writing. One study has shown, in addition, that bringing members of a writing faculty together to develop and score an assessment is the single most effective way to organize a faculty development program (White and Polin, 1986, pp. 215–220): since everyone needs to be involved and to discuss the purposes of the class, teachers learn more about the teaching of writing indirectly by working together on an assessment than they do directly in any number of retreats, lectures, and seminars.

Some students will be able to test out of the required course by demonstrating a high level of proficiency on a difficult written examination or through an expert portfolio. Such an examination or portfolio can be unabashedly demanding, requiring, for example, analytical skill and a substantial ability to use sources; to organize, demonstrate, and connect ideas; and to revise one's work. Since the standard means of certification is a course, the pressures to depreciate the assessment will not be difficult to resist. As long as the course is seen as the basic certification device, the challenge assessment can be appropriately demanding, designed for those special students who clearly do not need the course. Perhaps those who pass can form a special honors seminar or in some other way build on their demonstrated writing ability. Failing the assessment is no disgrace, since relatively few pass and most do not even attempt it. Most important, the challenge assessment now sinks in importance and prominence to a properly subordinate place to instruction. While the test or the portfolio will, of course, call for several kinds of writing, and show careful concern for validity and reliability, it need not carry the entire burden for institutional standards.

This procedure for certification, involving the introduction of a new general education requirement at the upper division and requiring assent from most of the faculty and participation by many of them, requires more than most universities are willing to give. As this book goes to press, I have completed a full decade as coordinator of such a program, so I know it is possible and practical, but no one should imagine it to be easy (see White, 1990, 1991). Establishment of the program is likely to take years of committee work, debate, and compromise, while maintenance calls for substantial resources and attention. Most of the university administrators and faculty concerned about the writing ability of their graduates do not want to confront the issue if it calls for so much trouble; they will prefer instead to complain (often about English teachers or the high schools) or to think that a test will make the problem go away. Some administrators and department chairs will neglect to ask why students can complete some courses of study without competence in writing. Others will point out, and genuinely believe, that writing is an outmoded or minor matter compared with the real business (whatever they take it to be) of the university. Still others will allege that certification of writing proficiency should be in the hands of the freshman English staff or the admissions office. Some may even regard the concern about writing ability as a passing fad, even now being replaced by worries about computer literacy and science training. For all these reasons, and many more, the stopgap and halfway measures I have been describing seem on many campuses to be a more reasonable response to pressures for certification of writing ability than the thorough reform I am recommending.

It is idle to imagine that the need for institutional certification of students' writing proficiency will disappear in the near future. Indeed, the democratic promise of expanded opportunity for less privileged populations and the renewed vigor of the community colleges should continue to provide most colleges in the United States with unconventionally trained upper-division students; there also seem to be no signs that the specializing majors in the college curriculum will ask their advanced students to return to the core of the liberal arts. Thus, the demands for the certification of students' writing proficiency outside the curriculum probably will continue and increase. Those responsible for such programs would do well to build upon the experience summarized in this chapter. In this area, as in most others, the close linking of assessment to teaching produces the most constructive solution to educational problems, which are never as simple as they appear to be. The basic problem of students' inadequate writing skill is so profound that only thorough solutions involving the entire faculty are likely to have much impact; the superficial and easy answers seem in general to create as many difficulties as they solve.

CHAPTER 9

Selecting
Appropriate
Writing Measures

The crucial decision of what measure to use often comes far too early in writing-assessment programs. Classroom practice is a useful model in this respect: even the most responsible teachers normally are busy constructing their final exams just a few days before they are to be given. If the final is to be valid, it needs to cover the material of the course, and coverage or emphases cannot be determined too far ahead of time; if the exam is to be fair to the students, it needs to deal with the actual curriculum, which has often shifted in emphasis as the term progressed. In addition, the final exam should be appropriate for this term's group of students, which may not be the same as last term's. Similarly, an assessment instrument must meet appropriate test specifications and must be right for the students involved, as well as for the material to be covered.

Unfortunately, in writing-assessment programs this process usually works backward. A test is often chosen first, not after the preliminary work is done, and decisions about its relation to instruction, its usefulness for the particular student population, and the meaning of its results follow and depend upon the particular test that has been prematurely chosen. In many cases, the test is selected for peculiar reasons—political or commercial or merely personal, for example—and the entire assessment is distorted as a result. It is as if teachers were to use someone else's final exam, with little relation to the courses they have actually taught.

As I was revising these words in 1993, a telephone call from the director of a writing program at a northwest university exemplified them. Would I help review the "outcomes assessment" of the freshman writing program? The existing assessment, I was informed, consists of a multiple-choice test of usage and punctuation, concocted by some forgotten faculty member decades ago. Students must pass this test to enter freshman composition and must score noticeably higher on it to pass the course. "Is the curriculum of the course," I asked with a sinking heart, "focused entirely on workbook mechanics?"

"Oh, no," the program director replied. "We focus on writing journals, the writing process, increasing student fluency, and developing critical thinking."

I felt some relief. As usual, the teaching was far ahead of the assessment. "In what way does your test relate to the outcomes of the course?" I asked.

There was a long pause. "Well, we've used this test for a long time and it is very convenient," came the reply. "And the rest of the faculty seem to like it very much."

I asked about the reaction of the composition staff.

"They try to ignore the test as best they can. But since so much is riding on it, they have to teach to it before the test dates."

I urged my caller to revise an assessment program that conflicted with the curriculum and to defer an "outcomes assessment" until she had reached consensus about what the outcomes of the program were supposed to be. Only then would it make sense to consider a measurement instrument.

This familiar disconnection between teaching and assessment leads to the odd complaint of "teaching to the test," a cliché in American education, a descriptor for distorted, even partially dishonest, instruction. The objection is inherently paradoxical, since virtually every classroom teacher does in fact teach to his or her own tests all the time and sees that as sensible and appropriate. Indeed, testing is so naturally a part of learning that no reasonable person questions the procedure. But when the testing seems, or in fact is, distant from or irrelevant to what is being taught and learned, "teaching to the test" suddenly becomes an issue. Some school administrators believe that mandating an inappropriate test (such as one normed on a wholly different population, using a wholly different curriculum) can raise academic standards and motivate greater performance. Such a procedure is, at best, a negative and damaging way to suggest curriculum reform. The primary mistake made in assessment programs is to begin by choosing a particular measure before developing the assessment goals, specifications, and uses. Since the assessment is a means of answering questions, to choose the measure prematurely is to decide on answers before understanding the questions.

Multiple-Choice Versus Essay Testing of Writing

A prime example of premature test selection emerges from the usual debate over multiple-choice testing of writing—an argument that usually ignores assessment goals and focuses on the convenience and economy of a particular test. Sometimes an active salesperson has gained commitments from a gullible administrator before the writing faculty are brought into the picture; at other times, key administrators may simply assume that multiple-choice tests are the only tests that can be depended on. Occasionally, the English department is so unwilling to invest time and effort in an assessment that it supports a multiple-choice test as the least objectionable alternative. But serious supporters of writing and writing programs will insist that no test should be chosen before goals and specifications have been developed; multiple-choice tests usually have little to do with what a writing program aims to accomplish.

Supporters of multiple-choice testing will argue that such tests are indirect measures of actual writing ability and that indirect measurement is often perfectly valid and appropriate. But traditionally and logically, an indirect measure is preferable to a direct measure only when it shows clear advantages over the direct measure. Until recently, advocates of indirect (usually multiple-choice) measurement of writing ability could point to the high cost and low reliability of scoring writing samples, as compared to the low cost and high efficiency of multiple-choice answer sheets. Now the argument has shifted: the high development costs of multiple-choice testing, the need for constant revision of multiple-choice tests under truth-in-testing laws, the lower validity of such tests, and the damage to curriculum such tests cause by devaluing actual writing—all suggest the weaknesses of multiple-choice measurement in the field of writing. Thus, the traditional argument about multiple-choice testing—namely, that it is similar to but less costly than direct measurement—no longer favors the fill-in-the-bubble tests.

But the larger objection most writers and writing teachers have to multiple-choice writing tests is that such tests examine an entirely different world than that of writing. When we enter the world of the multiple-choice test, we must accept a worldview in which questions (however complicated) have one (and only one) correct answer, to be selected from given options—a worldview unlike anyone's experience outside the testing room. When we write, we inhabit a quite different world, one in which we must generate and select from many options ourselves and in which most answers are at best partially true. However simple the writing task, we must select appropriate vocabulary, frame sentences, connect ideas, and express our own views. As writers, we know that life is complex and that simple answers are usually wrong. But if we use this perspective of the writer on a multiple-choice test, we are likely to get into trouble; we may see that, under some circumstances, the wrong answers could be right and the right answers wrong. But if we are good test takers, we sink those perceptions, along with all the other ambiguities and problems of life, and focus only on the single question that matters in the test world: what answer will the test maker define as correct?

When writers and writing teachers object to multiple-choice writing tests, then, they are not only protesting the validity of such tests in conventional ways. They believe that the entire world of those tests is so contrary to the world of writing that the results cannot be depended on to tell us what matters.

Everyone in education has a favorite "bad" multiple-choice test item. Here is mine, a question from a popular test designed to measure college-level competence in English composition:

English-speaking musicians use professionally a large
number of words from which one of the following
languages?
a. German
b. French
c. Spanish
d. Latin
e. Italian

The test makers are obviously looking in this question for a scrap
of information about the ways in which English uses foreign
words—in this case the Italian vocabulary for some aspects of musical notation. Some students may, in fact, pick up such information
in a composition course, though it seems unlikely; but the student
most able to darken the proper space on an answer sheet is probably
the one whose parents wanted to and could afford to give him or
her classical music lessons as a child. Those not so privileged (including, no doubt, some professional musicians) are not likely to
know the answer, regardless of their writing ability. And someone
who knew *too* much—for instance, a specialist in medieval music—
might even give the "wrong" answer, Latin.

It would be easy to select other unfair items from multiple-
choice tests (or any other kind), particularly items that are culture
linked, such as the one above, or based on dialect or usage differences that have no bearing on writing ability. The particular issue
here is not that unfair items exist but that multiple-choice test making encourages such items, since they "work" for certain convenient
norming populations. (Essay testing has its share, and more, of bad
questions, but they tend to be so difficult to score consistently that
they are rarely repeated; essay readers are much more opinionated
and vocal than are the computers that score multiple-choice answer
sheets.)

Those who are not specialists in testing sometimes fail to
realize that the most professional multiple-choice tests are very nar-
rowly and precisely conceived. I once asked an Educational Testing
Service test specialist about a particular item on the Scholastic Aptitude Test. "It's really a stupid question," I said to him, in some

exasperation. He cheerfully agreed. "Sure is. But those who succeed in the first year of college get it right, and those who don't succeed get it wrong. And that's what the test is all about." He was right, in a narrow sense, since ETS consistently tries to make those who use—and misuse—the SAT understand that its sole purpose is to predict success in the first year of college. But no amount of information seems to keep people from imagining that the SAT is a general intelligence test, a writing placement test, or (even worse) a measure of what should be learned in the freshman composition course.

A number of studies have attempted to relate the scores students receive on multiple-choice tests with those the same students receive on an impromptu writing sample (which is itself a problematic measure of writing ability). The correlations vary somewhat, as one would expect from the great number of variables involved (different kinds of students, multiple-choice tests, essay questions, scoring systems, and so on), but they tend to hover about the .5 range. The number, as usual, raises more questions than it answers. The correlation is roughly the same as that between the height and the weight of an adult American woman. That is, you can guess a woman's height from her weight with about the same accuracy that you can guess a student's essay test score from his or her multiple-choice score. Is that level of accuracy good enough? Partisans of multiple-choice testing will argue that the correlation is good enough to serve the purpose of a placement test and other measures, and good enough to support the inclusion of multiple-choice items on any writing test. Those opposed, many of them writing teachers, find such correlations too low, particularly in the light of evidence (described below) that the correlation drops markedly for racial minorities. Statisticians will remind us that a rough guide to the "overlap" of any two measures is the square of the correlation; by that principle, only about 25 percent of what is tested on most multiple-choice "writing" tests is also tested in a writing sample.

Nonetheless, particularly in the elementary and high schools, multiple-choice testing of usage or mechanics remains the standard way to assess writing ability. To be sure, some forward-looking state boards of education have begun experimenting with direct measurement: the California Assessment Program requires writing to set topics, for instance, and the Vermont schools assessment requires submission of portfolios. But, in general, those who argue for the economy and reliability of multiple-choice tests do not yet know that their arguments are outdated. How, the question arises at every turn, can informed teachers convince those in power to use and develop better types of measures? One intent of this book is to help those teachers marshal the evidence—through theories, arguments, and practices—to present a convincing case for an assessment program that uses direct measures of writing ability.

Ideally, the time to make such a case is in the planning stage of a new program or the evaluation stage of a continuing one; that is when a clear understanding of the issues surrounding multiple-choice and essay questions, placement and proficiency testing, and the strengths and problems of portfolios will help shape an assessment program. Knowledge, in this area as in most others, tends to destroy dogmatism and to promote a moderate and compromising stance. Perhaps the advocates of a multiple-choice test will be content to use it to examine some aspects of reading ability or critical thinking, while writing can be tested by a set of writing samples scored holistically according to carefully established criteria. Many of those who defend multiple-choice tests of writing have become defensive of their stance and will be ready to include writing if they can be shown that writing samples or portfolios can be properly constructed, reliably scored, and economically handled.

These debates can probably never be wholly avoided, but their acrimony can be substantially mitigated if the selection of a testing instrument is delayed until after careful program planning is under way. With a statement of goals, criteria, and uses, and with a clear connection between the instructional program and the assessment, it becomes possible to consider the assessment instruments within a context that encourages logical and purposeful discussion.

Bias in Writing Tests: The CSU Study

In recent years, the courts have become involved in the assessment of writing, most particularly in its fairness for various ethnic groups. In Florida, a high school proficiency-testing program had to be revised after a court found that it was testing for skills that had not been taught to substantial numbers of minority children. In Michigan, a similar legal quarrel developed over the legitimacy of a particular dialect ("black English") for testing purposes. (Attorney and English professor William Lutz is preparing a summary of legal issues in writing assessment for White, Lutz, and Kamasukiri, forthcoming.)

The entire history of mental measurement is marked by the questionable use of questionable data that support the prejudices of the time. Stephen Jay Gould's *The Mismeasure of Man* (1981) should be required reading for anyone involved in assessing others, on whatever scale. In the book, Gould documents a particularly inglorious history of distorted test results; and he claims, with what may be hyperbole, that science normally distorts facts in the interest of what it imagines to be the truth.

In this light, it is particularly interesting to review the comparative claims of essay and multiple-choice testing to fairness in the testing of ethnic minorities. The problem is complex, dealing as it does with the ambiguous and vexing definition of bias. Every test is, by definition, "biased" against those who do not know what is called for; the problem is to ensure that no unintended or illegal or immoral bias takes place (see Allan, Nassif, and Elliot, 1988). Those who believe that multiple-choice tests are objective are likely to assume that such tests are on the face of it more fair to minorities, since no humans (with intended or unintended prejudice) are part of the scoring. Evidence is beginning to accumulate, however, which casts doubt on that assumption.

The following study illustrates some of the difficulty of research in this area, particularly the very large numbers of students and tests that are required in order to have enough numbers of minority students for statistical purposes. The conclusions, which suggest that essay testing is substantially more fair to racial and ethnic minorities, are consistent with the view of writing and writing assessment taken throughout this book. In addition, subsequent research done by the Association of American Medical Colleges, comparing student performance on the multiple-choice portions of the Medical College Admissions Test with experimental essays, has come up with substantially similar results (Mitchell and Anderson, 1986; Koenig and Mitchell, 1988).

Overview of the Study

More than ten thousand students entering the California State University in the fall of 1977 took two tests, both designed for placement into either remedial or regular freshman composition programs. Almost 70 percent of that group identified themselves ethnically, a sufficient number for meaningful statistical analysis of test results by ethnicity. The study compared three different test score distributions—from a holistically scored essay, a multiple-choice usage test, and a measure that combined the essay with certain other multiple-choice portions—in order to ascertain whether ethnicity had any effect on these score distributions by the same individuals on different kinds of writing tests. Results were gathered, and five sets of graphs were prepared (Figures 9.1 through 9.5) under the direction of Leon L. Thomas, then associate dean of institutional research for the CSU. The findings showed that those identifying themselves as "white" had relatively little change from test to test, whereas those identifying themselves as one of three racial minorities had sharply differing scores. Furthermore, those who identified themselves as "black" had a radically different and lower score distribution from the multiple-choice usage test than they did from the holistically scored essay test.

The Tests

The students in the sample took both the Test of Standard Written English (TSWE), offered by the College Board as part of the Scholastic Aptitude Test, and the English Placement Test (EPT), offered by the California State University with the consultant support of the Educational Testing Service. While both tests have the same purpose, they are different in a number of important respects.

The TSWE is described by the College Board in its information brochure for students as follows:

The questions on the Test of Standard Written Enlish evaluate your ability to recognize standard written English, the language of most college textbooks and the English you will probably be expected to use in the papers you write for most college courses. The TSWE tests some basic principles of grammar and usage such as agreement of subject and verb and of pronoun and antecedent, and it also deals with more complicated writing problems such as whether or not the comparisons made in a sentence are logical. The test begins with 25 usage questions, then has 15 senence correction questions, and ends with 10 more usage questions.

The test as a whole consists of fifty questions, to be answered in thirty minutes. The questions are of the familiar error-hunting type, as in the sample question provided by the College Board:

He spoke <u>bluntly</u> and <u>angrily</u> to <u>we spectators</u>. <u>No error</u>
      A   B   C   D   E

Students are expected to blacken the bubble marked "C" to show they have found the error, one that appears only in the world of multiple-choice testing. The assumption is, of course, that students who can locate such errors in a test designer's prose will not make similar errors in their own writing, or, to be more fair to the correlational concept of indirect measurement, that students who can accurately find such errors are likely to be better writers than those who cannot.

The EPT is a much longer test (two and a half hours) and consists of four parts: an essay section calling for forty-five minutes of student writing, a multiple-choice reading test of thirty-five minutes, and two additional multiple-choice parts called "sentence construction" and "logic and organization." It is designed to be more diagnostic than the TSWE, though the description in the EPT student brochure shows a very similar purpose:

The English Placement Test has two purposes. The first is to provide an indication of your general skill in reading and in written communication, and the second, based on an analysis of the specific skills measured, is to provide a brief description of your strengths and weaknesses.

The multiple-choice portions of the EPT, which are not our concern here, tend to avoid error hunting because they attempt to measure what writers do (read texts, construct sentences, use logic), and there is no isolated usage test at all. The essay is generally based on personal experience and calls for organized description with a limited amount of abstraction. The following sample essay question is distributed to students applying for the examination:

Write an essay describing an occasion on which you privately or openly resisted a viewpoint that had become popular with your friends and acquaintances or one on which you felt that actions taken by them were wrong. (1) Describe the situation, (2) explain why you disagreed with the group, and (3) tell how you handled the situation.

The scoring guide for the essay is similar to the holistic scoring guide that appears as Resource A at the back of this book. The essay scoring was reported and is used here as a sum of the two ratings given by two separate readers on a six-point scale; the best score is two scores of 6, or a total of 12.

The two tests are similar enough in intention—to identify students who require extra work in writing before entering freshman composition courses—and different enough in concept and construction to allow for the study of ethnic differences on the different portions of the tests. The differences on the tests have nothing to do with "standards" or with the value of teaching students appropriate usage for formal writing situations. Both tests in the study agree on the need for high standards and appropriate usage. The EPT, which does not include a usage section, stresses that usage in context is an important component of the essay score: "Of course, the rating your essay receives from the faculty members who score it will, to some extent, also be dependent on how well you spell and punctuate and how carefully you follow such conventions of standard written English as subject-verb agreeement."

The Student Sample

The student sample is unusually well suited to the purpose of the study. A large number of students must participate if significant minority-majority comparisons are to be made. The California State University, with its nineteen campuses (then) in a variety of urban, suburban, and rural settings, its centralized data banks, and its huge number of students (approaching one third of a million), is one of the few institutions that provide the opportunity for such a study. The students who took both the EPT and the TSWE in preparation for admission in fall 1977 were in every way representative of the entire first-time freshman population that year. Entrants were then (as now) restricted to those in the top third of the high school graduating class, with the exception of a small percentage of special admissions under such programs as the Educational Opportunities Program.

Of the 10,719 students in the sample, 7,300 identified themselves ethnically, principally in the following four categories: 5,246 white, 585 black, 449 Mexican-American, 617 Asian-American. These numbers approximate the proportion of these minorities in the CSU entering class and are large enough for meaningful statistical analysis of test results by ethnicity.

Test Results

The charts presented below (Figures 9.1 to 9.5) offer an unusual opportunity to compare the performance of different ethnic groups on a multiple-choice usage test (TSWE) and on an essay test that includes usage in a writing context (EPT essay). Both tests are intended to make the most careful distinctions at the low end of the test scale. Students above the mean are to be considered ready for college-level work, and the tests give no further information of use to that group. The most useful measurement is designed to take

**Figure 9.1. Performance of All Participants in CSU Study
on Multiple-Choice and Essay Tests.**

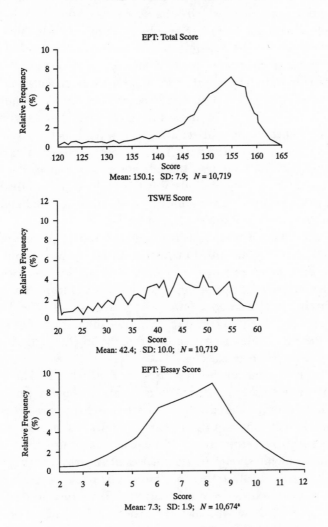

EPT: Total Score

Mean: 150.1; SD: 7.9; *N* = 10,719

TSWE Score

Mean: 42.4; SD: 10.0; *N* = 10,719

EPT: Essay Score

Mean: 7.3; SD: 1.9; *N* = 10,674[a]

[a] Essay score distributions do not include a few students who did not attempt the essay, although they completed the multiple-choice portions of the EPT (English Placement Test) as well as the TSWE (Test of Standard Written English).

Source: White and Thomas, 1981, p. 279. Reprinted by permission.

place in the scoring range where the decision about possible
remedial placement is likely to occur. Ordinarily, this means a
distribution that is skewed left—that is, stretched out and tailed off
in the lower range. The three graphs in Figure 9.1 all show this
characteristic in varying degrees.

The essay portion of the EPT shows a relatively more "normal" distribution than does the EPT total score. Such a distribution
is characteristic of most holistically scored tests; since its holistic
scoring develops its criteria in part from the papers in the sample,
its score distributions will tend more toward a bell curve than
strictly criterion-referenced tests. There is, nonetheless, a noticeable
left skew from the essay test, though not as much as in the EPT
total. The TSWE scale is considerably flatter than either of the EPT
scales, with curious concentrations of scores at the bottom and top
ends of the scale, but it is also skewed left.

Since the white students composed almost 72 percent of the
7,300 students who identified themselves by ethnicity, it is not surprising that the score patterns of these students are very close to
those achieved by the total group (see Figure 9.2). Mean scores tend
to be higher, and we notice fewer low scores overall. The TSWE
shows approximately 4 percent receiving the highest possible score.
While the EPT scales do not show as marked a shift upward, the
shift still may be observed.

So far, there are no surprises in these charts. The short
multiple-choice usage test seems to correlate reasonably well with
the writing sample, though the longer test seems rather better for
the purpose of distinguishing among the weak students. Those who
identify themselves ethnically as white score as a group better on the
test than nonwhites, reflecting an aspect of American society confirmed by virtually all testing programs. The patterns of scores on
all the charts are roughly similar. But when we turn to the score
distributions of those who identified themselves as black, we discover some radical differences of pattern and range of distribution.

The dramatic set of graphs in Figure 9.3 shows the different
score distributions black students received on the TSWE and the
EPT. The multiple-choice usage test not only groups over 11 percent of the black students at the lowest possible score but distributes
black students in a pattern of performance wholly different from

Figure 9.2. Performance of White Participants in CSU Study on Multiple-Choice and Essay Tests.

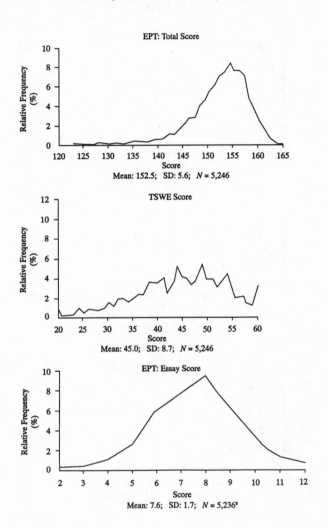

[a]Essay score distributions do not include a few students who did not attempt the essay, although they completed the multiple-choice portions of the EPT (English Placement Test) as well as the TSWE (Test of Standard Written English).

Source: White and Thomas, 1981, p. 279. Reprinted by permission.

Figure 9.3. Performance of Black Participants in CSU Study
on Multiple-Choice and Essay Tests.

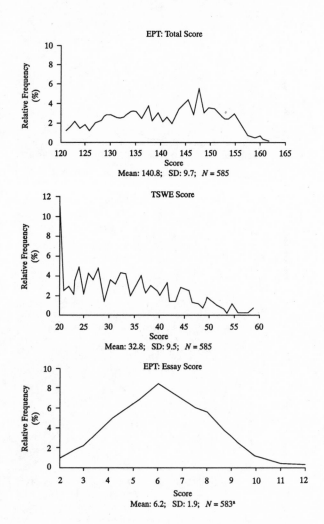

ᵃEssay score distributions do not include a few students who did not attempt the essay, although they completed the multiple-choice portions of the EPT (English Placement Test) as well as the TSWE (Test of Standard Written English).

Source: White and Thomas, 1981, p. 280. Reprinted by permission.

that shown by the same test for the majority (compare the TSWE scores in Figures 9.2 and 9.3). It might be argued that such a distribution reflects the writing ability of this group, but those same students—precisely the same individuals—scored quite differently on the EPT. While these students have a lower EPT total mean score than the white students, they are distributed along the whole range of scores, and their pattern reflects the left-skewedness that is desirable for placement testing.

After these charts were initially published (White and Thomas, 1981), some of those responsible for the TSWE argued that the graph showing TSWE scores in Figure 9.3 appears as it does because the test was too hard for this group of students; a revision of the test with easier questions would spread the bottom group out to the left in a pattern similar to the other patterns. That may be so, and I understand that the test was subsequently revised several times before ETS announced its intention to abandon it altogether. The issue, however, is not whether that particular test became better or worse than some others but, rather, the degree to which multiple-choice usage tests in general distribute minority students differently than direct measures of writing distribute them. The 1977 form and scoring of the TSWE—a highly professional test constructed by ETS and administered by the College Board to over a million students—clearly allow us to examine that issue, whatever the claimed virtues of revisions of that particular test. Indeed, the very high correlation of the TSWE scores with SAT scores suggests that the issue before us relates to certain aspects of multiple-choice tests in general.

Perhaps the most interesting comparison is between the performance of these students on the TSWE and their performance on the EPT essay test. We need to be cautious, since a single timed personal experience essay, even if scored with considerable reliability, should not be considered a definitive measure of writing ability. It does, however, serve as a direct measure of the characteristic indirectly measured by the multiple-choice test and must be considered a validity check for it. We have already seen that white students demonstrate a considerable similarity in score distributions on the TSWE usage and the EPT essay-writing tests. For black students, the dramatic dissimilarity casts some real doubt on the validity of usage testing as an indicator of writing ability.

Some defenders of the multiple-choice test have claimed that the faculty members grading the essay test were insensitive to the writing errors made by black students, and, in effect, showed a bias toward these students when they graded the papers. But this is unlikely for several reasons: readers would have had no way to distinguish the papers written by minorities from those written by the rest of the students (while deciding over 21,000 scores), strict quality-control measures (as described in Chapter Ten) have led to high inter-rater reliability for EPT essay readings, and the criteria for scoring papers do stress such matters as grammar, syntax, and diction.

The most likely explanation for the different patterns of performance on the TSWE and the EPT essay test, as shown in Figure 9.3, has to do with the significance of a multiple-choice usage test for determining the writing ability of black students. It is altogether likely that the *type* of question that usually appears on usage tests, and that dominates the TSWE, penalizes nonsignificant features of minority dialects. It is also possible that the ability to identify errors in a test maker's prose relates more strongly to the dialect learned as a young child (that is, the dialect spoken in the home and on the playground) than to a learned ability to write in prose acceptable to college professors as essay readers.

The College Board, of course, has a vital stake in demonstrating that its tests do not show racial bias and has published a number of reports dealing with such questions. Despite its general affiliation with the social values of the prestigious eastern private schools, the College Board has obvious good intentions in this regard and some real concern for the issue. It is well to be cautious about these reports, however, particularly in relation to the minority populations used in them. Research Bulletin RB-77-15, *Group Comparisons for the TSWE* (Breland, 1977a), for example, provides data on 9,144 students; however, not all minority groups are well represented in these data, since only eight of those students identified themselves as Mexican-American.

Figures 9.4 and 9.5 show the patterns of performance for two additional ethnic groups. Once again, we notice an important dif-

Figure 9.4. Performance of Mexican-American Participants in CSU Study on Multiple-Choice and Essay Tests.

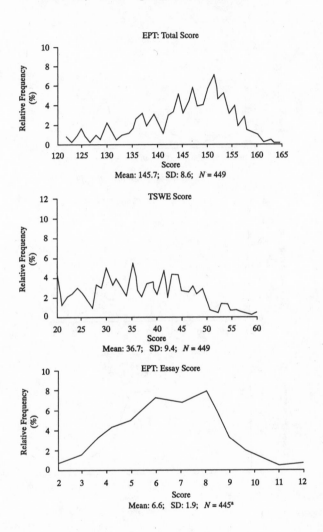

a Essay score distributions do not include a few students who did not attempt the essay, although they completed the multiple-choice portions of the EPT (English Placement Test) as well as the TSWE (Test of Standard Written English).

Source: White and Thomas, 1981, p. 281. Reprinted by permission.

Figure 9.5. Performance of Asian-American Participants in CSU Study on Multiple-Choice and Essay Tests.

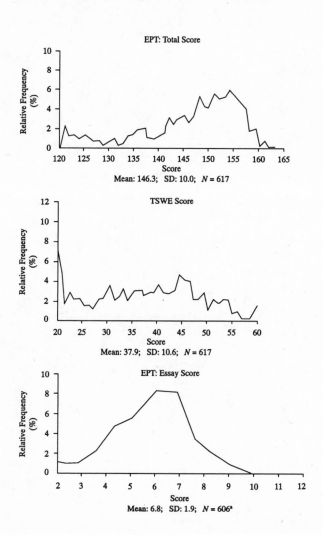

[a]Essay score distributions do not include a few students who did not attempt the essay, although they completed the multiple-choice portions of the EPT (English Placement Test) as well as the TSWE (Test of Standard Written English).

Source: White and Thomas, 1981, p. 281. Reprinted by permission.

ference in pattern of score distribution between the EPT, particularly the essay portion, and the TSWE. For these two groups of students, we may presume a certain amount of second-language interference rather than the dialect interference typical of the black group. The multiple-choice usage test once again rendered a much more negative judgment of these students' use of English than did the evaluators of their writing.

Conclusions

This study is by no means conclusive, though its replication by the medical colleges is confirmatory. But it does suggest a series of propositions and warnings. In the first place, it shows that the TSWE, a conventional multiple-choice usage test, does not distribute the scores of minority students the way that trained and accurate evaluators of writing samples do. Perhaps multiple-choice usage tests in general and even many other kinds of multiple-choice tests share this disparity. Those who use such tests (or any kind of test) should be aware of possible differences in measurement (unrelated to the subject supposedly being tested) for minority students.

The first major study of the correlation between essay and multiple-choice usage tests, published by the College Board, argued for the inclusion of both test types: "The combination of objective items (which measure accurately some skills involved in writing) with an essay (which measures directly, if somewhat less accurately, the writing itself) proved to be more valid than either type of item alone" (Godshalk, Swineford, and Coffman, 1966). A recent update of that study comes up with the same conclusions (Breland and others, 1987). The study of CSU entering freshmen tends to support that statement, by suggesting that the validity of multiple-choice tests may well vary according to the ethnic background of the student. A carefully devised and properly scored essay test seems not to contain that same problem of validity for minorities, and those seeking fairer treatment for minorities in testing would do well to argue for expanded use of essay testing. We can probably extrapolate these findings to portfolio assessment as well, though we must wait for studies to confirm that supposition.

The Process of Selecting a Writing Measure

In Chapter Eight I described various possible goals for college writing assessments and ways of reaching those goals. Here I will use the most common goal of writing assessments in colleges—the placement of students into a regular or a remedial freshman composition class—to exemplify the process of establishing goals and then selecting a writing measure.

Political and Social Issues Behind Placement

Although, on the surface, the goal of placement tests is to identify students who need special instruction in order to succeed in the regular program, below the surface lies the question of who is entitled to gain access to the privileges of college. Some institutions solve the placement problem in the admissions office. If admission is restricted to students prepared to succeed in the freshman program, a placement assessment is neither appropriate nor meaningful. This was the normal situation in what some take to be the good old days, when only "qualified" students showed up in college classrooms. These students usually were the well-conditioned and privileged sons (sometimes even daughters) of the upper middle class, with a few brilliant scholarship students recruited from the less privileged classes. Most of American higher education no longer inhabits that world, though many academics feel a powerful and not entirely covert longing for a return to it.

The vast majority of institutions now aver at least some concern for diversity. These schools, including most two-year colleges, have attempted to widen the paths to higher education. They soon found, however, that simply admitting a wider variety of students did not ensure their success; the "open door" they offered turned into a "revolving door" as students left in large numbers, for various reasons. Without substantial new supportive services, many of the new students could not succeed in the traditional programs; and numbers of those who could succeed chose to leave anyway, finding themselves not particularly welcome. But when the institutions did provide such services as writing placement into well-conceived remedial or developmental programs, students from social and ethnic groups outside of the white middle and upper classes performed successfully; unpublished data collected by the Chancellor's Office of the California State University and by the New Jersey Board of Higher Education showed that the persistence rate for poorly prepared students who had been placed in remedial courses surpassed the rate for students who had been placed in regular courses.

Many institutions that express a concern for diversity, and even provide support for untraditional students, ultimately undermine those programs, particularly under financial pressure. Before undertaking a placement assessment, an institution must be willing to fund a genuine program for those scoring at the low end of the scale; without such a program, placement is a waste of everyone's time. But these programs are always under attack, because they prepare students for college, presumably the job of the high schools. "Why should we pay for this stuff twice?" I was asked at a legislative hearing. "Because," I replied to the concerned lawmaker, "we have students on campus who have not learned it; without help, they will fail, and your fellow legislators have asked us to help such students succeeed."

The signs of a remedial program worth placing students into are obvious enough: qualified and supported faculty, up to date on recent research into ways to help untraditional students, with offices and time to meet with students. But when the remedial program is taught on the cheap, by retired high school teachers or untrained graduate students, using out-of-date workbook methods, without an institutional support structure that dignifies the enterprise, it serves as a holding tank for students who will not become part of the institution that has invited them to enter.

The first requirement, then, for a placement assessment is a writing program (in existence or in prospect) that will benefit the students. Without such a program, placement is simply negative labeling and not worth doing. The writing program, in turn, expresses the underlying political view of the institution, either welcoming and supporting diversity or seeking to screen it out.

Course and Assessment Specifications

Since an assessment develops information, the next step is to decide what information is needed for placement in writing courses. This question is much more complicated than it appears to be, since it depends on the curriculum of the writing courses on campus. Administrators or faculty outside of English are likely to believe that someone can come up with an objective definition of "remedial writing." It relates, they imagine, to the material taught in high school, which, of course, ought not to be college-level study. Thus, some mathematics faculty will argue, all math below calculus must be considered remedial. But American education is not structured sequentially, most particularly in its two foundation disciplines, English and mathematics. In both of these fields, the work done by, and expected of, the best high school seniors is at a higher level than we find in most first-year college courses. Only selective institutions can maintain the belief that all students unready for calculus are "remedial"; when we seek the parallel to that standard for writing, we wind up failing to meet the needs of many of the students in our classes.

The fact is that there is no single, context-free definition of "remedial writing." Since every institution, or system, needs to develop an operational definition of the term, the obvious place to start is with the regular freshman composition program. A remedial student is one who lacks whatever it is that is expected of those *entering* the regular program—not, we need to remind ourselves, of those *completing* the program. The answers to this question are easily obtained if one asks the right people: those who are teaching the students.

For example, after a series of meetings, the composition faculty from one moderately selective university gave a fairly simple response to the central question I kept asking them: "What distinguishes students who are ready to do the work in your regular course from those who are not?" The answer emerged after a serious curriculum review: basic sentence-level skills. I was surprised. This was not an open-enrollment institution; nonetheless, instruction in the regular composition course began with paragraph construction and focused on ways of demonstrating ideas in the paragraph and (later) in the essay. Besides, I was informed, a great many of the freshmen who met university entrance requirements had serious problems at the word and sentence level, so that there seemed no point in examining for more advanced skills.

The natural next step was to select or devise a placement examination that examined these word- and sentence-level skills. For the reasons I have set out in this chapter, the faculty did not want a multiple-choice test and were willing to undertake their own direct writing measure. But it did not have to be an elaborate examination, since all that was needed was a paragraph or two of prose. Writing topics that asked for analysis of arguments, explication of literature, or comparison and contrast of controversial positions were rejected as appropriate for the end of the composition course, not for the beginning. The faculty decided on a simple narrative topic, to emerge from the student's personal experience, as the best way to achieve the goal of the placement.

Within a year, such a test was created, pretested, and administered. True enough, nearly half of the entering students scored at the remedial level, as defined by that institution. But the story does not end there. The remedial course now had some clear goals, and the institution put some real resources behind the effort to reach those goals: class size was limited to twelve, renewed attention was given to the learning center, experimentation was encouraged, and regular faculty were rewarded for participating. The remedial course, under these encouraging conditions, was now able to bring most of its students not only up to the expected level but well beyond. Before five years had passed, those teaching the regular freshman course had reexamined and upgraded its curriculum, and the schools preparing students for the university were enhancing their writing programs in order to ensure that their students would pass the test. At this writing, the test is under review to see whether it should include more advanced skills, and a new course in study skills has been established for students who are not ready to begin work at the "remedial" level.

Those evaluating the effectiveness of placement testing in writing need to be particularly aware of the difference between placement and admissions testing, wholly different programs that are sometimes confused. Predictive validity is essential for admissions tests; their function is to separate potential winners from losers, and the results at the end of the freshman year should correlate highly with test scores. But placement tests exist to turn potential losers into winners. An effective remedial program will defeat the

predictions of placement testing; that is, it will help students succeed when (according to the predictions of placement) they were
supposed to fail. A naive evaluation of the placement program
based on simple predictive validity not only ignores the effects of
remedial instruction but declares that the program has the best statistics when it works the least well. Not all assessments are the same,
and the special purpose of placement should govern the evaluation
of the program as well as the selection of the measurement device.

Benefits of Local Development of Writing Assessment

The process of selecting an assessment device that I have just described offers much to the students, faculty, and curriculum of a
college. Institutions that seek to save money by adopting outside
placement tests normally gain only administrative sorting from
such tests—and sometimes not even that. But institutions that are
willing to see the placement test as functionally related to the writing program wind up not only with more appropriate tests but also
with a natural and continuing program review.

Moreover, placement tests deliver a powerful message to the
schools. If there is no writing on the placement test, the schools
preparing students for college have little incentive to require the
steady writing that leads to real improvement. This message function of placement has led some institutions to move beyond essay
testing to experiment with portfolio assessment. Certainly, many
years of multiple-choice testing have diminished the importance of
writing for college preparation, and portfolio assessment might reverse that message. Indeed, all writing assessment produces messages as well as scores, implications for curriculum as well as
sorting of students, definitions of the character of the institution
giving the assessment as well as repercussions for the students
involved.

CHAPTER 10

Organizing
and Managing
Holistic Essay
or Portfolio Readings

Those who are charged with organizing a scoring session for essay tests or portfolios can find little to help them in the literature. The procedure has developed so rapidly over the last two decades, and those involved have made themselves so generally available, that word of mouth and traveling consultants have satisfied much of the need. The basic source was the team that originated holistic essay scoring at the Educational Testing Service in Princeton, New Jersey. That team helped shape many holistic scorings, most prominently those begun on the West Coast in 1973 by the California State University English Equivalency Examination, whose director (the author of this book) made presentations at various places (such as the—then—Bay Area Writing Project), which further disseminated the concepts and procedures. The CSU English Placement Test readings, begun in 1977, were modeled on the previous CSU program and were widely copied; to complete a geographical circle, the CSU English Placement Test became the model for the New Jersey Basic Skills testing program and heavily influenced the essay test implemented at the City University of New York. Most holistic scorings have begun with help from those involved in these programs or those who attended workshops conducted by them. In addition, the first edition of this book (1985) set out the steps for conducting a scoring session, and many faculty have told me that their local work was based on those directions. By the early 1990s, hundreds of essay tests and a few portfolio assessments were being scored holistically.

The programs (and faculty) that have had the most experience with portfolio assessment, to my knowledge, are those in six institutions: the University of Michigan (William Condon), Miami University of Ohio (Donald Daiker), New Mexico State University (Chris Burnham), the University of Cincinnati (Russell Durst), the University of Alaska, Southeast (Joan K. Waters), and Alverno College (Marcia Mentkowski). The names in parentheses are scholars working to develop the validity and reliability of portfolios at their own institutions and to assist other colleges in mounting similar programs. Many other institutions are also developing portfolio programs for various purposes and are gaining valuable scoring experience. Two recent books have begun to disseminate this portfolio experience (Belanoff and Dickson, 1991; Yancey, 1992), and journal articles are focusing on specific issues (see, for instance, Hamp-Lyons and Condon, 1993).

The purpose of this chapter is to make generally available the experience of those who have been managing essay and portfolio readings. I will assume here that a placement or proficiency assessment has been given to a large group of students—the entering freshman class, say, or prospective graduating seniors fulfilling a proficiency requirement, or all students completing freshman English—and that a faculty member has been chosen to direct the scoring of the student materials. Whatever these materials may be— tests or portfolios or some combination—the inexperienced director confronts a surprisingly complicated task with many ulcerous traps. However, careful planning, with an awarenesss of the experience of others, can clear the way to a successful reading.

Planning the Scoring Session

Anyone who has been part of a badly planned scoring session will remember the irremediable sense of chaos it engendered. Before the scoring could begin, someone had to make the coffee (or find the coffee pot) and locate the pencils. Instead of being told where to record scores and how the first score will be concealed before the second reading takes place, the readers had to debate the procedure and come up with a system. The movement of papers from reader to reader was haphazard and uncertain. The chief reader scurried about finding materials and dealing with organizational matters instead of concentrating on developing a consensus on grading standards. The reading started late, and the last hour was as confused as the first, since no one seemed confident that the scoring would be finished before dinner. The experience seemed unprofessional and unsatisfying, and few would be ready to repeat it.

A well-run reading, in contrast, begins with a sense of calm and order. When readers appear, they find folders and name tags at their places and everything ready to start on time. They can concentrate on the taxing work at hand without being distracted by irrelevant detail, and they are kept informed about the pace of the reading and the expected finish time. The chief reader is calm and good-humored, confidently expecting agreement and ready to give full attention to the scoring. There is ample time for discussion of the sample papers or portfolios at hand, and some time is allowed for the readers to consider the implications of the assessment and the scoring procedure for teaching. Such matters as meals and honoraria are attended to by support staff in a way that makes the readers feel special. At the end of such a reading, faculty leave with a feeling of satisfaction, an enhanced sense of professionalism, and a willingness to repeat the experience.

The planning that makes the difference between a good and bad reading can be broken down into three categories: facilities, personnel, and materials. A well-planned scoring session shows care in all three areas.

Facilities

Typically, a room for a scoring session will be arranged with tables of readers as illustrated in Figure 10.1. This room arrangement will accommodate eighteen readers at three tables, with three table leaders. The chief reader, or room leader if there is more than one room, directs the reading from the front of the room. The aides need working space to distribute and collect portfolios or batches of papers, conceal the scores given on first readings, discover discrepancies, and check the count of tests or portfolios (to guard against misplac-

Figure 10.1. Room Arrangement for a Reading.

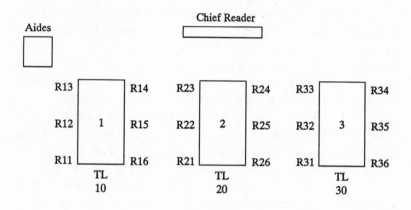

Note: R = reader; TL = table leader. Numbers are the individual identification numbers given to readers and table leaders.

ing one). The table leaders, whose function is to maintain a consistent grading standard at their tables, need room to walk around their tables to check randomly selected materials scored by readers.

Since all these activities require space and some whispered conversations, the room needs to be of ample size, with excellent lighting throughout, and, if possible, carpeted to reduce noise. The reading tables should be large enough for the readers to feel comfortable. Just outside the reading room should be an area for refreshments, with convenient rest rooms. A photocopy machine needs to be at hand, so that problematic student materials can be reproduced and made available for discussion; if no machine is nearby, one can be rented for a reading at low cost and installed at a convenient location.

Few schools have rooms suited for a scoring session. Classrooms and libraries cannot usually be rearranged suitably, and cafeterias or gymnasiums tend to be noisy and badly lit. Some universities will discover an appropriate location in a trustee meeting room or other conference room. Sometimes an auditorium can be made suitable, though lighting is often inadequate. The best facility may turn out to be a hotel meeting room or a local conference center. If compromises must be made, the highest priority should be lighting; second comes quiet; third is space.

Before the readers show up, the room should be prepared to receive them. Place cards help the readers find their seats quickly and allow the director to arrange readers to advantage. Inexperienced readers can be placed between helpful old hands or next to the table leader; noisy or gregarious personalities can be put next to unresponsive workaholics. Every reader and table leader should be assigned an individual number (as in Figure 10.1), to be written next to grades for record-keeping purposes and to ensure that second or third readings of a paper will always go to a new reader, preferably at a different table. A folder at each place could contain a copy of the essay question or the portfolio specifications (often forgotten), the scoring guide, sample papers, rosters of readers, pencils, and the like. The presence of coffee and doughnuts encourages early arrival and sets a pleasant tone.

Considerations of food and drink are by no means trivial for a longer reading. A hearty lunch on site saves reading time otherwise lost to restaurants, and a cocktail party planned at the end of the day keeps readers going through the long late-afternoon hours. Extra attention to these creature comforts says more loudly than words that the readers are special people doing a special task, and it reinforces the importance of the enterprise. The conversation at these social occasions and at breaks during the day (at least five minutes every hour or so) invariably centers around the task at hand, supporting the professional cohesion of the group and reinforcing the standards (and implications) of the reading.

For an essay test, only one question can be scored in a room at any one time. If the test consists of two or more questions, two or more rooms will need to be set up; or else readers in the same room can first complete the grading of question 1 and, after a break, undertake the grading of question 2. Only in this way can unwanted variables be kept out of the scoring process and reliable scoring be maintained. If portfolios are being scored holistically, they are usually treated as a single writing sample for scoring purposes and read in the same room. Although other scoring methods for portfolios (such as separate scores for each part, to be aggregated one way or another) have been considered, a single numerical score on overall quality is much less time-consuming. Moreover, since portfolios are usually considered units, whose whole is greater than the sum of their parts, holistic scoring remains theoretically as well as practically sound for them.

Of course, the perfect facilities may not be found or, in a small scoring session or a classroom scoring session, may not be needed. The teachers who involve their students in essay readings will group them in casual ways, and many of the strict procedures I am detailing in this chapter will give way before sensible compromises and alterations. I hope the classroom version of holistic scoring will not attempt to duplicate the machinery of large-scale assessment. At the same time, anyone who undertakes holistic scoring should be familiar with the strict procedures, even if they are not necessary at the moment; for the reasons behind the procedures do apply to any scoring session, however informal.

Personnel

Since a reading is only as effective as the people involved, particular care needs to be given to the selection of participants, particularly the chief reader, the table leaders, and the chief aide. Once chosen, these people should be given enough time to accomplish their tasks (not asked to add the scoring to already full teaching days or to volunteer weekends) and paid professionally for their extra time. Excuses for exploitation are always available and never convincing; the Educational Testing Service, for example, pays readers the merest token wages on the asserted grounds that it is a professional privilege to read essays eight hours a day for a commercial (if nonprofit) testing firm. But readers who are treated unprofessionally can scarcely be expected to develop the professional consensus and professional attitude that are absolutely essential for a reliable scoring session.

The chief reader, who is often but not always the program director, needs to possess a strong combination of flexibility and authority. This central person effectively runs the reading, choosing the sample papers or portfolios, moderating and ending debate over standards, arbitrating differences of opinion, and accepting final responsibility for a reliable scoring session. In the initial training session for readers, the chief reader needs to allow enough discussion of the scoring standards so that readers internalize and come to "own" the scoring guide; but discussion has to be cut off when it becomes unproductive. During the reading, the chief reader is constantly scoring papers or portfolios culled from the tables and discussing those scores with the table leaders; the essential task is to make sure that all table leaders have the same standards and that, therefore, the readers at the various tables do not drift up or down in their scoring.

From time to time during the reading, generally three or four times a day, additional brief training sessions will deal with particular problem papers or portfolios that have emerged. For example, a good essay test in bad handwriting will be distributed for scoring, or a good short paper will be contrasted with a weak long paper. Sometimes, superficial or empty papers with few mechanical errors will be receiving higher scores than they deserve, or unusual original approaches to the topic will be receiving lower scores than they should. Portfolios will sometimes show large variation in quality from one kind of writing to another or will demonstrate immense—perhaps suspicious—improvement from draft to draft, and the readers will need to agree on ways to handle such matters consistently. The chief reader will need to be alert to these potential problems and others like them and deal with them in a calm, authoritative way, eliciting rather than commanding assent.

Since there is no substitute for experience in a chief reader, those who are beginning new programs may want to import an experienced outsider for a first reading; the next chief reader can be chosen from the best of the table leaders. But sometimes it is politically wiser to select the most appropriate person available on campus as chief reader and let experience accumulate on the job. It is a rare academic who has the sensitivity, tact, self-confidence, and quick wit to accomplish this job well; a good first choice should be considered a lucky hit.

The table leaders need to have many of the same qualities as the chief reader. They need to be quick and steady readers, for it is their function to check-read papers or portfolios scored by readers at their tables throughout the entire scoring session. They must quickly locate the readers who are scoring higher or lower than the other readers, and it is their delicate job to ask these readers to adjust their standards; they must make these requests without damaging the self-confidence of sensitive professionals who are not accustomed to having their judgments evaluated or challenged.

It is easy to spot the good table leaders at a reading. They are seen as valuable allies by their readers, who will bring problem papers or portfolios to them for consultation. They establish a cordial tone at the table, even as they keep noise down, and they remain very busy check-reading papers or portfolios from each reader in turn. On the other hand, the inept table leaders see themselves—and are seen by their readers—as overseers; they tend to make everyone a bit edgy. These table leaders spot-check only occasionally and never seem to have much to do; their readers are unconvinced when asked to review or change scores that are out of line. An experienced chief reader knows that the quality and tone of a reading depends on the skill of the table leaders and will take particular pains to appoint the best that can be found.

The chief reader and the table leaders form a team that must work together comfortably. If they cannot reach agreement on the issues that emerge, the readers will never come to agree on consistent standards. But a team that works smoothly will be able to cope with problem questions or problem readers with aplomb and deliver reliable scores in a pleasant, professional environment. I hear many complaints about holistic scoring, which often fails to reach the ideal I have been describing; but no complaints are as severe as those about the chief reader and the table leaders. If readers feel that the people wielding power are coercing them into giving scores they do not believe in, the entire enterprise breaks down. The leadership team must take as its first responsibility the development of collegial consensus, not the rapid production of scores.

A competent chief aide is as important to an essay or portfolio reading as the chief reader and needs to be as carefully chosen. This aide will be responsible for the preparation of papers or portfolios for scoring, the movement of materials throughout the reading, the identification of papers or portfolios with discrepant readings (requiring a third reading), and the pacing of the scoring session. The aide prepares copies of all sample papers or portfolios, at the direction of the chief reader, and makes sure that readers are given the samples for scoring at the proper time. The aide usually oversees the preparation of travel reimbursements, payroll, time sheets, and the like, and sees to it that all supplies (including those for refreshment breaks) are at hand when needed. In short, the chief aide is responsible for all aspects of the reading outside of the actual scoring, and makes it possible for the readers to focus their attention on the scoring.

Chief aides thus belong to that bureacratic infrastructure that allows most enterprises in America to function: the special group that includes administrative assistants, department secretaries, assistants to the president, and so on. These people know how to fill in the forms, order the supplies, reserve the rooms, send out and monitor replies to appointment letters, and (when needed) make the coffee. No reading—no organization of any sort—can get along without such an aide, and one should be selected early, paid well, and honored fully. After two readings, the aide will know everything that needs to be done, maintain a small group of assistant aides as needed, require no instruction, and be indispensable. The only problem then becomes an occasional reminder to the aide that the chief reader must appear to be in charge and that the machinery of the reading must always support the reliability of the reading and not become an end in itself.

The choice of readers is fraught with difficulty, particularly for a new program; established programs will keep records of reader speed and accuracy, and so be more sure of a critical mass of good readers for any one scoring session. The ability to read essays or portfolios accurately and quickly demands a peculiar skill, not necessarily associated with other academic skills. Some excellent teachers never get the hang of it, while the least likely individuals sometimes turn out to be amazingly talented as readers. Excessively rigid teachers or those who are insecure often have difficulty adopting group standards, and faculty who take pride in their disagreements with their colleagues may resent the entire process. But even such apparently unsuited readers sometimes turn out to be delightful at readings, whereas some well-recommended people read erratically and inattentively. If an insufficient number of faculty members apply to be readers (probably because the pay and other rewards for reading are inadequate), the chief reader cannot make choices, and the reading will suffer in many ways.

Those who appoint readers should be careful about making premature judgments about them. Careful record keeping will identify those who read inaccurately or too slowly to carry their weight (though speed is much less important than accuracy and should not be overvalued). The experience of participating in a well-run reading is so valuable to faculty that rotation should allow virtually all those who are interested to take part. Sometimes a weak first reading will be followed by a strong second showing, as a teacher feels increasingly comfortable with the process. Over time, in a continuing program, the natural leaders will emerge to be chief readers and table leaders, and the best readers will form a steady cadre to help shape a new community each time a reading convenes. If the leaders of the reading have been well chosen, and if they can count on having a number of experienced readers at each table, the reading can accommodate as many as one-third new readers without losing control.

Materials

A scoring session is a specialized form of conference, and all the usual supplies for a conference need to be on hand: pens, pads of paper, aspirin, and the like. The chief aide should make up a list of such materials and add to it as needed. The special materials associated with a reading have to do with the arrangement of test booklets or portfolios for scoring, the preparation of sample papers and scoring guides used to develop consistent standards, the system of concealing prior grades for second and subsequent raters, and the plan for recording scores and other data from the reading for future use.

Arrangement of Test Materials for Scoring. I will speak first of essay test scoring and then of its adaptation for portfolios. It is so convenient to handle tests of uniform physical size and shape that virtually every essay testing program of any size requires students to write in a standard test booklet. Such "blue books" are available from every college bookstore, but many programs will design their own in order to develop a cover suited to their particular needs.

Such a cover will not only have spaces for the students to fill in identifying information but also locations for the assignment of grades. The lower half of such a cover (to be used by a reader who is scoring the test) may appear as in Figure 10.2.

This design allows readers to circle the scores they decide on, instead of writing them in more or less decipherable handwriting. The score of 9, meaning an off-topic or otherwise unscorable paper, may in some programs be given only by table leaders—in order to maintain consistency with papers uniquely different from those that meet scoring criteria. If the test booklet contains more than one question, additional boxes for scoring will be needed; if a third reader is used to resolve discrepancies between the first two, an additional set of boxes will be included for the reconciliation reader. In short, a well-designed booklet cover will allow for the needs of the particular test and simplify the recording of scores. Portfolio scoring sheets similar to these test booklet covers are often inserted as the first page in portfolios to be scored.

It is usually a good idea to randomize and batch test booklets in preparation for a reading. Batches of twenty or so can move from reader to reader as a unit much more conveniently than can individual tests; it is easier to keep track of 200 batches than 4,000 tests. Each batch should contain tests randomly chosen from the entire test group, so that certain groups will not be concentrated in special

Figure 10.2. Sample Test Booklet Cover Design (Bottom Half).

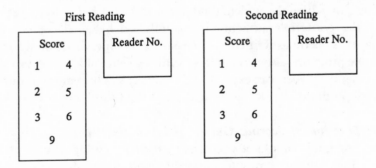

Note: The score of 9 is given for an unscorable paper.

batches. Even in a small campus reading of an exam from, say, eight sections of freshman composition (with twenty students in each section), the test booklets should be divided into ten batches of sixteen, with two papers from each section in each batch. Readers scoring randomized batches will not be distracted from the scoring guide by the peculiar characteristics of particular batches, and the reading will more fairly represent the group standards of the readers to all of those taking the test.

In a large essay reading, batches will be numbered, and every test booklet in the batch will also be stamped with the batch number. Any booklet removed from the batch (to serve as a sample, perhaps, or to be used during check-reading) can therefore be replaced. If batch numbers are included with final score reports, and if the batches are stored sequentially, any test can be easily located. In the last hour or so of a test reading, batches may have to be broken up, in order to even out the work that remains; if every test has a batch number, the booklets can be readily restored to order and counted at the end.

These well-established procedures for arranging test booklets for scoring have been adapted for portfolio scoring where appropriate. Unless the portfolios are small—at Miami University they may not exceed twelve pages—batching is not possible or desirable, so the portfolios move through the reading as individual units. But some attempts have been made to impose consistency and uniformity upon this basically open-ended format. Many portfolios require a cover sheet as the first item after the scoring page. This cover sheet, on which the student (and perhaps the teacher as well) testify to the portfolio's authenticity, is followed by a self-assessment paper, sometimes written under timed and supervised conditions. Some programs also mandate a specific sequence of kinds of papers, so that the readers can expect similar patterns as they move through each portfolio. (See Resource B at the back of this book.)

Preparation of Scoring Guides and Sample Papers. A tentative scoring guide should be prepared by the test development or portfolio assessment committee. Shortly before the reading, the chief reader and table leaders will meet to select sample papers or portfolios to illustrate the several score levels and to refine the scoring guide in the light of the actual student results. (Only the strictest purists require these samples to be scored again during the reading.) The final version of the scoring guide they approve will then be duplicated and made available to all readers, normally included in their folders at the table. Changes may be made in the scoring guide during the initial training session, but once actual scoring of the test has begun, no further changes can be made. All papers or portfolios need to be scored according to the same criteria. For examples of well-developed scoring guides, see Resource A and Resource B at the back of this book.

The length of the reading and the complexity of the question will determine the number of samples needed. An initial set of samples should be chosen to illustrate the range of quality, from the best to the worst, in the actual student writing samples and the distinctions in quality described by the scoring guide. Thus, a set of six samples would be chosen as the first set of "anchor papers" or "anchor portfolios" on a six-point scale, each one representing the most typical example of one of the scores. Some chief readers ask the readers to score this first set of samples, as a way to put the readers immediately on the spot making decisions. I prefer to distribute a scored first set, putting myself and the table leaders (who decided on those scores) on the spot, as a way to test the scoring guide and to ease the readers' tensions. After the scores for these samples are discussed in the light of the scoring guide, another set of typical unscored anchor papers or portfolios would follow, for further scoring and discussion.

If agreement is high and if there are few problems, relatively few additional samples will need to be used. But usually several additional groups of samples are needed in the initial training session. A set of four or five papers or portfolios may be used to clarify the distinctions between papers at the top of the bottom half of scores and those at the bottom of the top half. Another set may illustrate the difference between narratives that respond to the question and narratives that do not. Still another set may show readers the difference between papers that answer portions of the question indirectly and papers that do not answer portions of the question at all.

Training of portfolio scorers is much more complicated than

it is for scorers of essay tests. For example, portfolios designed to
evaluate the writing process run into contradictory assumptions on
the part of readers: some readers place a high value on improvements from draft to draft; other readers believe that any draft after
the first will reflect the influence of outsiders on the writer, and so
these readers disregard the improvements as inauthentic. The sample portfolios for such a program will need to provide examples of
revision, so that this matter can be brought into the open and resolved. The sheer bulk of portfolios extends training time, thus
tempting the leaders of the reading to abbreviate discussion; but the
complexity of portfolios suggests that substantial time must be
given to discussion of examples, or the scores will not be consistent.

At some point, the chief reader will decide that the readers
are ready for "live" batches or portfolios, and the scoring begins.
But additional samples will be used for training sessions after
breaks or meals, and the table leaders must be particularly alert to
problems that call for discussion during the early hours of a reading. A one-day essay test reading will often use twenty or more
sample papers before it is finished; the typical three-day reading
may well use forty. The bulk of portfolios reduces the number that
can be read but increases the representative importance of each
sample.

Samples are usually identified by letter, as sample "G" or
sample "BB." Aides should be prepared with sufficient copies of at
least fifteen samples at the start of an essay test reading, and they
will need to be ready to produce copies of additional samples rapidly throughout the reading. A minimum of twelve sample portfolios must be on hand for a portfolio reading on a six-point scale;
but, since test security is not an issue, these samples can be prepared
well in advance of the reading. If unexpected problems emerge, a
few portfolio samples may also need to be duplicated during the
reading.

At the end of Chapter Four, I mentioned the theoretical objections by critics of holistic scoring, who complain that this process of shaping a discourse community of like readers with
consistent standards falsifies the way people actually read. At many
readings, new readers are likely to voice this same complaint in
practical terms, particularly if they disagree with a group decision.

Certainly, readers who do not receive special training would normally apply different standards and criteria in scoring a student's paper, and a much wider spread of scores would result. But it seems absurd to me to argue that this variety of approaches to reading should be duplicated for test scoring. It is also naive to imagine that we are not already in discourse communities shaped in a variety of ways. An assessment has specific information to gather for specific purposes. The readers can work together to develop that information reliably if they form a temporary discourse community using common criteria. The world may indeed be inconsistent and unfair, but that does not mean our assessments should be so. I do not hear these critics arguing that the computers grading multiple-choice tests should be programmed for random errors, so that the test scoring can be more lifelike.

To be sure, some sacrifices are necessary to reach high reliabilities. Individual readers need to put aside their idiosyncrasies and agree with group judgments; a reader whose scores are different from everyone else's is scoring incorrectly. If the chief reader and table leaders are professional, this reader will not be made to feel uncomfortable or wicked; rather, he or she will be persuaded to change, at least for the sake and time of the reading. Unfortunately, some unprofessional holistic scoring sessions are in fact oppressive and uncollegial, enforcing scoring criteria that seem artificial and meaningless. Such readings are hateful, and I have no excuses to offer for them. But the more usual essay reading elicits from the readers a genuine consensus on the criteria for scoring and enforces that consensus, to everyone's benefit. I see no value in protecting the right of my more eccentric colleagues to fail brilliant essays with two spelling errors, or to rate every essay at the top of the scale because the students mean well. I have a cantankerous friend who declares with dreary regularity that for him to be forced to hear how his colleagues evaluate student work violates his "academic freedom" and his integrity. Such teachers, not to speak of their students, benefit from a certain amount of social coercion to use evaluation criteria their colleagues share.

The System for Concealing Scores. Every test paper or portfolio must receive at least two independent readings. If this basic rule is not followed—and economic pressures always urge this unprofessional shortcut—two serious problems occur. In the first place, the relative unreliability of any essay test or portfolio score will be exaggerated to the point that all scores will be open to question; in the second place, the essential data needed to demonstrate the reliability of the scoring will not exist. But it is not enough merely to generate two scores for each essay; those scores must be reached independently. Therefore, the score given by the first reader must somehow be concealed from the second reader. Furthermore, the system for concealing scores must allow for ready comparison of the two scores after the second score is registered, so that a reconciliation score may be added if necessary.

Small, informal essay readings can accomplish this goal in simple and informal ways. The first score can be written on the cover of the test booklet, which is then folded back; the second score is recorded on the now-exposed inside front cover. Or readers can privately record their first readings, which can be entered by a clerk after the second reading. However informal the arrangement may be, some system of concealment is necessary, since the temptation to look at the first reader's score is almost irresistible and will affect the second reader's score.

Larger readings have come to use more formal methods. Most commonly, aides will pick up a scored batch of papers from a reader and will cover all scores with a piece of specially constructed tape, unglued in the center. These tapes, nicknamed "Band-Aids" because of the perforations that allow the center portion covering the grade to be ripped away, come in rolls of 500 and are quickly and easily applied to the cover of the test booklet. The essay test office of the Educational Testing Service at Berkeley, California, has been a dependable and inexpensive source for those rolls.

Whatever system may be used will require special materials, and those materials need to be obtained well in advance of the reading.

Recording of Scores. When my colleagues and I get together to score the common examination we administer each term in the forty or so sections of our upper-division writing class, each of us brings a copy of the class roster. As the reading approaches the end, a graduate student aide busily unmasks first scores (we use Band-Aids), bringing discrepancies (a difference of more than one point on the six-point scale) to the chief reader for reconciliation, removing the scored tests from their randomized batches, and reorganizing them into class sets. Each instructor then receives the tests of his or her own students, records the scores on the extra roster for our records, and records them again on the class rollbook. At that point, the job is finished.

However, when the number of tests or portfolios reaches into the thousands or even the tens of thousands, more formal methods of recording scores are needed. In recent years, efficient computer record keeping has replace the cumbersome hand work of the past. The computer, when properly programmed, produces rosters in various kinds of order (such as alphabetical order by student name or numerical order from high to low score), individual score reports for each student, and various statistical data at the same time. Thus, score reporting and record keeping are part of the same operation, and files for additional score reporting can be easily kept and readily reproduced. Currently, this is the usual procedure for handling scores in large-scale testing programs.

Advances in technology suggest that much simpler procedures will soon become a new standard. As these new systems develop, they will require less and less complicated equipment, and the rather simple software will be available everywhere, as personal computers now are. Testing programs will not have to choose between simplicity and sophistication; every school and college campus will be able to manage records of essay and portfolio readings with ease. Any faculty director of an assessment program should involve the local computer specialist in planning for the use of scores. With careful communication and planning, the problem of what to do with scored materials and how to handle the mass of data produced by a scoring session can be solved. Without this proper and orderly planning, one can expect to be overwhelmed by tons of paper and unanswerable questions.

Conduct of the Reading

The central concern for a scoring session must be to establish what the literary critic Stanley Fish (1980) calls an "interpretive community": a community of readers responding in the same way to similar texts, as I described in Chapter Four and just above. The procedures involved in such a reading are all designed to set up such a community—within the constraints of a budget and a limited amount of time to accomplish a taxing and tedious job.

The most common mistake in the management of holistic essay readings is to lose sight of the need for collegiality. This delicate sense of joint participation and professional respect is difficult to maintain—especially when readings do not proceed by consensus and joint decision making. Some chief readers and administrators believe that discussions of standards for grading are a waste of time better spent in generating scores. Coffee breaks, cocktail parties, and the like, are seen as luxuries and frills instead of the community-forming activities they need to be. Gracious treatment of readers and professional pay for readers are considered to be expendable costs instead of essential ingredients for a professional working community. But readers are not merely employees; they must form a working team committed to group judgments and to the entire process of group scoring.

Even sensitive academics who run scoring sessions may make the same mistake if they are not careful, since the process of determining standards puts them in a position to coerce others in a good cause. Before readers come together to begin scoring, the chief reader and the table leaders will have met to read through many student papers or portfolios, in order to get a sense of the range of materials to be scored. These experienced readers will have spent a day or more reading several hundred test papers or dozens of portfolios, choosing materials to be duplicated for the readers to use as "range finders," and developing the scoring guide that describes the different points on the scale to be used at the reading. By the time the readers arrive, those responsible for the reliability of the reading will have already reached substantial agreement on standards. Every temptation exists, therefore, to tell the readers what to do and what standards to apply, so that the reading can get under way efficiently.

But to exercise authority in this fashion is to ignore the need for a community of assent, which is what a holistic reading must become if it is to function responsibly. Those who understand the process will exercise caution in using their advanced knowledge of the range of student writing. Readers must be given an opportunity to grade sample papers or portfolios, to argue out differences, to come to an understanding of the ranking system, and even to make changes in the scoring guide. The training of readers, or "calibration," as it is sometimes called, is not indoctrination into standards determined by those who know best (as it is too often imagined to be) but, rather, the formation of an assenting community that feels a sense of ownership of the standards and the process.

The standards of the reading and this sense of community must both be maintained throughout scoring sessions that may last many days. Retraining on new samples must occur from time to time, to prevent readers from drifting up or down in their scoring; and readers must see this process as a group endeavor to work together, not as a check by management on the accuracy of the workers. When leaders of a long reading organize social activities such as play readings, poetry readings, and special films, they are not serving as entertainment directors but, instead, are helping to hold the group together. When chief readers can use confident humor to acknowledge legitimate differences of opinion or admit that they might change their minds or even be wrong, they are not giving in to reader demands (as I heard one hard-nosed administrator call it); rather, they are admitting that they are human and part of the group, which must accept their leadership willingly.

In stressing the need for a sense of community, I do not mean to imply that the tone of a reading should be excessively casual. The best readings have a decidedly businesslike atmosphere, and the collegiality is part of the business to be accomplished. No one should regard the reading as a vacation or a social occasion. It is a hard and tedious job that must be done well in a limited amount of time. Establishing an "interpretive community" is simply the most efficient way to get the job done properly.

Visitors to a well-run holistic scoring session often are struck by the intensity of the work going on, usually with great rapidity, in an environment of relaxed cordiality. If an essay test is being scored, they will see a room of readers working through batches of essay booklets, at a rate of twenty-five to forty-five an hour (depending on the length and complexity of the question and the scoring guide). The table leaders will be standing by or moving around their tables, check-reading papers, or crouching beside a reader in a whispered conversation about the score of a troublesome essay. Aides will be picking up scored batches from readers and replacing them with batches to be scored; other aides will be masking scores at their work table or unmasking completed batches to discover discrepancies. The chief aide may be checking the pace of the reading and waiting to talk with the chief reader about how long the afternoon break can be. The chief reader may be talking quietly with the leader of table 2 about reader 24, who has been scoring consistently high and has had half a dozen discrepancies against reader 13. Meanwhile, one of the aides is duplicating a paper scored at the 2 level that ought to have received 4s; another aide is waiting to duplicate a hasty playbill for the play reading to occur after dinner (as it happens, a "world premier" of a new play to be produced by a major theater next month, directed by reader 36, who smuggled the script into the reading because he thought it would be just what the readers needed after a tedious day of scoring).

A portfolio reading will appear much the same, though there will be fewer aides, since portfolios are easier to keep track of. The fastest reading rate yet reported for portfolios is an average of six grades per hour; without controls on the quantity of materials, the pace can be as slow as one grade per hour. Anyone conducting a portfolio reading will need to run a pilot reading to measure pace, since standard measures have not yet been established for such readings, as they have for tests. The eighteen readers shown in Figure 10.1—if they are grading the typical college essay question, a forty-five-minute expressive or analytical paper—will average twenty-five essay tests per hour for a seven-hour workday (8:30 A.M. to 4:30 P.M.), including several training sessions with sample papers. That adds up to 175 scores a day for each reader, or 3,150 scores for the room. Since each test requires two readings, and about 10 percent of the scores will be more than one point apart and require a third reading, such a room will grade reliably about 1,500 tests a day. (The first day of such a reading will require about two hours for initial training and thus allow only a five-hour scoring day.) If the test consists of a twenty-minute writing sample, which allows for little development of ideas, the scoring pace will be almost twice that of the more complex test.

The budget for a scoring session often appears high at first glance. But a well-run holistic reading, besides producing scores at a reasonable price, has two additional advantages. First, the reading allows a writing assessment to be given and hence makes a major contribution to the educational enterprise at its most crucial point; the reading deserves funding support from the instructional budget for this reason. Second, a holistic reading is the most effective in-service training device yet discovered for the teaching of writing. It accomplishes more for the education and morale of the faculty involved than a series of lectures, seminars, and retreats; indeed, in a most creative way, it combines the virtues of various schemes for faculty development. The budget for faculty development or in-service training could hardly be better spent than in contributing to the costs of a scoring session.

Holistic readings, in common with any aspect of assessment, do not exist in a vacuum. Their influence on curriculum and teaching are what makes them important, and their positive effects on our work with our students are what make them valuable. Most readers of this book will not direct a scoring session and hence may not be able to take direct advantage of the technical experience summarized in this chapter. But many faculty members will take part in essay or portfolio scorings, and the better informed they are about what is happening and what ought to be happening, the better those readings are likely to be. This experience also will enrich their approach to whatever subject they may teach, at whatever level, and will encourage them to use writing as a means of learning—a means that can, if needed, serve as a refined and valuable measurement tool.

CHAPTER 11

Avoiding Pitfalls
in Writing Assessment

This chapter provides an overview of many of the issues dealt with in this book. The procedures and findings of writing assessment at various levels, from the large-scale test involving many thousands of students to a single classroom assignment, offer valuable experience to assessment directors and also useful applications to teachers of all subjects at all levels. The pitfalls present in these assessment programs also suggest important cautions to anyone involved in teaching or assessing writing. This chapter focuses on these pitfalls and shows readers how to avoid them at each stage of the assessment process. Thus, the first section deals with problems in planning, the second with test development and program administration, the third with scoring, and the last with pitfalls in both the evaluation and the use of assessment results.

Planning

The usual problem with the planning of portfolio or testing programs is simple: either there is not enough planning, or it takes place after problems develop instead of beforehand. The first large-scale test program I administered worked fine until the end of the essay-scoring session. As thousands of scored essay booklets emerged from the two separate reading rooms, I realized that no one had planned a system or location for combining and recording scores, and no one had reserved space for the ton or so of paper that we had to store and keep accessible for at least a year. We, of course, improvised. Our resourceful statistician came up with a workable solution to the first problem on the spot, and I took the tests home to store in my basement until a better place could be found. In succeeding years, we made sure to plan more carefully.

In the classroom as well, we often fail to give adequate attention to planning. Unclear and apparently purposeless assignments burden students in too many classrooms, and unreliable final exams are common. We teachers often receive bad writing from our students because that is what we ask for, in spite of ourselves. For example, our most frustrating task as writing teachers is the teaching of revision; yet few students take revision seriously because we often fail to plan time for the revision process and rarely plan to reward revisions as highly as first drafts.

An understanding of the kind of planning necessary for careful assessment will improve classroom practice in all these areas. The topics that follow (which are not intended to be inclusive; particular programs or classes will come up with different lists) illustrate the need for planning and the need to expand the team of planners, if the program is large, to include both faculty and staff specialists.

Goals

As Chapter Nine stresses, a common pitfall in writing assessment results from inattention to the purpose and function of the assessment. Classroom teachers generally have no trouble planning their exams, since their goal is clear: to find out whether students have learned what has been taught in class. But few teachers are as clear about the goals of the writing they ask students to complete outside of class, and they are even less clear about the goals of large-scale assessments. Some may even believe that a writing assessment— which they regard as an impromptu timed writing sample on a vague topic—does not require a clear definition of the purpose and meaning of the measure. But those who take assessment and its effects on teaching more seriously will insist that a goals statement with test specifications be established before, not after, a measurement procedure has been designed.

Sometimes assessment seeks to measure group performance, rather than individual ability. For instance, those seeking funds for a writing program, a research study, or an in-service project may need to demonstrate to a funding agency that the project has positive benefits. Chapter Twelve reviews in detail the various pitfalls involved in program evaluation, where the usual methods of measurement—a short multiple-choice or essay test given before a student enters the program and again after the student completes the program—are generally inadequate, since most such programs have many more effects than these short tests can show. Effective program evaluation calls for a multiple series of measures for the multiple effects, including the intangible ones (see the sample evaluation design shown as Resource C at the back of this book). This more complicated and extensive evaluation process need not, however, lead to exhaustive testing of individuals, since group scores are what count. For example, matrix testing, which divides a long test into short segments to be taken by different students, can provide reliable group scores even though no single individual takes the whole test; a three-hour test can be broken into six half-hour segments, and, if the groups are well chosen, no individual need write more than one segment. Whatever form of measurement may be used, if an evaluation is attempting to measure the comparative effectiveness of two programs or of a program in comparison with a control group, the measurement should focus on the aims of the program being evaluated and should avoid testing matters that are irrelevant to the programs. Thus, a freshman writing program that focuses on the development of analytical skills, say, ought not to be evaluated by a multiple-choice usage test or an expressive writing essay.

In all cases, the most important aspect of planning is to consider with care the goals of the assessment. When that complicated job is done, much of the rest of the work flows naturally from it. When that job is not done or is done badly, we can expect most of what follows to be confused, undefined, and ineffective.

Specifications

Specifications usually emerge from a direct and unambiguous written statement of the goals of an assessment listing those specifications. Those accustomed to putting together multiple-choice tests construct charts listing those goals, to be sure that all are tested. Thus, a reading test may have a list with specifications of skills down one side, such as "understands metaphors" or "comprehends implied meanings"; across the top will be a set of content specifications, such as "short poems" or "Shakespeare." Every item needs to fit both a skills and a content specification, and the more important specifications will be represented by proportionally more items.

Such a grid is not really appropriate for essay tests or portfolios, although the demand for precision of specification is always a worthy goal. Instead, the members of a writing faculty must develop clear specifications for writing assessments that require different kinds of abilities. These specifications, which are drawn from and related to their statement of goals, can then be used by a test development or portfolio specifications committee to evaluate its questions or content demands. For example, a specification such as "use concrete language in descriptive prose" would lead to different questions than would "analyze the structure of a modern poem" or "summarize and then evaluate a given complex argument." Similarly, a portfolio contents committee would need specifications in order to decide how much personal writing or revision to include. A failure to articulate clearly and to record in writing the assessment specifications (often because at the moment they seem self-evident) is an important omission that can lead to confusion or worse, particularly after some time has passed.

Here is an example of the way one college moved from general goals—in this case, for a required upper-division general education writing course—to more precise specifications for the outcomes of the class, and then to an assessment that examined whether or not students had met the specifications. The goals for the course were defined as follows: "to develop students' writing skills, not necessarily knowledge of any specific subject matter, at a higher level of competence and sophistication than in freshman composition." The goals were then clarified by the following specifications:

Students should learn to

1. Develop awareness of audience, control of tone, and appropriate use of individual style in various modes of discourse.

2. Define their intentions in a given rhetorical situation and organize and express ideas according to their purpose.
3. Use sources properly to support their ideas: synthesize source material, incorporate it into their writing, and document sources.
4. Demonstrate competence in recognizing and using conventions of edited American English.
5. Express and develop complex ideas in coherent, logical fashion.
6. Revise as well as edit their work, through regular rewriting of assignments.

A faculty committee set out to develop an assessment for upper-division and graduate students who claimed that they had already developed these abilities and hence did not need to take the class. The course specifications became assessment specifications. A multiple-choice test was out of the question, since it could not assess most of what was specified. Clearly, a short impromptu essay could not examine many of the specifications, as a portfolio assessment might, but just as clearly, the resources for a portfolio assessment were not available.

The committee's solution was a three-hour examination (to allow time for planning, use of sources, revision, and editing) focusing on two reading selections. Students enrolling for the examination were told to acquire a specific anthology of readings; a list of a dozen selections from the anthology was provided a month before the examination, so that although students could not write the test in advance, they could gain command over a limited number of readings before the test took place.

In the question given out at the beginning of the test, the students were asked to write a single coherent essay in which they developed an idea of their own, using comparison and contrast of two specific selections from the list. The students were to show their understanding of the selections through summary, analysis, and integration of material from the two readings into their own essays and, incidentally, demonstrate a consistent citation system for quotations.

Although the assessment proved to be a difficult one, between one-quarter and one-half of those taking it have passed each time it has been given. The clarity of the specifications led to a clear assessment design that limited the voluntary test takers to a small and generally able group. The assessment, now entering its second decade, retains strong support from the faculty and administration, since its specifications reflect campus agreement on the writing abilities to be expected of graduates. Furthermore, the scoring of the assessment has been straightforward and reliable, since the specifications led directly to a scoring guide that was easy to use.

Consultation and Personnel

A major destructive result of many badly planned assessment programs is the separation of teaching from assessment. Such programs fail to take advantage of the mutual support that teachers and test developers can give each other. (The College Board's Advanced Placement Program is a fine example of this mutual support; the high school courses generated by the tests are more important than the tests themselves.) When those who teach writing are carefully and regularly consulted, and when their ideas are both heard and used by those developing the assessment, there are many beneficial results: the assessment will be appropriate, the tone of classroom discussion of the assessment will be positive (since the teachers will gain a sense of ownership of it), and the students will find the test a meaningful part of their education. Those outside the field of education will wonder why this logical and obvious situation is exceedingly unusual in the assessment of writing; in fact, serious consultation among those working at different levels is rare in most American enterprises. If procedures for consultation are not built into the planning process, consulation will probably not occur, and potential support will turn into covert or even overt opposition.

Budget

No one ever forgets to deal with money during the planning of an assessment program. But there is never enough money to do all that one would like to do, and constant budgetary decision making threatens to dominate planning. Two national testing programs have cut budgets by eliminating second readings on test essays, thus reducing the scoring reliability of the tests. For a grueling day of scoring papers, another national testing service pays essay readers the salary earned by a journeyman plumber for an hour of pipe cleaning; those in charge of the essay scoring then wonder why some of the readers may act in less than professional ways.

After two decades of planning assessment programs, I have come to some highly personal conclusions about budgets. Since the difference in cost between a well-funded and a badly funded test program is relatively minor, budgeting in this area is almost always a statement of priority, not finance. If underfunding becomes a serious problem, it is a symptom, not a cause, of the weakness of the program. When the cost of a writing assessment, particularly its written part, is challenged, most often it is writing itself that is under attack. If possible, the assessment program should be abandoned rather than rendered ineffective or trivial by those who do not value writing. Those planning a program need to decide on the minimum funding allowable (including professional wages for essay or portfolio readers), and to arrange for appropriate action if the money available sinks below that figure.

Those in charge of budgets need to be reminded that assessment costs include development as well as scoring. Although multiple-choice tests cost far less to score than do essay tests or portfolios, it is far more costly to develop multiple-choice tests and to keep them current, secure, and valid. Thus, the relatively high cost of scoring writing can be balanced by the relatively low developmental costs and the benefits to faculty and the curriculum of such development. The weakest assessment programs can avoid development costs by purchasing out-of-date and inappropriate multiple-choice exams that have little to do with the local specifications or students; such tests are available everywhere. But responsible professionals will not participate in programs with such tests.

Reporting and Use of Assessment Results

From the outset, the planners of an assessment program need to determine how the results will be reported and used. It is pointless to gather more information than can be well used; it is mischievous to report results in ways that can (and hence will) be misinterpreted and misused. No one should underestimate the concealed power of a test score or the readiness of various publics and the press to misread, misunderstand, oversimplify, and distort assessment results.

Any apparent improvement in scores is likely to be heralded as evidence of a successful program, and an apparent decline in scores will confirm the doomsayers convinced that the younger generation is plunging into illiteracy; in both cases, the data will be used to appeal for additional funds. But unless planning has taken account of the difficulty of stabilizing scores from one assessment to the next, apparent trends in scores may just be the result of measurement error. Some programs do not report raw scores (such as the sum of two readings on a six-point scale) because changes in the difficulty level of the essay questions or in the standards of the readings may lead to score changes that do not reflect actual changes in students' writing ability. Instead, a statistician will convert the raw scores to a stable scaled score, one, for example, from 20 to 80, which can be used for valid comparisons. But such a scaled score does not solve all problems; it tends to conceal its source and magnify the meaning of minor changes.

Unfortunately, it is common to postpone planning for score reporting until much too late. It is even more common to forget that the results will be used to evaluate the assessment itself; as a result, many valuable data are lost before evaluation can occur. Evaluators for the assessment program should enter the planning process right from the start. They may, for example, suggest that information about writing ability should be gathered before a program begins, so that a comparison is possible later on; once a program is under way, such information can no longer be obtained. There may be ways of designing forms, such as portfolio covers, essay booklets, or test answer sheets, so that data are available when needed by the evaluator, instead of requiring an expensive later data collection effort. Finally, long before the assessment is begun, planners should attend to record keeping (distribution of rosters, machine-readable results, security, privacy laws, availability of transcripts) and storage. The sheer bulk of an essay test or of a portfolio assessment and the convoluted laws on the release of scores must be seen to be believed, and these matters ought not to come as surprises at the last moment, though they often do.

Scored essays or portfolios often impress those who have labored over them as precious resources for research, even after the scores have been recorded and reported. Unfortunately, researchers with funding for and interest in someone else's assessment are rare. In the meantime, great mounds of scored essays and portfolios sit in faculty offices and garages from coast to coast. Unless a local study is under way, faculty should return portfolios to their originators and ship tests more than a year old to a paper-recycling center.

Time Lines

Participants at initial planning meetings should develop overall strategies and should construct time lines for activities. This is the place to guard against a major pitfall in assessment programs: the failure to allow sufficient time, money, consultation, and energy for adequate attention to planning.

Planning committees will discover many options in laying out time lines. One time line might look like this:

1. Develop and print information about the assessment.
2. Distribute these materials.
3. Register students and collect fees.
4. Print and distribute test results.

A different time line, probably under the supervision of a different individual, might follow the selection and development of the measurement instrument itself; for example, if an essay test is to be given, this time line would look like this:

1. Designate a committee to draw up specifications.
2. Set up pretesting and printing schedules (with extra proofreading!).
3. Distribute the test to test centers.
4. Return materials to the central office.
5. Pay the proctors.

Yet another time line might consider the scoring of the test as the central temporal element.

If student writing is involved, a choice site for the reading needs to be reserved many months ahead of time; and a team should develop procedures for selecting current readers (including chief readers, room leaders, and table leaders), for identifying a cadre of future readers, and for determining all costs for the reading. As Chapter Ten points out, an essay or portfolio reading is in many ways similar to a substantial conference and requires at least as much attention. Any postassessment activities, such as publication of sample portfolios, papers, and scoring guides, should be included in these time lines, since nobody will automatically collect materials for such a purpose during the scoring session.

The preparation of time lines is important for any assessment program, for several reasons: it allows the cool consideration of tasks in advance (instead of during the confusion of other activities); it calls for the establishment of clear lines of responsibility, so that those involved will know who is supposed to do what and when; and it helps break down a complex job of administration into a series of discrete tasks with deadlines.

Planning sessions may sound cold and uncreative, but in practice they are quite the reverse: exciting, creative, contentious meetings, they blend people, theories, and practical activities into the pattern that becomes an assessment program. They turn the chaos of an idea into the order of a plan, they share responsibilities among those best suited for the various tasks, and they anticipate problems before they occur. Even in the best-planned program, of course, one will encounter unexpected turns and unpleasant surprises; planning can never obviate all problems, nor can it be expected to do so. But planners can set aside time and money to meet unanticipated problems. A program that has not been carefully planned is an inevitable disaster just waiting to begin.

Essay Test Development and Administration

A particular advantage of portfolio assessment is that it avoids the time and expense required for test development and test administration. Thus, portfolios are spared an entire set of pitfalls that testing programs must encounter.

Test Development

As Chapter Three describes in detail, test development requires time, money, and the appropriate people before it can work properly. The most common mistake in test development is to assume that it is easy and that most of us who teach (since we give tests regularly in our classrooms) can do it well. Unfortunately, test development is difficult to do well, and, even more unfortunately, most of us do it rather badly. One of the great if indirect benefits to an institution that moves into careful essay testing is that its faculty will learn better evaluation techniques.

Some institutions will ask faculty to develop a multiple-choice test of writing skill. But even professionally developed multiple-choice tests in this area tend to be uneven at best; the tests created without professional support tend to be unmitigated disasters. No individual should accept the responsibility of putting such a test together without a committee of colleagues. The members of this committee will need to work together for at least a year and should have at their disposal a professional test consultant, substantial computer support, clerical support for production and administration of sample test items and norming tests, and a very large budget. Unfortunately, these provisions guard against only the most obvious pitfalls of multiple-choice testing (ambiguity, invalidity, unreliability); they do not guarantee that a very good test will result. Instead, many of the problems with multiple-choice testing of writing that we have seen are still likely to appear.

The development costs of multiple-choice testing are not well known and are usually ignored when arguments for the economy of such testing are presented. As I pointed out in Chapter Nine, the validity problems of multiple-choice writing tests are severe, and the low cost of scoring is no compensation for an invalid test. Besides, multiple-choice tests, though cheaper to score than essay tests, are far more costly to put together; if we add in the necessary costs of multiple forms and revisions (required by many of the new truth-in-testing laws), essay tests turn out to be far more cost-effective.

And when we consider the advantages to the curriculum and to the professional development of the faculty from essay testing, such direct measurement of writing skill becomes a wise investment of resources. Portfolio assessment repeats these same arguments with even more force. Although its scoring costs can be five times greater than the scoring costs of essay tests, it can claim even greater validity and even lower development costs.

Under ordinary circumstances, then, test development will mean essay test development, and that is the test development procedure detailed in Chapter Three. The steps, from appointment of a test development committee through pretesting of the questions, allow systematic review of the test as it takes shape over a period of months.

The fact that test questions must themselves be tested is not well understood and leads to many pitfalls in testing. But, given sufficient time and support, test developers will come up with test questions that will work. With such a test in hand, scoring the questions reliably becomes a manageable matter. Unfortunately, most testing programs allot insufficient time to developing the questions, and then expect those scoring them to produce fair scores on an unfair test. Anyone who has been placed in such an unfortunate position will insist that those responsible for the question development need also to be present at the scoring. If readers are forced to score a stupid or impossible question, they have the right to be able to attack the perpetrators at the reading site, without delay.

Essay test development can never be considered finished as long as a testing program continues. Just as a conscientious classroom teacher is always revising his or her exams, improving, clarifying, updating, or expanding them, so test development committees can never rest. The challenge to these committees is not only to produce new topics, but also to keep abreast of writing research, which is now slowly moving into the area of measurement and cognition. We know much more about essay testing now than we did a decade ago, as this revised and expanded volume demonstrates; five or ten years from now, we will know much more than we do today. For example, as I pointed out in Chapter Two, we do not know why some students will perform much better on one kind of writing assignment than on another or why there is a surprisingly low correlation between scores on personal experience and on analytical topics. Research in this area will probably lead to tentative answers, and thus better tests than we can now produce. Even within single modes, the difficulty of topics can vary greatly. Furthermore, some experimental programs are attempting to include revision as part of essay testing; so we may soon be able to examine more than first drafting on such tests—thus removing a major objection from faculty who regard writing as a process.

Test Administration

Many institutions have diligent test officers, sometimes with statistical or psychometric training, who can be trusted to see to the many details involved in the administration of tests. The test officer should identify and deal with such matters as the appropriate time and place for the test, the proper handling of test materials, the control of the testing environment, the hiring and paying of proctors, and the handling of dishonest test takers.

But there are other matters in this general area of test administration to deal with. How long should the test be? How many essay questions should there be, and what kinds of questions should be used? Is there to be a multiple-choice portion of the test? If so, how much weight should it have in the total test score? What kind of information about the test should be distributed to students ahead of time, and when? If there is a test fee, what is it to be, how is it to be managed, and under what circumstances are there to be refunds?

A portfolio assessment does not remove the need for a test professional, but it shifts somewhat the concerns to be dealt with. Instead of test security and proctors, the concern must be for the authenticity of the writing in the portfolio. Some programs require that a teacher countersign every paper, including revisions, giving a telephone number for a follow-up inquiry if suspicions are aroused. Students will have many more questions about a portfolio assessment than they will about an essay test, since tests are much more familiar to them; the test officer will need to handle most of these questions. The portfolio-reading fee is usually higher than a usual test fee, and the testing office will have additional financial matters to attend to.

In addition, a test professional can support the portfolio reading in many ways. For example, translating the specifications for the assessment into a scoring guide is always difficult, but essay tests require a relatively simple and focused one; portfolios offer many more possible specifications and hence may develop much more complicated scoring guides. But the more complex the scoring guide, the less attention paid to it by readers, who are, after all, attending to the student writing. A test professional should be on hand during pilot readings, checking the reliability of the readings and suggesting revisions to the scoring guide when necessary. I worked with one group of portfolio readers that had spent a full year developing the scoring guide for the assessment; only after a full day of reading did they agree to cut the scoring guide from three pages to one. Much as they valued the elaborate scoring guide they had labored so hard to produce, nobody could actually use it. The wise and sensitive test officer convinced them that for the scoring guide, as for so much in life, less turns out to be more.

Portfolio and Test Scoring

The first edition of this book (1985) devoted an entire chapter to the theory of holistic scoring. This theory argues that, since we do not know enough about the supposed subskills of writing and since writing as a whole is more than the sum of its parts, writing should be evaluated for its overall quality. The theory is so well accepted by now that a few paragraphs can substitute for that chapter, though there is still considerable controversy about practice. The practical aspects of holistic scoring—question development, scoring guides, sample papers, controlled scoring sessions—have been detailed throughout this book, and the history and future of this approach are discussed in Chapter Thirteen.

Holistic Scoring Versus Other Scoring Methods

The major theoretical difficulty with holistic scoring emerges from the limitations of the single score, which gives useful and reliable ranking information but no details. Teachers usually want to know more about their students' writing than where their test papers stand in relation to each other; they want diagnostic information to let them know what aspects of writing should be taught. We can score papers holistically but we cannot teach holistically; we must teach one thing at a time. In addition, research projects that focus on particular aspects of writing do not find holistic scoring useful; we cannot know whether a high holistic score is the result of focused teaching of coherence, say, or of concentrated work in sentence combining, or of native fluency and imagination unaffected by teaching. Many research projects require scores on the features that are of particular concern.

Two methods of scoring have emerged to deal with these needs: primary-trait scoring, which is a variation of holistic scoring, and analytic scoring, which is directly opposed to holistic scoring. Neither one is widely used, but they are available for special purposes.

Primary-trait scoring is like holistic scoring, since it yields a single score for student writing to a set topic. However, a primary-trait scoring guide seeks to describe not the overall quality of the writing but rather the variations in quality for the single trait of concern: coherence, say, or sentence complexity, or imagination. Those who score the writing must follow the scoring guide and ignore all other matters besides the one (or two if there is a secondary trait) on which the score depends. If coherence is the primary trait, a coherent paper would achieve a high score despite major problems with spelling, grammar, and vocabulary; if sentence complexity is the primary trait, a wholly incoherent and confused paper could score at the top, as long as it contained enough complex sentences. Such scoring requires much training of readers, who must read in a way quite different from any other reading or teaching experience. But information about the primary trait can be developed with considerable reliability—after strenuous and costly labor.

Analytic scoring reverses the holistic assumption that the whole is greater than the sum of its parts. Analytic readings proceed by requiring readers to score individual subskills, such as spelling, sentence structure, coherence, or imagination. Those scores are then added to provide a total score. Since the scored subskills are not of equal importance, each usually receives a multiplier or "K factor"; thus, the spelling score may be multiplied by 1, the sentence structure score by 3, and so on. In theory, analytic scoring should provide the diagnostic information that holistic scoring fails to provide and in the process yield a desirable increase in information from the writing sample. In practice, three major problems have so far restricted analytic scoring to small projects with very few readers: (1) There is as yet no agreement (except among the uninformed) about what, if any, separable subskills exist in writing. (2) Reliable analytic writing scores are extremely difficult to obtain, because of the lack of professional consensus about the definition and importance of subskills. (3) Readers must make many scoring decisions about each piece of writing, so that scoring is slow and the cost is high.

So we return here to holistic scoring, which is used in the vast majority of essay and portfolio readings. It not only yields economical and reliable ranking of papers for various purposes but has the unique capacity to combine norm-referenced and criterion-referenced test theories. Norm referencing means that the score a student achieves has meaning only in reference to the scores obtained by other students, those in the norm group; a percentile score of 75 means that the paper scored higher than three-quarters of the others. Holistic scoring is basically norm referenced, since it uses sample papers or portfolios from the assessment group as one way to establish the standards for the reading. But the scoring guide is not norm referenced; it states the criteria for scoring, the goals of the program, without reference to the actual performance of students. In theory, only those portfolios or papers that meet the scoring criteria should achieve high scores, however many or few of them there may be. The scoring guide (sometimes called a "rubric" by those who enjoy jargon) describes the qualities to be found in papers at different score points. It is normally drafted by the test or portfolio committee to reflect the assessment criteria; it is then revised just before the reading by those in charge after they have read and ranked a large sample of the writings to be scored. In practice, a holistic scoring modifies the criteria of the scoring guide by the achieved performance of the group; at the same time, it modifies the strict norm reference of the group by assertion of the importance of the scoring guide. This flexibility in both theory and practice has been a major advantage for holistic scoring and is a primary reason for its dissemination throughout education at all levels.

Our concern here is with the pitfalls into which those directing holistic scoring may fall. Problems in essay and portfolio scoring can be divided into three areas: procedures, personnel, and statistics.

Procedures

The most common pitfall in the management of holistic essay or portfolio readings is the loss of collegiality among the readers. Chapters Four and Ten speak in detail about the importance of maintaining the essential community of a reading.

A second procedural problem often centers around the use and origin of the scoring guide. (Examples of scoring guides for essays and portfolios appear as Resource A and Resource B at the back of this book.) Some readings proceed without a scoring guide, in the mistaken conviction that debates over abstract descriptions will distract readers from practical decisions. Since readers will rarely refer to the scoring guide after the reading is well under way (the goal of the training period is to help readers internalize the standards), some practical administrators argue that a scoring guide is a waste of time and money. All readers, the argument goes, can intuit common standards from sample papers or portfolios just as well as the table leaders can.

But the scoring guide is particularly valuable for several reasons: it explicitly sets out the standards for judgment, so that they can be discussed and accepted; it establishes the theoretical grounds for the ranking; and (since it is influenced by norm referencing) it encourages the use of the full range of scores by giving reasonable descriptions of the strongest and the weakest papers. Since the scoring guide is derived in part from the actual range of papers written to the particular question, it reinforces the particular job to be done—that is, to rank the student materials at hand according to specific criteria devised for the writing topic or portfolios at hand.

Furthermore, the argument against scoring guides ignores

the need for an assenting community, one that can act in agreement because its members have reached agreement. The scoring guide not only accomplishes the useful tasks I have summarized; it also symbolizes this community agreement by its explicit statement of standards. The discussion of those standards welds the community together and gives individual readers ownership of and a stake in the outcome of the reading. My most uncomfortable readings have been those without a scoring guide; I felt more like an employee trying to follow established but unstated rules than a professional using delicate judgment for a goal I understood and approved.

A variety of pitfalls await the chief reader who mistakenly imagines that a scoring session should be like a department meeting, with its endless unresolved debate, fixed positions, and personal agendas. A reading has much more specific goals than a department meeting: agreement must be reached, and all the papers or portfolios must be scored within the time allowed. The purposeful work and collegiality of a well-run scoring session might in fact be productively copied by many English departments, whose meetings are often agony to experience. The detailed description of a scoring session given in Chapter Ten is designed to help those responsible avoid the pitfalls of the department meeting, so that the session will be a pleasant and productive experience for participants.

Personnel

If the process of selecting personnel for the scoring sessions is given careful attention, many of the pitfalls of bad choices can be avoided. Of course, one can use academic position or other existing structures, such as elections or selection committees, to select appropriate people. But one needs to be sure that the qualifications of those selected in fact match the demands of the job; often the existing procedures do not take into account the special nature of essay or portfolio readings. For example, I witnessed a school district essay reading in which English teachers handled the statistics, secretaries scored the papers, and an able statistician was put to work hauling boxes of essay booklets.

At another scoring session that I observed, confusion reigned because some of the personnel were spectacularly unsuited for their tasks. The dean was chief reader, the department chairs were table leaders, and the faculty had been required to be the readers, grouped at tables by departments. The hierarchy continued with the aides: the dean's secretary was chief aide, and lesser secretaries were table aides. Unfortunately, the dean was extremely soft-spoken and mild and could not make himself heard in the reading room; at some of the tables, long-standing departmental quarrels continued unabated while student papers remained unread; and the readers from a vocational educational department looked askance at their unlettered chair, who, in turn, looked helplessly back as they attempted to read the work before them. The dean's secretary disappeared in the middle of the reading, never to return, and the movement of test papers ground to a halt. Fortunately, a small number of diligent graduate students were on hand to learn from their professors; they quickly sized up the situation, took over, and made things work.

It is usually a good idea to convene a small and informed committee to choose the personnel for a reading. This committee should develop a set of criteria for the various jobs and then seek the best available candidates, wherever they may be found. Choosing the chief reader is always the most difficult task. The individual chosen needs to be a firm and forceful leader who understands the goals and criteria for the program. He or she must take charge of meetings, work effectively with and through the table leaders, and serve as the final authority on scores. Since the chief reader in fact runs the reading, setting the tone and making key decisions, he or she needs a sense of proportion and humor, an ability to work comfortably with sensitive colleagues, and the capacity to juggle competing important demands for attention. Such individuals are rare indeed, and the temptation to settle for less than the very best available should be resisted. No one can earn a position as chief reader by longevity, publications, or academic title.

The criteria for selecting the chief reader, table leaders, readers, and the chief aide were discussed in Chapter Ten. All these jobs are difficult and responsible working positions, not to be seen as honorific. An abrasive or indecisive table leader will cause an unreliable reading; an inefficient chief aide will waste much time and money; a seriously disruptive reader will have to be dismissed.

While some personnel difficulties are to be expected during

a large reading, no matter how careful the selection process, serious attention to choosing the right people for the various jobs is the best way to avoid major problems. Every faculty and every support staff have good candidates for these jobs, and every test program can recruit them to work in a scoring session, under the right conditions and with enough planning.

Statistics

Many pitfalls are associated with the use of statistics in scoring sessions, but two particular problems are so common that they deserve special mention here: the temptation to score papers or portfolios only once and the confusion between ranking papers and deciding on the meaning of the ranking.

Standard practice in scoring requires two independent readings of each paper or portfolio (see Chapter Ten). Whatever the system, the second reader must be unaware of the first score. When the two scores disagree (at many readings this means more than one point apart), a third reading then takes place to resolve the discrepancy. Continuing programs use these comparisons, as they accumulate, to gather data on the reliability of the reading itself, as well as on the accuracy of individual readers. Without double readings, it is impossible to gather these figures or to verify the consistency of the test scoring. Although there is a constant temptation to reduce costs by reducing the second readings to samples or by eliminating second readings altogether, such an economy renders the reading unaccountable and unprofessional.

The second problem has to do with the setting of passing scores. Those who prefer an entirely criterion-referenced reading use the same scoring guide for all scorings for a particular program, in the belief that the various scores on the guide will represent the same level of writing ability even though the test question, portfolio contents, or student group may differ. Under these circumstances, the passing score can be set in advance and can even be part of the scoring guide itself. However, those who prefer to introduce some norm-referenced aspects into the reading or who are uneasy at the differences among questions, portfolios, and student groups will argue that the meaning of the holistic ranking must be determined after the ranking, not before. Statements of scoring criteria that include references to passing and failing, this group argues, invite readers to go outside the scoring criteria into their own individual experience, and so reduce scoring reliability; it is a difficult enough job to rank papers or portfolios reliably, according to the criteria of a given reading, and that job should not be confounded with matters beyond the ranking.

Certainly, if the program is including a norming sample in the scoring (to see, for example, how freshmen with certain grades score on a placement test), referring to previous pass-fail rates, comparing percentile scores, or using other norm-referenced concepts, the decision on passing scores should be delayed until the ranking is completed. And if you suspect, as I do, that this year's total score of 7 may represent the same level of ability as last year's score of 8 and next year's score of 6, you will want to decide on passing scores after reviewing score distributions and norming data and whatever else may be available.

Special Problems of Portfolio Scoring

The most serious pitfall in portfolio assessment is the time and cost of scoring, a problem that was dramatized recently at a large midwestern state university. An official announced at a press conference that the university was replacing its freshman English placement test with a portfolio requirement. Each of its many thousands of applicants would now need to accumulate a binder of writing done in high school, which would be evaluated to designate the appropriate starting place for college English studies.

The proposed advantages were clear: instead of using an artificial, timed, first-draft piece of prose, the faculty could examine a range of writing of various sorts, including revisions, produced under natural circumstances. Even better, the high school students would begin to request writing tasks from their teachers (so they could present thick portfolios), instead of avoiding writing, as they now did, and so the university would be supporting the best instruction in the schools. With enhanced writing instruction in the schools, the university would have few remedial students, and the entire level of education in the state would improve. The portfolio assessment would benefit everyone.

Two years later, the thousands of portfolios collected remained unfiled and unread in storage. The resources and plans needed for dealing with this mountain of paper never materialized, and the university is counting on the short memory of the newspaper readers in the state (not to speak of more prominent university scandals) to mitigate its embarrassment over the failed portfolio project. The previous placement system, dropped with some fanfare, has never been restored, so entering students place themselves into freshman or remedial English, according to their self-confidence. The quality of the freshman writing program has thus dropped, but the part-timers and teaching assistants who handle the course have little voice, so no one notices. The lack of attention to the complex job of scoring has wound up not only undermining the advantages of the assessment but actually damaging the program it was designed to benefit.

Wiser institutions move slowly into portfolio assessment, using small pilot programs to develop scoring systems that can then be expanded. Since the most expeditious portfolio readings—with writing limited to twelve typed double-spaced pages—average under six scores from each reader per hour, and since reader training must proceed more slowly than for essays because of the bulk of the writing, too ambitious a project is bound to fail. Even fifty readers cannot score more than about six hundred portfolios in a hard day's work after training; the eighteen readers shown in Figure 10.1 will be able to score little more than two hundred.

Aside from the extra problems caused by the bulk of the student writing, portfolios present the same pitfalls as essay tests. A reading needs to be planned carefully, scoring guides and sample portfolios need to be prepared in advance, and the usual pitfalls of a scoring session need to be avoided.

Scoring of Multiple-Choice Tests

The great convenience of multiple-choice testing is, of course, ease of scoring. With sensible planning, well-designed answer sheets will produce a computer printout with scores arranged in several different ways (high to low, alphabetical by last name of student, and so on), with such student information as file number or mailing address listed next to the scores. In addition, the printout can provide a statistical package with all kinds of useful numbers about the score distribution and correlations among parts of the test.

It is tempting to believe that an impressive list of numbers provides everything we need to know about the test. However, the printout merely provides the raw material for what we need to know; those responsible for the test still have a great deal of work to do after the production of the numbers. They have to determine the meaning of those numbers and their appropriate use in the context of the measurement of writing ability.

For example, one number to be examined closely is the Standard Error of Measurement. This rarely discussed statistic is enormously important for the responsible use of a multiple-choice test score: it sets out the range of meaningful score differences. Even highly reliable multiple-choice tests, such as the Scholastic Aptitude Test, yield only rough approximations of student rankings, not absolute measurements, and the scores should be read as the center of a band of scores rather than as a single point. The Standard Error of Measurement describes the width of the band, and the possibility of greater error is always present.

People who are unfamiliar with multiple-choice test statistics sometimes fail to notice how wide the range of error is, even on the best of these tests. Everyone knows that essay test scores are approximate, but many people attribute an altogether unwarranted precision to what they like to call "objective tests." We ought to avoid that term *objective*, which is a judgment rather than a description, and remain aware that multiple-choice tests are a useful yet fallible method of testing some matters; they are no better than the questions they contain, which were themselves composed and evaluated by subjective human beings, just as essay tests are.

Anyone using multiple-choice test scores, then, needs to consider them as bands of scores, rather than absolute points, and as approximations of the skills they measure, which are likely to have an undetermined relation to writing skill. The best use of multiple-choice scores, if they *must* be employed in the area of writing, is as a portion of a test, rather than as the assessment itself. The results of a careful multiple-choice test, when combined with the results of a single essay test, will yield a fairer and more accurate measure of writing ability than will either test when used by itself, according to research done at the Educational Testing Service (see Godshalk, Swineford, and Coffman, 1966, p. vi; Breland and others, 1987). A preferable alternative is to score more than one writing sample, either in paired essay tests or in portfolios.

If a writing score from essay testing or portfolio assessment is to be combined with a multiple-choice test score to produce a single total score, a statistician will need to perform a simple operation called scale matching. This operation ensures that the differences in numerical scale on different kinds of tests do not distort the weight each score should have in the total score. Scale matching puts different kinds of scores on the same scales, so that they can be combined properly. However, someone still must decide whether the different parts of the test are to have equal weight or some proportional weight. Should a twenty-minute multiple-choice portion weigh as much as a ninety-minute essay portion in determining the final score? Half as much? One-sixth as much? And how much weight should a short multiple-choice test have in combination with a portfolio that may represent hundreds of hours of work? As always, the numbers will serve those who understand how to use them.

An additional burden falls on those receiving the numbers from multiple-choice tests: relating the numbers to decisions about the students. The numbers will not say who fails a proficiency requirement or who should be placed in a remedial class; only informed faculty can make that decision after reviewing everything relevant to an assessment, including the numbers. It is tempting to imagine that the numbers, or those who report them, can make that decision, but such a reliance on numbers avoids responsibility. Test results, after all, are only data; the most important responsibility of those administering assessment programs is to make appropriate use of the data produced.

Evaluation and Use of Assessment Results

There is a wide gulf between the message intended by most assessments and the message received by those who use or hear about the test scores that assessments usually produce. This sad fact is true in classrooms, where students are ever ready to interpret grades and the teacher's comments on their work as judgments of their personality or of their relationship to the teacher. Many studies have documented the gap between what professors say or think they are saying in their commentaries on papers and what students actually perceive (see Chapter Five). Large-scale writing-assessment programs suffer the same distortions in score reporting—only, of course, on a much larger scale.

The desire to gain simple answers to complex questions leads to misunderstanding and distortion of many test results. Schools receive test reports designed to help them assess their programs and will use the information solely to argue that they are more (or less) effective than other schools and hence more deserving of increased funds. Writing tests at the upper-division college level, designed to warn juniors who are poor writers to develop their skills so they will write better papers as seniors, turn into barriers for seniors who have met all other degree requirements. The full range of information provided by some national college entrance tests is always in danger of being read by students and admissions officers as a simple pass-fail cutoff score. Public school administrators in a few states, looking for an easy way to combine economy with the appearance of high standards, mandate particular scores on the National Teachers Examination (an entry-level test for credential candidates) for experienced classroom teachers looking for raises in salary. Multitest programs, such as the College Board Admission Testing Program or the College-Level Examination Program (CLEP), merge in many instances into a single conflated score or a hazily understood single test. Some college administrators will talk about a student's "CLEP score," without awareness that more than forty tests exist in that program—about half a dozen in English alone.

Since the principal pitfall in reporting assessment results, whether in individual classrooms, or schoolwide, statewide, or national settings, is the misunderstanding and misuse of scores, institutions and faculty must pay particular attention to proper reading and interpretation of scores. Sometimes they will have to develop graphs as well as numbers, or present several kinds of comparative or normative data, or explain just what the assessment is or is not examining. A number of writing tests with essay portions include the essay score in a total score and then, in addition, give the essay raw score, the sum, perhaps, of two readings on a given scale. This useful separate report for the essay portion allows those receiving the score to understand how that particular score was reached and to use it separately if they wish. But the danger here is that some audiences are likely to exaggerate the reliability of an essay score if they get one; like any test score, an essay score is an approximation and should not be regarded as absolute truth. Therefore, it may be more responsible for test reports to bury that score in a composite score. Portfolio assessments can be spared some of these pitfalls if they restrict their score reports to descriptive information about the portolios evaluated; but too simple a score report is likely to be dismissed as insufficiently meaningful.

To complicate matters further, an assessment program that affects students must provide some machinery for students who want to review the assessment and their performance on it. Just as a classroom teacher who gives a test cannot refuse to hold office hours afterward, those who administer large-scale assessments cannot (as new legislation has made clear) refuse to allow students to challenge questions, assignments, or scores. Some large campus assessment programs include in a test fee a charge for advising after the scoring, and even ETS has been persuaded to change some scores after students have had their say. Writing measures are not devised solely for the purpose of failing students, and the best programs consider carefully how to make information from an assessment clear, meaningful, and useful.

Follow-Up Studies

Tests and other assessment programs must themselves be tested. If they do not pass the test, they should be failed and discontinued. Again, the classroom can serve as a model: if a test does not "work," it is abandoned and replaced by a better one. Many teachers never stop experimenting with their tests, so keenly do they feel the difference between their knowledge of their students, gained over a semester, and the final test grade. Large-scale assessments require large-scale evaluations, but the same principle holds.

The differing purposes of assessments will require different kinds of evaluations. Someone evaluating a college entrance test, for example, will try to determine its predictive validity: most of those passing the test should succeed in college. The evaluator of a college placement test, on the other hand, will seek to discover the accuracy of the placement, through such means as surveying the faculty to discover obvious misplacements. Predictive validity is a tempting but disastrous method of evaluating a placement test, since a placement test is designed to change predictions; weak students are placed in a program to help them succeed, and their success will lower the predictive validity of the test, whose prediction of failure the curriculum attempts to forestall. Thus, anyone using predictive validity to evaluate a placement testing program is using the success of the writing program as a way to document the supposed failure of the test. A placement testing program has different goals from an admissions testing program and should be evaluated differently.

Proficiency testing and equivalency testing will require follow-up studies, sometimes over many years, for evaluation. What happens, we may want to find out, to students who receive credit by examination for freshman English as they move through their college years? If the credit is too easily earned, we would expect these students to perform less well than similar students who had the benefit of the freshman English course. If the test is appropriately encouraging to the best students, we might expect to find them taking more English courses, at a higher level, than their counterparts—and doing better in them. The only way to know for sure is to design a follow-up study to trace the students through college and to compare them with a group of students who have similar ability.

A proficiency test calls for a different kind of follow-up study. Those identified as not proficient on a writing test had better not be publishing articles and books or editing newpapers; proficient writers, according to the test, should also be proficient writers according to other measures, such as their grades in writing-related courses and their success in professions calling for writing skill. A recent court ruling in Florida has required the public schools to show that they are in fact teaching the skills examined on their proficiency tests. In similar cases, various professions have been required to show that the tests given to prospective employees are relevant to the job skills actually involved in the profession: firefighters, for instance, cannot be examined in English literature.

The people selected to evaluate tests and assessment programs should not include those who devise the tests, direct the programs, or have demonstrable commitments to them. At the same time, evaluators who have little knowledge of the purpose or setting of the program will bring their own assumptions and biases to bear on programs they do not understand (despite the claims of objectivity made by "goal-free" evaluators). Among all the other pitfalls to avoid in the assessment of writing, those responsible for such assessments must seek out evaluators who are in fact neutral and uninvolved, as well as informed. Since programs that receive no evaluation, insufficiently rigorous evaluation, or negative evaluation are not likely to survive, those responsible should not take lightly the selection of the evaluator and the evaluation design.

Political Pitfalls

The teaching and assessing of writing are, in a large sense, political acts. Those who devise tests for the public schools are not likely to forget this fact, faced as they are with vocal parents, elected school boards, and public financing. College faculties, however, are more likely to imagine that the assessments they choose or create deal only with academic matters. That may be so for an individual instructor, who often claims that academic freedom (which protects the scholar's right to speak freely without professional punishment) should extend to a right to grade students without interference from others. But assessment programs are inevitably political, and college-level assessments sometimes have high political stakes attending them. Indeed, as I stressed in discussing multiple-choice tests and placement and proficiency testing in Chapters Eight and Nine, the very act of giving an assessment represents political decisions about values of education and about what classes of people are to be offered opportunity for economic and social privilege.

These political matters exist at all phases of an assessment program, from the planning of goals statements (which require general assent), to test development and scoring (which require funding and general participation), to evaluation (which is often prepared for the use of public funding agencies). Power over assessment programs often resides with administrators or others who control funds, and these people's goals may differ from those of the people who develop the programs. Sometimes, unfortunately, the political needs of these administrators, or even their personal career goals, lead them to assume control over assessment programs and to change them radically. For example, a placement testing program designed to help bright but poorly prepared students succeed can be changed all too easily into an admissions program designed to exclude such students altogether. Faculty administrators of successful assessment programs neglect these perennial political issues at their peril, since power over dollars—combined with personal ambition—can overwhelm academic concerns, academic due process, and even academic courtesy.

Finally, assessment is power, and power is a root political issue. In our classrooms, we need to use that power with decency and humanity. In large programs, that power remains at our backs and over our shoulders, always to be reckoned with. Those who ignore the politics of assessment may well find themselves replaced by better and smoother politicians, and even those who are alert to the power pressures and power drives of administrative and political figures or of the public may wind up defeated by forces with little concern for academic matters. No one should imagine that a test is above politics or that an assessment program is outside the political arena.

The Pervasiveness of Pitfalls

In the long run, the pitfalls that await writing-assessment programs do not differ significantly from those that await any major educational program. At every stage, from initial planning through reporting and evaluation, opportunities for confusion of purpose, improper action, and unprofessional influence offer themselves to the unwary. Fewer such dangers are open to classroom teachers, although it would be quite wrong to imagine that this difference in scope is a difference in kind. Classroom abuses of assessment are no less to be condemned than public ones and, since they are usually less readily rectified, may even be more heinous. As the size of a program increases, so does the chance of encountering (or, more usually, failing to avoid) one of the many problems I have discussed in this chapter. The surprise is not that pitfalls occur in the assessment of writing; the wonder is that—given the general lack of understanding of these issues and the general lack of communication among those involved in evaluation—so much assessment goes on so competently and intelligently at large and small institutions throughout the country.

CHAPTER 12

Evaluating
Writing Programs

The typical evaluation of writing programs (including writing projects, writing-across-the-curriculum programs, research and grant
designs, in-service training seminars, and regular instructional programs) usually fails to obtain statistically meaningful results. This
failure should not be taken to mean that writing programs are failures. The inability to get results ought, in general, to be seen as a
conceptual failure, deriving, in part, from a failure to understand
the state of the art in the measurement of writing ability. For example, if you go on a diet and lose ten or fifteen pounds, take in
your belt two notches, and fit nicely into an outfit you previously
could not button, you have pretty good evidence that your diet has
been a success. But suppose that you had decided to employ a more
quantitative pretest/posttest model as an added rigorous statistical
check and had used the truck scale beside an interstate highway as
your measure before and after your diet. Since the truck scale weighs
in hundred-pound increments, it does not register your weight loss.
Alas! you would say—if you were to follow the usual unsophisti-
cated program evaluation model—I must have been deceiving myself; I have not lost any weight, since the truck scale does not show
that I have, and the truck scale is, after all, an objective measure.

Strange as it may seem, this truck scale measurement model
is still the dominant form of program evaluation, and it has led to

much absurdity. For example, about thirty years ago, a study of the composition program at Dartmouth College (Kitzhaber, 1963) gave much evidence to demonstrate that graduating seniors wrote worse than they did as entering freshmen. The definition and measure of writing skill consisted of an elaborate error count in student prose. The evaluation showed that Dartmouth seniors make more errors in writing than freshmen do (an unsurprising finding, since many writers who handle complex subjects tend, at least on early drafts, to make more errors than they would if they were writing on simple subjects); but the measure, elaborate though it was, made little attempt to evaluate complexity of idea, depth of thought, integration of knowledge and opinion, or any of the other higher-order skills that are presumably part of a Dartmouth education. Nor did the study consider other possible program effects beyond the reduction of errors in student prose. An inappropriate measurement device was used to "demonstrate" a finding contrary to much available evidence (and to common experience). Nonetheless, those findings are still widely cited and have entered academic folklore.

Program evaluation is a serious matter, and serious financial and personnel decisions often depend on its results. Most grants require at least a gesture toward evaluation, research findings require validation before dissemination, and instructional programs of all sorts depend for their funding on a demonstration of their value. Since the more sophisticated measurement models frequently seem to be as ineffective as the simple-minded ones, we need to look closely at the usual evaluation models in order to avoid committing the same mistakes. A program evaluation that fails to show results is a damaging document, and it is far better to avoid such an evaluation than to engage in one that will seem to demonstrate that no measurable good is being done by an effective composition course, writing-across-the-curriculum program, grant program, or research hypothesis.

Program Evaluation Models

We will look first at four general models of program evaluation that can be applied to writing programs. In the first place, we need to review, and dismiss, the norm-referenced pretest/posttest evaluation model, which is certain to show no results. Second, we will look at the criterion-referenced pretest/posttest model, which is much more supportive of the curriculum but also normally is still not sensitive enough to show results. A third model often obtains results, but it does so by avoiding the gathering or evaluation of data, using instead the impressions of outside experts or of participants responding to survey devices. The final model uses a variety of measures, is not irrevocably tied to the pretest/posttest model, and is very likely to yield results if they are there to be found.

Certain Failure: Norm-Referenced Testing

The great appeal of a standard norm-referenced test is its supposed objectivity. Some publisher or testing service produces a multiple-choice instrument with an impressive name, such as the Test of Standard English Usage, and, even better, publishes norms and statistical tables along with the test. Furthermore, some local education professor has been heard to say that the test is unexceptionable, or something like it, so it must be good. So the institutional research office of the college or the assistant superintendent for instruction of a school district administers the test to students before and after the composition course, only to find that scores do not change. When the results are published, the composition teachers find themselves in a difficult defensive position.

The basic problem with using someone else's norm-referenced test is that it is probably not the right test for a particular program. It may define writing as spelling and punctuation, whereas this program defines writing as originality and coherence; it may be normed on a population with characteristics quite different from those of the students in the program. In addition, it has probably been constructed according to the usual procedures for norm-referenced tests—that is, so that it will yield a bell-shaped curve. Such test construction needs a preponderance of questions of middle-range difficulty, since the bell curve is its goal, and hence tends inevitably toward the kind of question suitable for aptitude rather than achievement testing. It is the nature and goal of many norm-referenced tests (the Scholastic Aptitude Test is the best-known example) *not* to show the effects of short-term instruction.

Thus, the use of a norm-referenced, multiple-choice test, following the pretest/posttest model (the kind of program evaluation that seems to come first to the minds of the uninformed), gives an almost certain negative prognosis. The test is designed *not* to show what is sought, it will most likely examine something that has not been taught, and it is probably normed on an inappropriate population. Furthermore, it defines the effects of a writing program in the narrowest possible terms. And all this is accepted in the name of "objectivity"! We should certainly demand of any instrument used in program evaluation that it be appropriate to the material and the population in the program and that it be designed to measure the specific kinds of improvement that the program is designed to bring about.

Probable Failure: A Single Essay Test

More sophisticated program evaluation in writing will respond to the problems I have just summarized. Careful evaluators will bring together the administrators and faculty responsible for the classes, work out test specifications that correspond to the writing skills being taught, develop and pretest writing topics, and grade the writing test according to the state of the art of holistic or primary-trait scoring. More and more program evaluators are following this more responsible model, which they then use as part of the pretest/posttest design in order to show (as they fully expect) that the students' writing performance as they define it has improved as a result of that particular writing program.

Such evaluators deserve applause. The faculty benefit from the discussion of and added sophistication in the assignment and measurement of writing; the students benefit from a consistent emphasis in class and in assessment on actual writing; the program itself benefits from the considerable evaluation of goals and procedures that must take place. Only one important benefit is missing: normally, the posttest shows that no statistically significant improvement has taken place in the students' test scores.

The disappointment brought about by this kind of result, after all the work of the assessment, can be devastating. Sometimes it becomes hard to realize that the fault is still with the evaluation design, since all the problems with norm-referenced multiple-choice testing have been avoided: the essay test is a criterion-referenced device, designed specifically for the local population and for the goals of the particular program. Why has it failed to measure the improvement in student writing that every teacher in the program knows has occurred? Or is it (the hidden fear buried in every American intellectual) all a delusion that education has an effect, that students can be taught to write, that we have really earned our salaries, such as they are?

No, the problem remains with the evaluation model—the pretest/posttest model, to be precise—with its assumption that the only program effect worth measuring is the short-term learning that may show up in first draft products on a writing test. Although such a model may well be effective for lower-order skills, such as counting or spelling, or for limited kinds of learning, such as the declensions of Latin nouns or theorems in geometry, writing is in itself too complex and multifaceted to be measured in such a way. The amount of improvement that can occur in so complex a skill in a few months is likely to be submerged by such statistical facts as regression to the mean or less than ideal reliability.

A carefully designed essay test is an appropriate part of many composition programs' evaluation designs. The more careful it is, the more likely it is to show the effects of instruction (see Sanders and Littlefield, 1975). But everyone involved in the evaluation should be aware of the strong odds against obtaining statistically meaningful results from this one instrument. Therefore, a simple pretest/posttest model using actual writing scored holistically should never be the entire evaluation design. As *part* of the design, such a test has many beneficial effects and just might document the improvement that has taken place; as the *whole* design, the test is asked to carry more weight and more responsibility than it can well bear.

Those using a writing sample as part of the evaluation design should attend to the following procedures, in order to give themselves the best chance at obtaining results:

1. Those teaching the classes must be involved in developing the test specifications, and at least some of them should take part in selecting the writing topics. If the test is to be truly criterion

referenced, energy, time, and money will have to be spent on test development. A primary-trait scoring guide will help those scoring the test focus on the aspects of writing that are being taught in the program.

2. Unless the program being evaluated teaches only one mode of discourse (as some business or research-writing courses do), the test should give all students an opportunity to do their best by requiring at least two different kinds of prose: for example, a personal experience essay and an analytical essay. The test should recognize that some students learn some kinds of writing much more quickly than other kinds.

3. Two separate forms of the test should be prepared, so that each half of the student group can take different forms as pretest and posttest. Thus, half the group will take Form A as the pretest and Form B as the posttest, whereas the other half will take Form B as the pretest and Form A as the posttest. Raters will then be unable to distinguish pretests from posttests by topic.

4. After all tests have been coded, all identifying marks should be removed from them, and all the tests (pretests and posttests) should be scored at the *same* controlled essay reading. After the scoring has been completed, the tests should be grouped once again by test date, school, class, and so on, so that statistical processing can take place. Pretests should never be scored separately from posttests.

5. The test needs to have enough administrative, clerical, statistical, and computer support so that its various components can be carried out professionally. It is a foolish economy to ask an English professor to do statistical work or to ask secretaries to grade compositions. In testing, as in life, we get what we ask for and usually what we pay for. Those elected or chosen to direct this limited evaluation design need to recognize the strong odds against achieving results and to resist the kinds of economies that lower reliability and validity.

Anecdotal Results: Outside Experts and Opinion Surveys

Just as the pretest/posttest model seems to come readily to the minds of those with little assessment experience, so do two other means of simplifying the complex questions of program evaluation: hiring an outside consultant and administering an opinion survey. Although these devices are not improper in themselves as part of an overall evaluation plan, they are sometimes adopted as substitutes for an evaluation plan. They usually will produce positive results, whether the program is an effective one or not. For this reason, the results may not be convincing to some important audiences, particularly those looking for data rather than opinions.

Outside experts are often chosen rather haphazardly, often by the English department chair or someone else without much awareness of assessment issues. The experts are often longtime English faculty who may have some expertness (or may not) in some aspects of composition and may even have some experience in evaluation, but all too often the outsider has less expertness than good will. Some genuine experts are available, such as those trained by the Council of Writing Program Administrators; they have some systematic questions to ask and will require substantial in-house evaluation work to precede a visit (see the WPA guidelines shown as Resource C at the back of this book). While training and qualifications may or may not matter to those selecting the expert, two characteristics are almost invariable: the expert must be from out of town, preferably out of state, and the expert must be friendly to the program being evaluated.

The outside expert, for a nominal fee, is usually expected to spend a day or two on campus and to write a brief report about the program in question. An astute and experienced visitor can discover a great deal about a program even under such disadvantageous circumstances and can prepare a modest document for the use of the program administrators. Such documents are usually highly laudatory of the professionalism of the program, citing its best features and most qualified personnel. Negative matters, if reported at all, are likely to be only hinted at—buried in the praise and covered with qualifiers—unless these items can be used by program administrators to gain more funds or other advantages in future negotiations with campus officials.

The reports produced by most outside experts, particularly by those without discernible expertness, should really be called subjective impressions of a program rather than program evaluations.

In many cases, the reports use the evaluator's home campus as if it were the best model to be followed, a sure irritant to the campus that asked for a responsive evaluation of its own circumstances. But no one expects to take such reports too seriously. Since the expert is making a brief visit from out of town, he or she can hardly be expected to understand the program in detail in the time allowed; so recommendations can easily be ignored if they are not convenient.

It is possible, of course, to contract for a serious evaluation by an experienced evaluator or evaluation team, and the WPA consultant-evaluator service is the most prominent source for such evaluations. But even the WPA team, which brings a national perspective and regular training to the job, in the interests of economy will produce only one report, usually relying on the materials that the campus supplies and a day or two of campus interviews. More elaborate evaluations will generate their own studies and data over a period of months or years. But few institutions are willing to find the large amount of money such an evaluation team demands (running into the tens or even hundreds of thousands of dollars) or the time such an effort would take. Those seeking serious but economical evaluation prefer to use evaluators who already know the program and its context and who can find legitimate evaluation devices at modest cost.

Surveys of faculty and students about writing programs are often part of responsible program evaluations, but they cannot substitute for such evaluation. Those without much experience at such surveys imagine them to be much easier to prepare and analyze than they in fact are and often will ask local faculty to prepare one on short notice. Such quick and cheap surveys are almost sure to have numerous flaws; most prominently, the wording of the questions will lead respondents to give answers that the evaluators are hoping to obtain. It is relatively easy to accumulate favorable opinions of a writing program from those teaching in it and from the students who have invested time and labor in it; even faculty and administrators who have little contact with the program are often ready to say positive things about their friends and colleagues if a questionnaire urges them to do so.

Those who develop questionnaires and surveys professionally have learned how to protect such instruments from the usual abuses: ambiguity, suggested or even forced choices, oversimplification, and so on. They develop the instruments over a considerable period of time—pretesting, evaluating, and revising them—and subject the results of the drafts to intense analysis for reliability and validity. Even after such labor, however, the data produced by surveys must be regarded only as statements of belief, not as program descriptions or progam effects, although opinions sometimes may reflect or anticipate behavior.

Thus, outside experts and surveys of opinion do not, by themselves, solve the problems of program evaluation. Indeed, since they are easy substitutes for a program evaluation, and since they are even occasionally used as if they were program evaluation, they may be even more deceptive than the pretest/posttest models. The worst one can say about these latter models is that they generally do not live up to the expectations of those who employ them, whereas experts and surveys are often sympathetically misleading.

Probable Results: Evaluation by Varied Measures

Writing programs have many goals, all of which have something to do with improving student writing. An evaluation design that attempts to define and acquire information about a wide range of these goals—such as those discussed in the following sections—will be more responsible and much more likely to identify measurable results.

Student Outcomes. No instructional program evaluation will be taken seriously if it does not attempt to identify the benefits to students—either by coming up with "gain scores" or by devising some other measure. This book argues for the value of measuring students' writing skills by means of several holistically graded writing samples or by portfolios; unfortunately, this type of assessment rarely produces a "gain score," since only a fairly narrow improvement can be expected as a result of a relatively short writing program. Another approach to student outcomes through direct measurement would be to set program goals and seek to measure the proportion of students who reach them as time goes by; if an increasing percentage of students achieve these goals each year, the program is clearly attaining success, even if individual gain scores cannot be obtained.

An early indication of improvement to come is an attitude change. Measures of student attitudes may show that students have more positive feelings about writing after they complete the program, even if their writing skills have not yet improved very much. Other desirable student outcomes might be improved grades in some or all other classes, a lower dropout rate, or a willingness to take other courses requiring writing. Long-range outcomes, such as changed attitudes and behavior years after the program has been completed, have not been much attended to, but they offer real possibilities under the right circumstances.

Faculty Effects. Although the effects of a program on teachers are generally ignored, programs that value and challenge the faculty, that make them feel efficacious and appreciated, usually are successful programs. Teachers' feelings about a program can be discerned in their attitudes toward the subject and the students, morale, conference attendance, pedagogical research and publication, classroom assignments, syllabi, and exams.

Faculty effects have received the most attention in writing-across-the-curriculum (WAC) programs, which encourage faculty in all areas to use writing as part of their teaching. As Gail Hughes has shown, WAC programs proceed in three stages: in the faculty development stage, faculty are shown how to use writing in their courses; in the classroom implementation phase, faculty attempt to increase or improve their writing assignments in the classroom; and in the student impact phase, students improve their attitudes about and skill in writing and increase their learning in all their classes through writing. Hughes argues that program assessments cannot stop with the first phase, since faculty may be delighted with the faculty development workshops or retreats but may fail to change their teaching in any way; an evaluation of classroom implementation is therefore crucial. If the first two phases are taking place successfully, the third phase can be shown to occur.

According to Hughes, program evaluation for WAC does not address the apparent question "Does it work?" Rather, it seeks to deal with two more relevant questions: *"Can* it work?" and *"How* can I get it to work at my college?" To answer these questions, a program evaluation must be highly detailed and descriptive, using an "eclectic, multimethod, and multidisciplinary approach" (Hughes, forthcoming; also Hughes-Wiener and Jensen-Cekalla, 1991). (See the research design shown in Resource D in the back of this book.)

Spread of Effect. Writing programs, particularly the most successful ones, may have a wide circle of effects beyond the immediate impact on students and faculty in the program. Sometimes faculty outside the program show their support by adding writing assignments or essay tests to their own curricula. Perhaps a special college writing program at the freshman level calls forth other programs at the upper-division level, or an extraordinary program at a junior high school elicits changes in the school district's elementary schools and high school. Sometimes writing programs lead to changes in the way that students, or even their parents, deal with writing or reading outside the classroom.

A further advantage to an evaluation design not limited merely to a pretest/posttest model is the formative effect the evaluation itself can have. The very act of gathering information from a variety of sources leads to new lines of communication and new thinking about the program. There is no need to wait years for data analysis; some findings result directly from the evaluation activity. The principal of the school discovers that the new creative software he or she proudly ordered is still not in use; the freshman composition director is dismayed to find out that half the staff are teaching literature instead of writing; the English teachers are amazed to hear that they are held in high esteem by their colleagues in the sciences, many of whom require writing in their classes.

Steps in Program Evaluation

Much of the literature on evaluating writing programs consists of warnings, bad examples, and explanations of ineffective procedures (for example, Davis, Scriven, and Thomas, 1987; Witte and Faigley, 1983). Valuable as these ill omens may be, they are not much help to the faculty member directing the evaluation of a writing program; something, after all, must get done, and successful evaluation designs, while difficult, are not impossible. The following steps outline the procedures that can lead to a successful evaluation.

Initial Planning and Personnel

At the outset, those responsible for the program should consider the scope, funding, audience, and function of the evaluation design; they should then give the evaluator they engage a precise description of the task. If resources allow only a gesture toward assessment and if the audience for the report is sympathetic, evaluation can consist of a survey or two or a friendly outside expert's report. To be most useful, such an evaluation should be essentially formative— that is, aimed at the improvement of the program. The primary audience for this evaluation would be those who can effect such improvement. Since less rigorous procedures can be used (as long as they are sufficiently convincing to the participants), even sparse resources will allow for enough formative evaluation to indicate that the program goals and procedures might (or might not) need to be reconsidered. For example, a visiting expert with high credibility could prepare a brief report that could have substantial impact on the program despite its paucity of data.

However, an evaluation designed primarily for the improvement of the program may turn out to be exactly the wrong plan for a funding agency looking for demonstrated results. In this case, the limited resources must be devoted to a summative evaluation, documenting the effectiveness of the program. Many funding agencies expect 10 percent of a grant to be used in evaluation, for example, and will expect some statistical verification of the findings.

A final task in the initial planning stage is to select the persons who will be responsible for the evaluation. There is some professional difference of opinion here. I have suggested that outside experts might be used for consultation but should not be made primarily responsible for the evaluation, and Witte and Faigley support that position in the strongest terms (1983, pp. 5-7). However, Michael Scriven, a professional outside expert, disputes that view, arguing, in effect, that only a "goal-free" outsider is in a position to distinguish what is in fact occurring (1973). Those close to a program are inevitably corrupted by their knowledge of or even commitment to intended effects, according to this view, and thus have trouble seeing with the needed clarity. The handbook produced by the Scriven team takes a more moderate position, calling for evaluation teams with maximum credibility, containing both insiders and outsiders (Davis, Scriven, and Thomas, 1987).

Under most circumstances, the best solution is to select as evaluator someone with expertness in the field who knows the program involved but is not directly connected with it. An evaluator who knows little about the teaching of writing cannot be expected to understand the issues involved in evaluating a writing program; an expert who needs to spend a great deal of time learning the context of the program is less valuable than one who can begin right away. Thus, someone usually can be found locally to direct the evaluation effort. As mentioned, this person should have little direct connection with the program being evaluated. If, as sometimes happens, the only one available to serve as evaluator is the director of the program, unusual steps (such as use of an outside statistician) need to be taken to establish the authenticity of the final report. An evaluation team representing various perspectives is an obvious advantage, if one can be recruited. However, a team needs a leader, and some one individual needs to be responsible for the entire evaluation effort.

Goal Definition

Once the basic decisions about the purpose and audience of the evaluation plan have been made, and an evaluator has been selected who has enough knowledge and experience to avoid the most obvious pitfalls, the next step is to develop a clear sense of the goals of the program itself, in as precise terms as possible. If improved student writing is a goal, it is well to ask what "improved" means to the participants; if better teaching of writing is called for, the ways to identify (if not to measure) that teaching must be determined and specified.

The discussion of goals is central to the evaluation process and requires a substantial amount of time and thought. The evaluator should keep in mind the "Framework for Evaluating College

Writing Programs" developed by Witte and Faigley (1983, chap. 3), a wide-ranging view of five components moving from the instructional activity itself outward to the social and cultural context. The list of over thirty "questions for evaluators" with which the booklet concludes (pp. 74-78) should keep any evaluator from taking too narrow a view of the subject.

The evaluator needs to compile a list of goals, including unintended goals and spread of effect, before setting out a plan for measuring the program's effect. Since most writing programs will have more—and more complicated—goals than evaluation funding can encompass, these goals will have to be arranged in some sort of hierarchy of importance. The most important goals should be given particular attention in the evaluation report, though all goals should be listed, along with any available evidence of their achievement.

The Evaluation Design

In constructing the evaluation design, every evaluator is constrained by time and money, so it makes sense to use what is already at hand. Before attempting to generate new sources of data, the evaluator should see what "found" data may already be available. (Davis, Scriven, and Thomas, 1987, pp. 78-97, make several useful suggestions for finding such materials.) Certain baseline data often are on hand from, say, placement tests or admissions tests of one sort or another. Instead of developing an end-of-course essay test for all freshmen taking composition classes, the evaluator may be able to use or adapt one instructor's course final examination. There is usually no need to develop questionnaires, since questionnaires for almost any occasion are already available.

As the evaluator decides among the most important goals for detailed examination, he or she needs to consider available resources, data, time, and cooperation (teachers will give up only a little class time for evaluation). The most important principle to keep in mind is to use a variety of measures that reflect the various goals of the program and not to put all the funds in one measure or narrow the goals of a complex program. Witte and Faigley are very clear on this point: "No matter how carefully conceived and constructed the design or how sophisticated the methods of analysis, evaluations must be based on more than pretest and posttest writing samples. Evaluations of writing programs and courses, if they are to result in valid and reliable judgments, must employ a variety of methods and procedures" (1983, p. 38).

Follow-Through

Since most program evaluations cover an extended period of time, sometimes years, the evaluator and the evaluating team must keep written records of discussions, decisions, and plans—in short, enough documentation for the design so that it can proceed in their absence. Frequently, new evaluators who come on the scene have little to guide them: data have been misplaced or destroyed by accident; evaluation reports covering years of work wind up patched together hastily at the last minute. Since the most energy, creativity, and support for evaluation usually occur at the beginning, that is the time to prepare background chapters of the final report, time lines for later evaluation activity, and detailed descriptions of how the design is to proceed.

Empirical and Nonempirical Research Designs

As Ann Ruggles Gere (1985) has shown, empirical research has been part of American composition studies nearly from their beginning. The tradition began with the first Harvard report in 1892, assessing English A; flowered in the 1960s with Kitzhaber's study at Dartmouth (1963) and the Braddock team's summary of research (Braddock, Lloyd-Jones, and Schoer, 1963); and continues unabated in the 1990s. Our relatively new concern for reliability and validity in writing assessment might even be seen as one tide in this continuing empirical sea of composition research. Those committed to empirical research, or to its ethnographic and clinical offshoots, have dominated the field and arrogated the very term *research* for their own particular methodology.

But empirical research in program evaluation has not given us direct answers—or even clear ways of reaching answers—to our questions about the effectiveness of writing programs. Despite its strong appeal as a dominant method of research, it has not been able to deliver the certainties that we long for. (See North, 1987, pp. 141-196, for a critical review of the method; and Flower, 1989, for a rebuttal defending "observational" methodology.) There is no replicated design in existence for demonstrating that any writing instructional program in fact improves student writing (if we define writing in a sophisticated way). Although there are isolated examples here and there, usually without much statistical sophistication, of some measurable student improvement, we have not, despite massive efforts, come up with an experimental model we can point to and say, "Yes, this is how we demonstrate that student writing has been improved by this particular program." Hillocks's (1986) elaborate meta-analysis must be seen as the latest in a series of heroic efforts to achieve some conclusions by this method. Richard Larson's (1987) dry question in his review of the book captures the reaction neatly: "After such promise, what fulfillment?" The review provides the expected answer: Not much.

The most dramatic example of this depressing inability of empirical research to provide us with convincing program evaluation is Witte and Faigley's *Evaluating College Writing Programs* (1983). The book has an unintended dramatic structure. In its opening sections, it examines closely a series of empirical program evaluations that failed. The authors select the best empirical precedents and mercilessly detail exactly where these efforts went wrong. At the center of the book is the promise that the authors, who are planning their own program evaluation, will avoid all past errors in their own design. The drama builds as we see the new and more perfect plan they evolve and proceed to implement. And then, the denouement, the reward of hubris, the fate of those who challenge the gods: the even more spectacular failure of the new design, with an assessment of the new and more sophisticated errors they committed. It is hard to know which to admire more—the honesty and writing skill of the authors, as they show that they too have failed at writing program evaluation, or the damnable recalcitrance of the problem they tried in vain to solve.

The nonfinding of this Witte-Faigley study, by the way, replicates the nonresults of the exceedingly well-funded Carnegie Foundation evaluation of the (then) Bay Area Writing Project. That evaluation, headed by Michael Scriven, produced no less than thirty-two separate reports, "none of which," according to the *Carnegie Quarterly,* "was able to present direct cause-and-effect statistics" ("Teaching and Learning the Art of Composition," 1979, p. 7).

To be sure, if we reduce the scope of the problem sufficiently, we can come up with something. Hillocks (1986) summarizes certain kinds of results and, in his meta-analyses, gives certain kinds of confirmation about effective and ineffective teaching "modes" and "foci" in writing programs (see White, 1989, chap. 3, for a critical summary and analysis of those findings). We can take a small part of writing, such as spelling or syntax, and show that some kinds of class work can improve scores on certain narrow kinds of tests. We can imagine that T-units are in fact (as they are in some theories) a way of defining writing quality and then show how to lengthen students' T-units. We can use sentence combining to lengthen sentences, and we can drill on active verbs to shorten sentences. We can use error counts, as Kitzhaber's 1963 study at Dartmouth did, to show that freshmen write better than seniors; we can use six-way scoring of complicated essays on three kinds of scales, as the California project (White and Polin, 1986) did, to show that weak student writers perform better on campuses where there are upper-division writing requirements. But empirical methods seem always to circle about and get no closer to the "simple" question of whether this or that writing program actually makes students write better or not. Why?

In the first place, we need to recognize that empirical program evaluation takes place at several removes from reality. There is, on the first level, the student—thinking, learning, daydreaming. On the second level is the written expression of that student's mental activity: a first-draft writing product, a survey or multiple-choice test of some sort, a demonstration of the writing process, a portfolio of processes and products. Then we have the third remove from reality, the evaluation of that second level. This evaluation may be a number, a letter grade, a statement of some sort, a profile of scores, or any combination. Then comes the fourth level, for we are concerned not with individuals but with groups: we must aggregate these measures somehow to come up with group measures. Furthermore, we must have comparable group measures over time, for a single group measure can tell us little; we need to compare performance in order to show improvement. But we have seen the perils of pretesting and posttesting. On this treacherous shoal have foundered virtually all the hopeful empirical evaluation barks that have been launched. But yet a further remove into abstraction and metaphor awaits. We must now apply statistical tests of reliability, validity, and significance to whatever group comparative data may still be afloat. Then, and only then, can we measure the probability (*never* in this method the certainty) that our findings are not the result of chance. Only after these tests have battered our work can we stand up and assert that our program has indeed proven itself to be of value. But we can't seem to get the numbers people to perform their psychomagic (as a statistician I know calls it) for us; they usually abandon ship well before we stand naked and alone on the farther shore declaring that our programs work.

But, of course, we and our colleagues have known the value of our work from the beginning of the measurement effort. We know it because we have seen our students improve, year after year, and they come back to thank us for the help we have given them. But although we know that our students write better and we have all kinds of unofficial nonempirical evidence to show that our programs are valuable, we seem unable to come up with data to prove it to outsiders.

We thus find ourselves like Dr. Johnson, kicking the stone to demonstrate reality, despite the arguments of the philosophers. But, like the philosophers, the granting agencies and the trustees smile at our naiveté and then award the spoils of statistically demonstrated value elsewhere.

So let us return to the catalogue of problems we face in the empirical evaluation of writing programs. We share the many removes from reality I have just described with some other disciplines; our problem of definition, however, is almost unique. What is this thing that we are measuring, and how do these different meanings affect our comparisons of group performance?

This question returns us to the central problem of defining what we mean by "writing" or "writing skill" or "writing program"—the first step in implementing a research design. But we know that even among writing teachers there is little agreement. We are familiar with the reactions of untrained graders of student writing; as we have seen for decades, without efforts to reach agreement on standards, all papers get all scores. We have learned how, on a single test, to cope with the fact that writing is for some readers a structural concept, for others a stylistic one, for others a mysteriously creative one, for others a conventional or mechanical one, and for still others a moral one. The recent developments in the testing of writing require a clear, focused, and forced agreement on the definition of writing for a particular test or portfolio assessment.

But our ability to cope with this definitional problem on a particular writing assessment is by no means a sign that we have really solved the problem or that it can be solved or even that it ought to be solved in general. Even though scoring guides, anchor papers, and similar methods to force consensus have put order into our group scoring of tests and portfolios, a serious attempt at program evaluation throws us back into the primal chaos once more. In this chaos, the multiple and conflicting definitions of writing are both our despair (they keep us from giving simple answers) and our hope; indeed, it is through this complexity of definition that we are likely to find the answers we seek.

Thus, we cannot use holistic scoring very effectively in the area of program evaluation. We must recognize and allow others to recognize that writing is all the aspects of learning and expression that I have briefly summarized, and more. That is, for program evaluation purposes, we need to develop new theories about the meaning of writing—theories that define writing more inclusively than our holistic scoring guides and other assessment documents do. For example, a simple pretest/posttest evaluation design, even using sophisticated question development and careful holistic scoring, normally yields no gain scores for groups across an academic year. We know that the students are writing better, but the measurement device does not show it. Why? The reasons have become plain: the relatively small improvement in writing ability that occurs even in a first-rate writing program (when compared with a lifetime of language use) tends not to show up in the rough and relatively unreliable scores of a single test of first-draft writing. Furthermore, many aspects of what has been taught, from revision and editing procedures to reading and library research skills, are not tested by the timed essay. In addition, such a set of tests does not even attempt to look at certain long-range benefits that we sometimes claim for writing, such as intellectual or moral growth, increased ability to learn, and enhanced understanding of the self. We cannot simply import routine test procedures into program evaluation and expect them to yield results. Instead of trimming down what we measure, so that we can measure it accurately, we need to expand our procedures, so that we can catch improvements of all sorts wherever they may show up.

My point here is that we need to think differently about these basic matters when we shift contexts. Program evaluation is not just large-scale writing assessment; it is a wholly different, if related, activity. And if writing assessment is difficult and complex, program evaluation is even more so.

The problems with empirical methodology that I have been alluding to are profoundly important, because they lead us to the crucial questions for assessment of writing programs: How can we improve composition programs to the point that they can justify their claim to a position at the center of postsecondary education? How can a concerned faculty and administration improve the campus climate for writing, and thus for thinking and learning? If our most trusted means of generating information—that is, the inductive reasoning and empirical methodology that have led to modern science and technology—will not reliably confirm the value of writing programs, can we really believe that writing does what we claim?

One response to these perplexities is to remember Einstein's proverb about research: "Everything should be as simple as possible—but no simpler." Empirical methodologies require relatively uncomplicated and clear phenomena, so that experiments can be run with sufficient controls. If the phenomenon we are studying is complicated, we need to isolate one or two variables for examination while we hold everything else constant. Furthermore, the method is more attuned to what North (1987, p. 145) calls *"disconfirming* possible explanations" than to discovery of truth; since empiricism must leap to generalizations from a limited number of cases, it confirms theories by failing to deny them, and its inferences must always be tentative. In addition, a kind of positivism lies behind the empirical quest: the world is assumed to be orderly, definable, and knowable. When the investigator discovers the rules that govern the world, they hold in all similar cases; thus, empirical experiments must be replicable if they reveal truth.

Writing programs certainly seem ill suited for this kind of inquiry. While any modern person must grant empirical inquiry enormous power in the investigation of the physical world, it is not necessarily the best method for inquiry into either the process or the success of writing programs. Certainly, the results of empirical program evaluation are discouraging—as, indeed, are the results of empirical research on writing in general. An enormous investment of time, energy, and money has produced mainly survey data, tending to organize what every thoughtful person knew all along.

In program evaluation, as in all other aspects of writing programs, we need to resist using or accepting simple and reductive definitions, procedures, tests, and inferences. It is surely a wise instinct that leads us to trust writing instruction more to poets than to scientists, or even to logicians. The resistant reality of learning to think, to write, to create, to revise and re-create, and to understand does not yield its secrets readily. Our primary job, in program evaluation as in many other aspects of our work, is to help others see the complexity and importance of writing, to distinguish between the simple and the not so simple, to be willing to accept the evidence of many kinds of serious inquiry into the nature of creative thought.

The Value of Evaluation

While a negative program evaluation, or a badly done evaluation report, can be most damaging, a well-handled evaluation has many advantages. The sheer consideration of goals and ways of approaching those goals that evaluation demands is a formative activity; it asks those who teach writing to consider what they are doing and why—questions that need to be asked far more often than they usually are. The gathering of information for an evaluation is itself a creative activity; it not only forces those producing the information to see it with new eyes but also makes statements about the importance of the information being collected. (Imagine an item on a faculty questionnaire asking about the number of professional conferences on the teaching of writing attended, or the number of conference papers read on pedagogy.)

Finally, of course, a careful evaluation leads to a reexamination of the way things are being done, the way human and financial resources are being spent. It may suggest that some of us have found more successful ways of doing our jobs. It may even suggest that we are so enormously effective at what we do that we should spend rather more time than we do at self-congratulation. Or it may suggest that we are not very effective at all. In any case, the evaluation of writing programs need not be threatening or destructive; if it is done in a sensitive and intelligent way, using a wide range of measures and involving those teaching in the program in the substantive issues of the evaluation, it can be a valuable experience for everyone.

Program evaluation ought never to be seen as a mere measurement issue, unrelated to conceptual, contextual, and curricular issues that define the writing program. Behind program evaluation lies our responsibility to our students and to the central role of writing, in all its complexity, in education. Whenever writing teachers involve themselves, as they should, with program evaluation, they must be fully alert both to the dangers of oversimplification and to the large possibilities for constructive change offered by any evaluation program.

CHAPTER 13

The Politics of Assessment: Past and Future

Those of us who began advocating and using holistic scoring for student essays in the 1970s believed that we had discovered the ideal method of assessing writing. By developing careful essay questions, administering and scoring them under controlled testing conditions, and recording a single accurate score for the quality of writing as a whole (with scoring guides and sample papers defining quality), we had become committed to a flexible, accurate, and responsive measurement method, one that could come under the control of teachers. The rapid and widespread acceptance of such scoring, and the kind of testing that led to it, let us take a relatively uncritical stance. We were promulgating a kind of religious belief in an approach to writing as well as a testing device, and we were more interested in converting unbelievers than in questioning the faith—or the political issues behind the faith.

But as we move through the 1990s, with holistic scoring more or less routine, we have a belated scholarly obligation to step back and see it in perspective. Those of us who were personally involved need to convey the flavor and personal touches as well as the history of this minor revolution in a profession's approach to writing measurement and writing instruction. But these personal matters are interesting only as they convey underlying truths of a discipline in flux. What, we ought to ask, were the historical and political forces that allowed a lethargic profession to change so radically the way it evaluated students, within a single decade? Furthermore, technology has taught us that every solution brings new problems; what are the new problems that holistic scoring has (inevitably) produced? Finally, we need to consider the challenges to holistic scoring that have recently emerged from the profession. Portfolio assessment, for instance, proposes itself as a new solution to the problems raised by holistic scoring; yet it seems to be repeating many of the problems and solutions of its predecessor. What have we learned from the profession's experience with holistic scoring that will be useful for new assessment methods?

Some Personal Background

When I published an article entitled "Holisticism" in *College Composition and Communication* in 1984, I summarized, indeed exaggerated, the arguments for holistic scoring of student writing. Though that article has often been cited, and though I still stand behind the essence of what it says, some qualifications are by now in order. Miles Myers has told me that my assertion that I conducted the first holistic scoring on the West Coast in 1973 is incorrect; some San Francisco Bay Area teachers had carried the concept and procedure from Advanced Placement readings back home before that time. More significantly, the editor for the first edition of this book, to whom I had proudly sent the article (which was being revised into the second chapter), was decidedly unimpressed by the title; every serious writer, the late Kenneth Eble wrote me, has an obligation to refrain from inventing new and barbarous words. He also suggested that I was making rather too much of a fuss over what any sensible person is likely to use at times in grading or teaching. By turning a simple scoring procedure into an "ism," I was creating ideologies without good reason. I could not fully agree that things were quite that simple. The remarkable triumph of holistic scoring was bound to be theoretically interesting, and was probably ideological as well. Surely, though, he was right that one should discuss these matters in clear and direct language, however profound their implications turned out to be. I can see now that my inflated language, as I began to write about holistic scoring, expressed an understandably inflated view of the uniqueness of the enterprise.

When those of us who accidentally became the apostles of holistic approaches to writing measurement began our work, we had no such elaborate sense of what we were doing. A few key players—such as Paul Diederich, Evans Alloway, and Trudy Conlon of Educational Testing Service (ETS)—were members of the testing community and were simply going about their jobs as researchers or test administrators. Albert Serling of ETS was directing the College-Level Examination Program and saw essay testing as a way to give substance and academic respectability to a testing program sorely in need of both. Alan Seder of the Berkeley ETS office, a superb administrator, was stimulated by the sheer challenge of managing the complex programs that emerged, and John Bianchini, also of the Berkeley ETS office, became involved in the statistical challenges that holistic scoring presented. Some of us (such as Rex Burbank of San Jose State, Richard Lid of California State University, Northridge, William Lutz of Rutgers, and Karen Greenberg and Marie Lederman of the City College of New York) were English teachers, trained as literary scholars, unwilling to accept the reductive concepts of reading and writing that were dominant in writing testing at the time; and we found ourselves in administrative positions that let us try to do something to better the situation. We gave ourselves crash courses in testing procedures and statistics, and we tried to handle test administration the way we handled departmental administration: we expected to take a few years to do necessary but boring clerical duties that could be handled by anyone with common sense and basic intelligence.

My first clue that I was into something bigger than that occurred during the summer of 1972, when I undertook to prepare a report for what became the California State University system on what was known about the measurement of writing ability at the college level. Aside from one book published by the College Board (Godshalk, Swineford, and Coffman, 1966) and a series of in-house documents at the Educational Testing Service, I found only material of questionable use and relevance in statistics and education. Various college English faculty on three continents were rumored to be knowledgeable in measurement, and I assiduously gathered their names and requested their help; but each of them hastily denied the allegation, pointing to others as expert; the others repeated the same lateral-passing movement. Aside from a few Advanced Placement readers and table leaders with valuable practical experience, no one in college English knew anything about the measurement of writing ability. I nonetheless had committed myself to directing a major statewide testing program using holistic scoring. I received some willing help from ETS, most notably from Paul Diederich and Albert Serling, but scholars in my own field were silent, though supportive. For some years, I felt myself in an alien world, exposed, ignorant, and almost alone, an odd position for one whose major scholarly energies had been expended on Jane Austen's novels, Thackeray's journalism, and two notably unsuccessful freshman composition textbooks.

Combat in the 1970s

In the early 1970s, hardly anyone had heard of holistic scoring, and the term had a faddist ring to it, akin to holistic health or holistic physics. Sometimes its Greek roots of unity disappeared before an awkwardly anglicized "wholistic" spelling. English teachers found it unsettling: its emphasis on reading and scoring a piece of student writing as a whole flew in the face of an overwhelming professional nit-picking at parts, while its attention to what student writing does well (as opposed to the customary focus on what it does badly, the usual error hunting) seemed weak-willed and slack in the face of the predominant negativism of teacher grading. At the same time, most of those in the testing and assessment communities smiled patronizingly at one more effort by poetic subjectivists to resist the cold numbers of multiple-choice tests, the sure truth-givers for hard-headed behaviorists.

Even the institutional core of ETS, the originator of holistic scoring, saw it (indeed, still sees it) as a bone to throw to English teachers, while the multiple-choice tests were delivering the data; the essay-testing (and, now, portfolio assessment) defenders at ETS have always been a beleaguered crew, with relatively little influence. The few scholars and test administrators who were using holistic scoring were spending all their energies on confronting the problems of cost and scoring reliability, as practical aspects of the large testing programs they were supervising. Writing researchers were still using error counts, T-units, and other neatly quantifiable measures of doubtful validity for college writers.

So a small group of English faculty apostles set out to promote the word of holistic scoring, quickly developing missionary zeal. While I and my colleagues in the California State University were proselytizing in the West, Karen Greenberg and Maria Lederman (along with Harvey Wiener and Richard Donovan) did the same in the East; with the endearing presumption of New Yorkers, they established an organization they called the National Testing Network in Writing and developed it into a thriving institution whose newsletter, book (Greenberg, Wiener, and Donovan, 1986), and annual conferences have had an important influence on all measurement of writing. We were justifiably self-righteous, on the side of the angels and opposed to a host of devils: the reductionism of multiple-choice usage testing, the hostility to students and point-less negativism of contemporary paper-grading, the domination of teachers and curriculum by insensitive tests and testing agencies, the distortions introduced into teaching by socially biased tests over which nobody seemed to have control. Holistic scoring did not defeat these destructive influences wholly, by any means; they can still be seen everywhere in American education. But college English faculties and many college administrators were fed up with the dominance of multiple-choice testing. To our surprise, the opposition melted before us. Podiums and journal space were made available by every professional organization, government moneys flowed like red ink, and every essay scoring produced new converts to spread the message. By the time the first edition of this book appeared in 1985, I could say, "In the early 1980s, a survey of English departments conducted by a committee of the College Conference on Composition and Communication showed an amazing change: Not only did almost 90 percent of responding English departments state that they used holistic scoring, but nowhere did either the committee chair or the responding parties feel the need to define the term by more than a parenthetical reminder. In one decade, in a notoriously conservative and slow-moving profession, a new concept in testing and (hence) in teaching writing became accepted while no one was watching" (p. 19). The triumph seemed complete. It was not actually complete, of course, but it was a sufficiently impressive victory to demand analysis of its causes.

During the 1970s, holistic scoring became a focus for a variety of ideas and conditions that had been impinging on the traditional teaching of English for some time: awareness of the social and economic bases of privileged language and "correctness," development of poststructural theories of reading and process theories of writing, emergence of writing research as a field of inquiry, and appearance of a vocal proletariat of regular as well as part-time writing faculty for whom writing was a serious business, not merely a path to literature seminars. (The founders of the Council of Writing Program Administrators in 1980 took some pleasure in the New Deal proletarian ring of the new group's initials: WPA.) Some of these developments were related to the virtual disappearance of tenure-track positions in university English departments; others had to do with a new attempt on the part of higher education to enroll student populations traditionally barred from college, as symbolized by the traumatic switch to open enrollment by the City University of New York in 1970. In addition, the force of the student rebellions of the 1960s could still be felt, particularly in their demand for connections and meaning in education, and in their protests against atomization of knowledge, impersonal bureaucracy, subordination of liberal education to economic or government concerns, and rote memorization rather than critical thought.

Multiple-choice testing, particularly in the area of English, became a powerful symbol of what was wrong with education from each of the perspectives I have just listed. Part of our zeal, which caused some distortions still evident today, emerged from our opposition to these fill-in-the-bubble tests; as with many another reformation, our language and concerns bore a striking resemblance to those of the enemy. (Thus, the overriding concern for scoring reliability on the part of holistic research is a direct result of frustrating combat with the perfect scoring reliability of the machine-scored tests, a combat largely conducted on foreign soil.) While it was clear that multiple-choice testing is merely a human tool (not necessarily the devil's handiwork), and that it could be useful under appropriate circumstances, the uses of those tests to grade, label, place, and screen out students seemed then (as now) to demean education in general and writing in particular.

The two multiple-choice tests that focused the opposition most pointedly at the college level were both produced by ETS: the Test of Standard Written English (TSWE) and the College-Level Examination Program (CLEP) General Examination in English. Though the tests had different purposes, they both drew on the same ETS item bank of dreary questions, examining for "correct" answers, according to the school dialect and the test makers' social perspective (see the sample question in Chapter Nine). Since these two tests did more to promote holistic scoring than any or all of the missionaries, we should pause to consider why they elicited—and continue to elicit—outrage.

The TSWE was put together by decent and well-meaning ETS people to meet the demand from colleges for a quick and convenient means of placing the new and untraditional students in remedial courses, where all right-thinking people in power knew they belonged. Although the TSWE is technically separate from the Scholastic Aptitude Test, it is administered at the same time and place, and TSWE scores are reported along with the SAT. Since the massive numbers of students taking the SAT made essay testing cumbersome and costly, the TSWE remains even now a fill-in-the-bubble test of "correct" English, which is by association defined as scholastic aptitude. To this day, some of the ETS people involved do not understand why the community of writing teachers and writing researchers were—and are—so opposed to their socially and linguistically naive work. The test serves one buried and inglorious purpose of the institutions that award college degrees in America: it designates as "remedial" most students who grew up in homes where English was spoken in any dialect other than that used by the white upper-middle class. The ETS defense is simple: national tests exist to reflect college needs, not to crusade for change. Since colleges generally demand skill in using the school dialect and since students must learn that dialect to succeed, ETS will test for editing skills in that dialect (which is defined as "standard") and provide that information as part of what the College Board defines as "scholastic aptitude." This response simply accepts as fact that a major component of such scholastic aptitude involves being born into an upper-middle-class white family; that is the way the world works.

Aside from the test's unquestioning acceptance of one of the most elitist aspects of American society, it also accepts as fact that an ability to identify correctness of dialect is an acceptable definition of writing ability. While the ETS staff are well aware that editing is not the same as writing, those defending the TSWE point to high score correlations (among middle-class white students, of course) between editing and writing tests. Thus, there is no need to spend money to ask students to write or to pay faculty to read that writing; by giving scores based on the family dialect of students, obtained cheaply, ETS helps colleges identify those who require remedial help in "writing."

I was present at two encounters between English faculty and ETS personnel during the mid 1970s at which these arguments were presented and disputed. The first of these was a special session of the Executive Committee of the Conference on College Composition and Communication (CCCC), to which I had been elected. Incredibly, the ETS developers of the TSWE were asking the CCCC, which represents those who teach composition courses in American colleges and universities, to approve the test, as a needed support to college writing programs. Only in retrospect does the lack of communication at that meeting seem comic; powerful emotions and strong language dominated at the time. The CCCC leaders talked of sociolinguistics and the importance of writing as a central form of critical thinking on tests and in the schools; the ETS staff talked of administrative convenience and the practical needs of writing programs. CCCC representatives talked about helping students learn, whereas ETS staff talked about inexpensive testing of standard English. My memory of just how things concluded is a bit dim, clouded not only by time but also by my own fervor and rhetoric as a participant. I think the ETS staff finally stormed out of the room, while the Executive Committee unanimously passed a strong resolution condemning the new test. Subsequently, virtually every other professional organization in English endorsed that resolution or passed one like it. Despite this opposition, the test became, and still remains, a steady thorn in the side of writing faculty, demeaning their work wherever it is used. As a gesture, ETS does include a halfhearted recommendation that, for increased validity, institutions may want to add a writing test to the TSWE usage items, if it is not too terribly inconvenient to the test officer. To its credit, ETS has recently announced that it will phase out the TSWE, and many of us will be watching to celebrate its demise—and to see what may replace it.

The second incident is clearer in my mind, since it was a private conversation I had with an ETS vice president, a statistical specialist who had become administratively responsible for the TSWE in its second year. I had requested the meeting to clear up a statistical problem with a wholly different test, an issue he resolved directly and easily, as befitted the national expert in the area. Now it was time for social talk before leaving. Smiling graciously, he asked, "What do you think of our new Test of Standard Written English?"

"I'm sorry to say this," I replied, trying to smile back, "but I don't know anyone in the field of writing who respects that test."

His smile disappeared abruptly. I watched his neck and jowls turn bright red; and when he spoke, his voice had turned harsh. "Oh, you mean the student's right to his own language and all that nonsense, don't you?" His reference was to a CCCC document arguing against requiring all students to succeed in the school dialect in order to succeed in college composition. I was a bit uncomfortable with the document, since it did not take sufficient account of social reality, but I was even more uncomfortable with the implicit accusation in his tone. He knew of my Ivy League background, and he was calling me a traitor to my class!

"I think it is wrong to call the dialect you and I grew up speaking 'scholastic aptitude,' " I continued. "It's simply unfair to score kids according to social class, and we've been doing that for too long in this country."

Now he was furious. "Don't you think that students should be able to read the literature of the past?" he shouted. I turned to leave, stunned at what I took to be a thundering non sequitur. "I don't see what that has to do with it," I said. He turned away from me, and our meeting was at an end.

Remembering that conversation today, after almost a decade of national debate about "cultural literacy," "reclaiming a legacy," and "the closing of the American mind," I realize that I was wrong to take the vice president's statement as a non sequitur. I could not have foreseen that those who ridiculed the rhetoric of "political correctness" would seek to portray an overwhelmingly conservative faculty as a supposed beleaguered minority. Like the authors of the reports, slogans, and books I have alluded to, he believed that the traditions of the West were in peril, under attack from barbarian hordes. For him, as for the test he administered, education and educational standards depended on the indoctrination of students into his dialect. Those who were different could be accepted only if they gave away their differences and adopted his traditions and language. Here was education as socialization, with a vengeance. This was another version of what a white inner-city high school principal told me once, with self-righteous assurance: "It's impossible to be intelligent in that black dialect; all it is is a bunch of grunts and coughs."

With the TSWE expressing and codifying these attitudes, the forces in education seeking to open the process and offer new opportunities to the excluded rallied around holistic scoring. Here was a procedure that defined writing as producing a text, that could award scores for originality, creativity, intelligence, or organization, as well as for mechanical correctness. Most educators in the humanities and many college administrators were, and are, uncomfortable with the simple class barriers made apparent by the TSWE; they additionally feel a responsibility to help the schools teach writing as well as skills at coping with fill-in-the-bubble tests. The TSWE, then, has spurred the growth of writing tests and holistic scoring, in part because it everywhere raises the banner of low-level class warfare.

The CLEP test is small potatoes compared to the TSWE, since it must be sought out by students who hope that their college will accept a high score in place of freshman English. Nonetheless, that test raised more violent emotions from English faculty in the 1970s than did any other single measurement device. Since those who passed it supposedly had achieved the goals of freshman English, it presented a definition of the foundation course for most English departments in the country. That definition turned out to be even worse than the definition given by the TSWE. If the TSWE presumed to place students into freshman English by examining their dialects and editing skills, the CLEP test declared it could recommend the award of college credits by testing the same things. English faculties looking at the test were thunderstruck. Here was a definition of freshman English that did not include reading (aside from the reading of test questions) or writing.

The protests against the CLEP General Examination in English reverberated from coast to coast. When the chancellor of the California State University sought to award college credits for the test, and for the other CLEP General Examinations, the CSU English faculties revolted, and the *Los Angeles Times* supported the faculties with editorials and front-page stories mocking the "instant sophomores" created by short fill- in-the-bubble tests. The Florida English Council echoed the California protests (ironically, without acknowledging its source). To complete the geographical coverage, a major conference on "The Politics of CLEP" took place in Peoria, Illinois, sponsored by Bradley University, and the National Council of Teachers of English published the proceedings (Burt and King, 1974). In every case, the opposition to the demeaning multiple-choice test focused on essay testing and holistic scoring as the creative response.

A curious version of the conflict occurred even within the ivied walls of the bucolic ETS campus in Princeton. There, the Advanced Placement Program had considerable stake in the essay portions of AP exams (a stake somewhat diminished these days under financial pressure). The AP exams themselves had become a center for experiment and dissemination of information about holistic scoring. The AP bureaucracy at ETS, and even more so at the College Board, regarded—and attacked—the CLEP exams as low-level competition for the same market: award of college credit by examination. The developers of the CLEP exams, embattled within as well as without, were eventually forced to improve them—to add optional essay portions and even (with the English General Examination) some token holistic essay scoring. But long before that occurred, the rallying cry of CLEP had led English departments to create competing essay tests with holistic scoring, most notably the Freshman English Equivalency Examination in California (White, 1973–1981), now into its third decade.

The triumph of holistic scoring, then, had principally to do with the enemies it faced. To the atomization of education, it brought a sense of connection, unity, wholeness; to the bureaucratic machinery of fill-in-the-bubble testing, it brought human writers and human readers; to a true-false world of memorized answers to simplified questions, it brought the possibility of complexity; to socially biased correctness, it brought critical thinking. On behalf of students, it had the human decency to ask them what they thought as well as what they had memorized; on behalf of teachers, it asked them to make complex community judgments as well as to give grades. Most political of all, despite its ETS parentage, holistic scoring represented a partly successful attempt on the part of teachers to wrest control of the goals of education from the ETS-Industrial Complex; any success at all on this front had been for decades as unlikely as the breakup of the Soviet Union.

Holistic Scoring: The Triumph of the Human

But holistic scoring triumphed for personal as well as institutional reasons. In a lonely profession, holistic scoring requires the scarcest of environments: community. I argue in Chapter Four that the literary theory developed by Stanley Fish—namely, that an "interpretive community" of readers determines the meaning as well as the value of a text—is embodied by every holistic reading. But here I am using the term almost the way Paolo Freire does, as a community whose work is made meaningful by a joint social purpose. ETS recognized early on that it would have to bring Advanced Placement readers together for some days in order to generate scores; perforce, a community developed, shaped in part by the common grind of scoring during the day and in part by the alcohol that flowed in the evening. ETS has an internal conflict with the requirements of community during holistic readings; with an eye to the bottom line, it tends to see too much debate about scores (or anything else) as time taken away from production of scores. But as campus and other faculty-run holistic scorings became more and more common, the warmth and fellowship they generated became one of their most valuable features. Discussions of scores became discussions of what one valued about writing, which, in turn, became discussions of teaching writing. With its necessary emphasis on agreement, the holistic scoring session provides a wholesome atmosphere for such conversations, as opposed to the contentious jockeying that normally occurs within English departments. Good fellowship, good food and drink, good conversation, constructive community work: this is a rare combination for writing teachers, or for anyone else, and if the price is the generation of grades on a test, that is a small price to pay. Even ETS, with its slave wages and empty pretense that an appointment as ETS reader is a professional plum, has a steady waiting list of eager applicants to read for various tests; that is a sign, I take it, of the hunger for community by isolated writing teachers.

When these same writing teachers returned to their classrooms, they found that their teaching had changed. As I point out in Chapter One and throughout Part One, with newfound confidence in their ability to give consistent and fair grades, they have been able to use evaluation as part of teaching, a great change from the customary empty whining about their responsibility for grading and testing. Some teachers brought scoring guides, sample papers, and peer evaluation directly into their teaching of writing. Other teachers realized that the careful questions they had been scoring at holistic readings usually put to shame their own casual and vague writing assignments. Particularly if they had served on question development committees, they learned to think systematically about what they wanted their students to do, why the tasks were worth doing, and how writing assignments related to each other. Most important of all, they became able to teach revision of writing, since their grading standards could become public, understandable, accountable, and clear. With new attention to evaluation, writing classes could attend to the writing process as a way of meeting clearly stated standards. Holistic scoring has become a significant, perhaps the most significant, in-service training project in the profession, its power deriving from its indirectness.

As we move through the 1990s, evaluation of college writing no longer means the kind of fill-in-the-bubble test represented by the TSWE or the CLEP. True, it might mean that, and in the public schools it usually still does mean that. But when a university or college opens discussion of the measurement of writing ability these days, the point of departure is usually a holistically scored essay test. The clearest sign of this change emerged, curiously, from the medical schools. The Association of American Medical Colleges, which administers the Medical College Admissions Test, funded a five-year pilot study of ways of testing writing, as part of an overall attempt to enhance the liberal arts preparation of medical students (Koenig and Mitchell, 1988). At the conclusion of the study, early in 1989, the AAMC announced that the forthcoming revision of the MCAT would contain two essay tests, which would be scored holistically. When college English departments generally accept holistic scoring for placement, credit, course exit, and university exit exams (as they now do), a major triumph may be declared. When the medical schools look up from their serums and viruses to make the same statement, perhaps we could justly call it an achieved revolution.

Problems with Holistic Scoring

Nonetheless, holistic scoring remains a technique, a means of obtaining information from a test, one of many possible scoring mechanisms. Although it embodies a particular humanistic attitude toward teaching, writing, and students, it is not, after all, a religious experience. It may be more or less appropriate to different circumstances; it may be done more or less creatively; it may or may not yield the needed information. Now that we have done with celebrating its successes, it is time to turn to the problems and limitations of holistic scoring. I will proceed here as I did in Chapter One, using the concepts of validity and reliability to focus the issues.

Validity

Validity, you remember, has to do with honesty and accuracy, with a demonstrated connection between what a test proclaims it is measuring and what it in fact measures. Holistic scoring has posited its technical claims on its face validity: it is a direct measure of writing, measuring the real thing, and hence is more valid than indirect measures, such as fill-in-the-bubble tests of correct editing. Indeed, this single claim has been persuasive enough to lead to many a decision to use holistic scoring; as a political argument, it has no peer. But when we look at it closely, the validity of holistic scoring poses a series of problems.

In the first place, the claim that the student writing presented for holistic scoring is "real writing" requires a special definition of writing. Students producing prose during a test *are* doing a kind of writing, but its "reality" is of a peculiar kind: first draft (usually), pressured, driven by external motivation rather than an internal need to say something, designed to meet someone else's topic and grading criteria. It is not "unreal" writing; surely pressured first-draft work, for evaluation purposes, has enough reality for most definitions. And the attempts to make the writing on tests more like "real writing" are generally unsuccessful. Some tests provide time for leisurely revision; but since most students do not learn how to revise, they tend merely to recopy a draft in better penmanship. Other tests supply fake supposed audiences for the prose; but students know that the test will be scored by faculty, so the pretend audience only complicates the artificial writing problem. Still other tests provide choices of questions, but students do not know which choice will work best for them; or they provide opening sentences for students to use, but that demands that they write to someone else's pattern. When these efforts lead to more careful and precise question development, as they usually do, they are useful; but they never can turn a test into a picnic, test questions into self-expression, or test scorers into Aunt Sally.

We may as well recognize, then, that writing to a test is an artificial situation, as is most writing, and take it for what it is. Some good writers freeze under pressure, or need more time than our test allows, or just can't handle the particular question, or have a bad hangover, or whatever. Most students will write better when they are not taking a timed test, so we do not need to be overly punitive in our scoring, particularly of minor errors, and we can afford to reward good work despite some glaring errors. In short, we had best moderate our claims that test questions and test conditions produce uniquely valid real writing.

Once we recognize that the "real" writing under test conditions represents a severely limited kind of reality, we can take a more relaxed posture in relation to some of the objections to holistic scoring. We need not feel compromised by combining scores on a responsible multiple-choice test of reading (which represents another kind of limited reality) with our essay scores; a combination of measures is usually more accurate and more fair than single measures of any kind. When our colleagues protest that the holistic score does not measure the writing process, we can cheerfully agree; it only measures what it measures, and it has certain correlations with other kinds of tests. There are many aspects of college writing, such as learning to use the library or to appreciate complexity in reading or to revise repeatedly, that cannot be measured easily and directly on any test.

One aspect of the "reality" of the writing on a writing test is particularly troublesome if one believes that writing is a process, not a product. Clearly, on a holistically scored exam, we are grading a first-draft writing product rather than the process by which that writing emerged. But I think that the slogan is a false simplification: every writer knows that writing is both a process and a product. We must resist narrowing writing to only one kind of activity, just as we must resist imagining that one score reflects all possible writing abilities. Writing as product is a serious and common form, from professional published work to job applications and reports to term papers and essay exams. All these products count, and we make ourselves foolish if we pretend that they do not exist. Holistically scored essays measure writing products, and they only hint at the writing process. And if our colleagues protest that we are not measuring the writing process, and therefore are not measuring the only kind of writing that matters, we must answer "of course" to the first and "nonsense" to the second.

It is also extreme to pretend that holistic measurement of writing is a talisman and the only right way to proceed. Sometimes, specific information about particular traits should be measured, and for such needs primary-trait scoring and other kinds of trait scoring are available (see Chapter Eleven, the section headed "Holistic Scoring Versus Other Scoring Methods"). These methods are akin to holistic measurement, since they render a single score, ranking students against each other; but they are focused sharply on particular traits: coherence, logic and organization, sentence sense, or whatever. When special instructional information is required, such as for diagnosis or measurement in relation to a section of a curriculum, a holistic score is too general to be useful. Under such circumstances, a trait scoring, focusing entirely on the material taught, will make the best sense. On some occasions, researchers may even want to use analytic scoring, with its improbable assumption that a series of scores on supposed subskills will add up to a total writing measure. Those developing portfolio measurement are coming up with new scoring schemes, responsive to the particular needs of the many kinds of portfolios. Just as there is no firm consensus on the best scale for holistic scorings (though the four-point and six-point scales are most common), we cannot expect holistic scoring to be the best kind of measure for all writing.

Sometimes the validity problem with holistic scoring emerges from weak question development. One of the most consistent complaints about holistic approaches is that the writing tasks are both trivial and personal (not the same thing), variations on "What did you do last summer?" I have seen such questions on testing programs that have lost energy; the faculty team that originated and developed appropriate and valid questions has gone on to other things and left the test in the hands of staff, unaware of the complexity of and the need for question development. Or sometimes the program began with borrowed questions, which seemed to work pretty well, and the faculty never got around to developing questions more relevant to their instructional goals. Since holistic scoring can apply to any kind of writing product, including argument and exposition of all kinds, we ought to be particularly careful about question development; everyone expects a few silly questions on even the best multiple-choice tests, but when the only question on an essay test is an embarrassment, the entire test—and testing method—becomes invalid.

With all these variations of scoring and all these objections to the validity of holistic scoring, what can we say with confidence? In the first place, we need to restrict holistic scoring to overall measures of writing ability, defined as clearly as possible for a particular program and a particular student population. These definitions appear in the written scoring guide and are exemplified in the sample papers used in the reading. Furthermore, these definitions and samples need to represent a clear, developed consensus by the teachers and others using the results of the test. Test questions should be carefully developed—with an eye to the stated test criteria—by a committee constantly refreshed by new members. Then, validity studies, relating the scores on the test to other useful measures, need to be undertaken. For example, students who fail a university upper-division writing test should also be failing other courses that require writing, and should be avoiding writing in general. If students with low test scores are getting high grades in English and philosophy, publishing work in the student paper, and otherwise succeeding with the written word, something is wrong with the test. We cannot assume that an essay test is, by definition, valid. We need to work carefully to ensure its validity, and then, as we would ask of outsiders, we need to produce some evidence to show that it is indeed valid.

Finally, we ought not to overstate the validity of holistic measurement. The power and success of holistic scoring normally lead faculty and administrators to imagine that the test results mean more than they do. While we ought to make the writing test, or any test, as valid as possible (using multiple measures, conducting validity studies to gather data, and so on), we should know that any test gives only an approximate score and is subject to error. Far too often, a single essay score is used to make important decisions about a student, a procedure that is indefensible. Holistic scoring in no way relieves us of the special obligation to use test results carefully and responsibly.

Reliability

Reliability—the underlying problem for holistic scoring since its origins—is a technical way of talking about simple fairness to those being assessed; and if we are not interested in fairness, we have no business giving assessments or using their results. A few matters relating to reliability are entirely in the hands of the director of an assessment program: test development, scoring reliability, score reporting (see Chapter Ten and Eleven); but certain matters are beyond their control: variations in testing conditions, student health on the testing day, or the test taker's test-wiseness, for example. These matters affect the reliability of all tests, which can never be perfect, and we should do our best to level the playing field but not fret too much about some inevitable tilt. I know I can increase my students' scores on essay tests with some practical tips (see Chapter Three). For instance, the clever writer learns how to write a second draft on a test, despite the lack of time for a first draft; anyone who leaves the first page blank, to be written after the entire essay has been completed, will gain a point or two on coherence and organization; a writer who saves a few minutes for editing and inserting the (inevitable) missing words will also improve the score. Oddly enough, most students seem not to know or to use these techniques, and so score a bit lower than they should. We should have no illusions about achieving perfect reliability in such an imperfect world.

More problematic still are those matters which are unique to essay testing and other kinds of performance or subjective measures of ability. These are complex matters that call for some speculation about the meaning of what we are measuring and how. What is the difference between measuring ability in writing or musical performance or artistic production and measuring the weight of a cow or the knowledge of German strong verbs? What, we need to ask, changes about the concept of reliability when we move into necessarily subjective areas? I am not aware of good answers to these questions.

So reliability remains an underlying theoretical and practical problem for essay testing in general and holistic scoring in particular. We cannot dismiss the issue, as many would prefer to do, because it is a statistical way of talking about simple fairness and accuracy, matters we would be foolish to ignore. Yet we cannot be bound to a narrow and mechanical version of reliability, designed for simpler measurement; for such limits diminish and trivialize what essay testing can accomplish. Perhaps some card-carrying statistician with an interest in essay testing will emerge before the century is over, to produce new theories and practices for the statistical analysis of reliability of holistic scoring (see Shale, forthcoming, for such an attempt).

Meanwhile, we need to be alert to the uncertain reliability of holistic scores, in order to ensure that these scores will not be misused, particularly when they are used alone to damage students.

Too many institutions use holistic scores (indeed, all test scores) as if they were handed to them by the gods and were infallible measures. For example, numbers of freshman composition programs require students not only to receive a passing grade from their instructors but also to pass a writing test, holistically scored. When some students fail the test, despite good or even excellent grades from their instructors, the natural reaction is to deprecate the low standards of the faculty. Although some instructors may have standards that are too low, and the test may, over some years, show a pattern that suggests problems with standards, one test score is simply not reliable enough to warrant such a conclusion. It is far more likely that the instructor's grade, based on multiple measures, will be accurate than that the holistic score will be a reliable single measure. The comedian Richard Pryor once said that cocaine is God's way of telling you that you have too much money; perhaps reliability statistics are a similar message about too much academic arrogance.

Teaching and Assessing Writing in the Future

The future, according to the old joke, is not what it used to be. Some two decades ago, when I gave my first talk on teaching and assessing writing, the teaching of writing was emerging from its dark period of product-oriented and linguistically naive correctness into a new era of process-oriented creativity, discovery, and critical thinking. Writing programs were receiving new funding from institutions and granting agencies. New creative faculty, driven in part by the near disappearance of tenure-track jobs in English departments but also by a new concern for rhetoric and pedagogy, were taking the field in new directions.

Assessment of writing also seemed to have a clear and bright future, as teachers and test makers began working together to clear away the repressive and invalid old multiple-choice tests and come up with the essay tests that would empower both students and teachers. Teaching and assessing writing would combine, we predicted, both in the classroom and outside it, to help students internalize and apply criteria that would improve their work and make it more meaningful.

Only a little of that bright future has been realized to date, and it is easy to be cynical about the ideals of yesteryear in these much harder days of budget cuts, value-added assessment, and disillusion with essay testing. In the last two decades, we have taken ten steps forward and five backward, and the going seems harder all the time. At the same time, the bright new star of portfolios shines on the horizon, or at least flickers, with promise renewed. The future will depend in large part on the past; so it is appropriate to end this book with some speculations on what the future may hold for the teaching and assessing of writing.

Essay Tests

Essay tests will be around for the foreseeable future, and they have many advantages: students must invent, think, organize, compose, even edit a bit, rather than fill in bubbles. They must, in short, respond actively rather than passively when they are taking an essay test. But much of what seemed promising about essay testing has been undermined by the validity problem as the teaching of writing has developed under process theories. In the 1970s, we knew, and reminded ourselves repeatedly, that teachers will inevitably teach to tests, and we promoted writing on tests so that teachers would teach writing instead of multiple-choice testing techniques. But we failed to see that most essay tests emphasize first-draft writing to set topics—an advance over the fill-in-the-bubble tests, to be sure, but hardly the "real writing" we claimed it to be at the time. And teachers—most obviously, Advanced Placement teachers in the high schools or upper-division writing teachers in colleges with graduation writing tests—are now drilling students in ways to produce acceptable first-draft writing to set topics. Let us celebrate with only one hand clapping. Today's essay test does not really support today's teaching of writing. When we attempt to teach the writing process, the essay test more powerfully whispers that the first draft is the only draft; when we direct workshops for teachers in ways to foster creative assignments, the essay test urges teachers to go out and drill students in the five-paragraph theme. Writing as discovery, as delight, as revision, as self-awareness is rarely encouraged by the writing assessment when it is only a short, impromptu essay test.

Furthermore, the assessment process, through which teachers were supposed to gain control over testing by creating and scoring educationally appropriate topics, seems to be slipping back into the hands of the efficient test specialists. More and more writing teachers raise their hands when I ask if they have participated in a controlled essay scoring; but when I ask how many of them found it a collegial and useful experience, most of the hands go down. Essay test development—through which teachers come up with writing tasks appropriate for their students and their curricula, pretesting and refining the questions until they are really good—seems almost to have disappeared. Writers or writing teachers rarely direct testing programs these days, and the chief readers of essay readings rarely take the time to develop a genuine community of readers with internal assent to scoring standards. We insisted that writing assessment must be a function of a developed discourse community, an empowered teacher scoring team; but now the chief reader from ETS or even on campus, in the interest of efficiency and consistency, often requires readers of essays—without discussion—to score according to standardized scoring guides that may not fit the current test.

Portfolios

Although essay tests can still be collegial, responsive to the curriculum, and creative, most of the funding and energy that are required to make that happen seem now to be going into portfolio assessment. Those pressing for portfolio assessment in the present and future should learn from assessment experience. Chapter Six points out that portfolios conflate two different activities: the collection of materials and the assessment of them. The collection activities are quite new for writing assessment beyond the classroom and call for new solutions. The assessment part is not at all new, except in its physical dimensions, and calls for understanding of the assessment issues I have been describing throughout this book.

If portfolio assessment is to be taken seriously outside of our classrooms, it must connect with the language and the realities of the assessment community in general. It is futile to argue, as Peter Elbow does in his imaginative introduction to a collection of essays on portfolios (Belanoff and Dickson, 1991), that validity and reliability are in opposition and that we can ignore the problem of reliability, or fairness and consistency, in measurement. To argue that we need not concern ourselves with fairness in measurement is to make ourselves irrelevant to the future of assessment. True, portfolios have much stronger claims to validity than do essay tests, because portfolios provide a much larger universe for measurement; they also can support process theories of writing and of the teaching of writing. But portfolio assessment should not repeat the naiveté of an earlier generation of English faculty by ignoring reliability while it claims validity, a claim that nobody in measurement can take seriously.

If portfolios are to continue their movement beyond individual classrooms into larger assessments, they will have to demonstrate both reliabiity and cost-effectiveness. This is exactly the task that essay testing faced—and met—during the 1970s. Some parallels give cause for optimism: an infusion of grant money, substantial faculty enthusiasm, a cadre of devotees with considerable status, a clearly felt need. But some important differences suggest that portfolios will have much harder sledding. The lack of a prominent and visible prototype—such as the Advanced Placement Program was for essay testing—is a major handicap, and the competition for education funds is much tighter in the 1990s.

Assessment and Power

Something happened to the essay test on the way to the millennium, and I think it was a matter of power as well as naiveté. By calling for essay testing and more recently for portfolio assessment, teachers have hoped to gain power over assessment and hence over the definition of what is to be valued in education. They have attempted to impose the educational vision of assessment as a vital support for the learner onto the institutional vision of assessment as a sorting and certifying device. This was a bold power grab indeed, far more subversive to institutional purposes and structures than any of us realized. Compared to such a power move, collective bargaining over salaries or faculty control over curriculum is trivial. Make no mistake: assessment defines goals and expresses values. When our students ask us whether a class topic will be on the test, they are expressing this same view: if you really value it, you will assess it. The converse is also true: what you assess *is* what you value. A transfer of real power over institutional goals, values, and priorities from those who now wield it to actual teachers would seem to many, as a California State University trustee put it in a frank moment, like letting the inmates run the asylum. We should not be surprised to see such a drive for power frustrated.

We as teachers are naive if we imagine that we can by ourselves define the goals of education in this country. The business of America is business, and education is funded not for the purposes Thomas Jefferson set out but to keep America supplied with trained workers. If we are to get better assessments, we will need to convince the managers of our institutions that trained workers in the next century must be critical thinkers, problem solvers, and imaginative creators of ideas. We need, for instance, to point out some connections between the multiple-choice tests and the disappearing assembly lines in the rust belt; we also need to point out that the universities of our international competitors depend on oral and written examinations and laugh at American reliance on multiple-choice tests. We must, in short, connect the future of writing with the future of the nation, so that we can have the allies we need in furthering our assessment agenda.

In October 1991, I presented a position paper arguing for portfolio assessment (White, 1993) at a conference near Washington called by the United States Department of Education, as part of the President's "Education 2000" plan. Briefly and oversimply, the conference participants were supposed to consider and endorse some kind of national test for college graduates in three skills, skills that the organizers imagined to be distinct: critical thinking, problem solving, and communication. (Only in Washington, D.C., could anyone imagine that critical thinking and problem solving have nothing to do with effective communication—or that effective communication could go on without any kind of thinking at all.) The imagined national test would allow ready and simple comparison of the accomplishments represented by college degrees at different institutions, according to the plan, and, not incidentally, allow a self-proclaimed Education President to appear to take action with little investment or thought. A change in administration has not led to a change in policy, though the name of the program will be different; national assessment programs are clearly in the future, whatever political party may dominate. A brief note in the *Chronicle of Higher Education* (1993, p. A20) reports that the National Education Goals Panel still seeks to create such a test; the debate is over whether the results should be published by institution or by state.

Many of those at the conference registered alarm at the concept of a single national test in such areas; one group prepared a counterproposal for a national assessment *system*, which could develop and sponsor sensitive local assessments for program improvement. But the officials running the conference and many of the conferees betrayed the real goal by speaking regularly of "the test" as if it were a foregone conclusion, the only serious way to accomplish the task. As at most conferences on assessment, the educational values of assessment were seen as niceties that classroom teachers can play with but that could have no effect on the information gathering that was necessary. For big-time comparisons, the assumption was, we need big-time numbers. No one took portfolio assessment seriously, since it has unproven reliability and high cost; essay testing was seen as a minor part of the assessment, a kind of sop to teachers. The real stuff of this kind of assessment—massive in scope, cheap in cost, manipulative and illiberal in purpose— would have to be multiple choice.

This particular hairbrained scheme probably will not come to pass, for its problems and cost are overwhelming. But my point is that assessment is a high-stakes activity in government, a locus of major political power, just as it is in a local way on our home campuses. We will be allowed to play at defining writing skill as, say, imaginative discovery of ideas in a series of drafts, to pick an attractive definition; but we should not fool ourselves about what assessment means to those who fund it and use it. Institutional assessment means the picking (or, often, confirming the social and economic picking) of winners from losers. We need not and should not accept these definitions, but if we want to bring educational and enlightened social values into play on this field, we have to recognize the rules of the game. Assessment is power, and power has to do with political, social, and economic issues of the highest order.

In the future, as in the past, we are likely to see steady conflict between educational and institutional goals for assessment. As teachers, we will be pressing for assessments that help us teach and help students learn; we will resist the numerical reductionism of test scores and resist the simple sorting of winners and losers through simplified tests. After all, an important part of our business is helping those born losers become winners, or redefining the terms themselves so they relate to more than economic or social values. But our resistance to assessment will not be particularly powerful, since we too often make ourselves irrelevant to the discussion by arguing only educational goals, or, worse still, attempting to oppose all assessment. If we resist using our most creative ideas to produce the information our institutions need, assessment will go on without us. If we attempt to defeat all assessment, we just make ourselves foolish, since we need assessment as teachers in order to do our jobs.

Portfolio assessments seem to express our educational goals most fully these days, but unless we are able to link portfolios somehow to institutional assessment needs, they will have little influence outside of our classrooms. We need to find ways to shape portfolio assessment so that it can yield data, so that the best new idea in writing assessment can begin to affect the assessments that express institutional goals. If we can adapt portfolios so that they can yield reliable data at reasonable cost, they have a chance of revolutionalizing assessment in the future. But no one knows yet how to do this on a large scale.

I saw this problem clearly in a conversation I had recently with a high education official from the state of Washington. He was a great supporter of portfolio assessment, he told me, and he knew I was as well. But I was uneasy about his support. He was so supportive, he told me, that he was dead set against trying to quantify portfolio assessment; it should not produce numbers, only feedback to students. Very well, I responded, but then where do you get your information for setting budgets? Oh for that, he replied, we use our old assessments, the multiple-choice ones that yield numbers. I left the conversation with a heavy heart. This great supporter of portfolios had defined them as only a teaching device, without institutional value. The assessments that inform and shape funding and policy would come from the usual inexpensive institutional tests and readily quantifiable measures.

This conflict in values will not be settled easily or quickly. It must be coped with by faculty with eyes opened to stark political realities. We should note how much essay testing has had to sacrifice to become institutional, and we should consider how we can best protect our students and our writing programs from the assessments that do not value what we must value. Only through a change in institutional goals can we replace multiple-choice testing, or the simpler forms of essay testing, with writing assessments that reflect educational values—that is, with well-developed essay tests and portfolios. In my more pessimistic moments, I see portfolios and essays limited to classroom use, while the fill-in-the-bubble tests dominate the future of education.

But we are entitled to imagine and hope for a better world than this as we enter the next century. Large-scale essay tests will remain, I think, as a midpoint between the mechanical and the creative; and many faculties will struggle to maintain them, in order to stave off the multiple-choice alternative. Essay tests continue to offer possibilities for creativity, both for the teachers creating and scoring them and for the students writing them. They allow us to measure and therefore value such matters as analysis of written texts, reflection on the meaning of personal experience, and ordering and structuring a response to an idea.

But the brightest future, as I suggested earlier, lies with portfolio assessment. The excitement, energy, and (most encouraging) funding that recently have gone into portfolio assessment suggest that educational values still have a strong constituency, even among those most concerned with institutional evaluation. In a sense, portfolios represent an attempt to restore essay evaluation to its original purpose, under fuller and more vital definitions of writing. If portfolios can be shown to be reliable, valid, and cost-effective measures of student performance, they could lead to a basic transformation of the measures, and hence the goals, of American education itself. Portfolios promise to bring into institutional use and governmental policy the educational values of writing teachers. These are high stakes indeed.

Portfolios will be tested in the next decade. Part of the test will be taken by the large community of energetic faculty working to make portfolios effective; an even larger test will be given to the society as a whole, which must decide whether education is to foster the thinking and writing process or merely train workers for piecework. The future of assessment is bound up with the future of education, and the future of education is a function of the values of an entire society. But we as a profession can affect the way our society defines and measures its goals, and the evaluation of writing has an important, perhaps central, role to play in that process.

Teaching and assessing writing in the future can offer a troubled society a vision of active learning, creative thinking, and a much-needed blend of skills with imagination. We cannot be confident that such a vision will be welcome in the future, but we can be absolutely certain that teachers of writing will be among those struggling to achieve it.

Sample Holistic Scoring Guide

Score of 6: Superior

- Addresses the question fully and explores the issues thoughtfully
- Shows substantial depth, fullness, and complexity of thought
- Demonstrates clear, focused, unified, and coherent organization
- Is fully developed and detailed
- Evidences superior control of diction, syntactic variety, and transition; may have a few minor flaws

Score of 5: Strong

- Clearly addresses the question and explores the issues
- Shows some depth and complexity of thought
- Is effectively organized
- Is well developed, with supporting detail
- Demonstrates control of diction, syntactic variety, and transition; may have a few flaws

Score of 4: Competent

- Adequately addresses the question and explores the issues
- Shows clarity of thought but may lack complexity

Note: This scoring guide was prepared by committees in the California State University English departments, 1988.

- Is organized
- Is adequately developed, with some detail
- Demonstrates competent writing; may have some flaws

Score of 3: Weak

- May distort or neglect parts of the question
- May be simplistic or stereotyped in thought
- May demonstrate problems in organization
- May have generalizations without supporting detail or detail without generalizations; may be undeveloped
- May show patterns of flaws in language, syntax, or mechanics

Score of 2: Inadequate

- Will demonstrate *serious* inadequacy in one or more of the areas specified for the 3 paper

Score of 1: Incompetent

- Fails in its attempt to discuss the topic
- May be deliberately off-topic
- Is so incompletely developed as to suggest or demonstrate incompetence
- Is wholly incompetent mechanically

Submission Guidelines and Scoring Guide for Portfolios

1993 Guidelines for Portfolio Submission

1. All materials must be mailed on or before June 1, 1993, by your supervising teacher—the English teacher most familiar with the pieces in your portfolio. The supervising teacher signs a form that, to the best of her or his knowledge, all writing in the portfolio is your own. You sign a similar statement.

2. Arrange your portfolio items in this order: (a) completed information form; (b) reflective letter; (c) story or description; (d) explanatory, exploratory, or persuasive essay; and (e) response to a written text.

3. Your written work—not counting the information form and not counting the draft materials requested in 4 below—should *in no case* exceed twelve typed, double-spaced pages (8½ × 11").

4. For any one piece, include all draft material (paper-clipped at the end of the appropriate essay).

Note: Guidelines and Scoring Guide for Portfolios were prepared by Donald Daiker and the members of the Department of English, Miami University, Oxford, Ohio, 1992–93.

5. All items—except the draft material of item 4 above—must be free of teachers' comments, grades, and markings.

6. Do not write your name anywhere except on the information form, but do write your social security number in the upper right corner of each page. Items 2c, 2d, and 2e should have a title.

7. No staples should be used. The five-item portfolio should be fastened with a paper clip.

8. Papers written in class or out of school, including college application essays, are acceptable. Papers may be revised after being returned by a teacher.

9. You will be rewarded for originality and variety so long as you observe all items listed in 2 above.

10. Portfolio submission costs $21, but you will receive a $10 gift certificate from Follett's Miami Coop Bookstore and you will not be billed until the summer. Results will be available by mid-June—in time for registration at summer orientation.

Scoring Guide for Portfolios

General Directions: Each portfolio should be read holistically and given a single comprehensive score on a six-point scale ("6" is high and "1" is low). In determining that single score, do not average the four pieces but judge the quality of the portfolio as a whole. In doing so, give greater weight to the longer and more substantial pieces, and reward variety and creativity. Please consult the chief reader if you believe a portfolio does not meet the stated requirements or if for any other reason you have trouble scoring it.

6   A portfolio that is *excellent* in overall quality. It is characteristically substantial in content (both length and development) and mature in style. It demonstrates an ability to handle varied prose tasks successfully and to use language creatively and effectively. Voice tends to be strong, and there is usually a clear sense of audience and context. Often, there is a close connection between the writer's sense of self and the writing—and/or a sense of thematic unity within the four separate portfolio pieces. A "6'" portfolio typically takes risks that work—either in content or form—and challenges the reader by trying something new.

5   A portfolio that is *very good* in overall quality. It suggests the excellence that the "6" portfolio demonstrates. Typically, a "5" portfolio is substantial in content, although its pieces are not as fully developed as a "6," and it uses language effectively but not as creatively as a "6." It suggests an ability to handle varied prose tasks successfully, and its voice is clear and distinct if not powerful. Sense of audience and context is clearly present if not always firm. A "5" portfolio tends not to take as many risks as a "6."

4   A portfolio that is *good* in overall quality. The writing is competent both in content and style. There are more strengths than weaknesses, but there may be an unevenness of quality or underdevelopment in one or two pieces. The reader may want "more" to be fully convinced of the writer's ability to handle varied prose tasks successfully and to use language effectively. There is a sense of audience and context, but some of the writing may seem formulaic or lack strong voice. There tends to be minimal risk-taking or originality.

3   A portfolio that is *fair* in overall quality. It suggests the competence that a "4" portfolio demonstrates. Strengths and weaknesses tend to be evenly balanced—either within or among the four pieces. One or more of the pieces may be too brief or underdeveloped. There is some evidence of the writer's ability to handle varied prose tasks successfully and to use language effectively, but it is offset by recurring problems in either or both content and style. A "3" portfolio often lacks both a clear sense of audience and a distinctive voice.

2   A portfolio that is *below average* in overall quality. It does not suggest the writing competence that a "3" portfolio does. Weaknesses clearly predominate over strengths. The writing may be clear,

focused, and error-free, but is usually thin in substance and undistinguished in style. Two or more of the pieces may be either short and undeveloped or abstract and vague. Moreover, the writer rarely takes risks, relying instead on formulas and clichés. There is little evidence of the writer's ability to handle varied prose tasks successfully. The few strengths of a "2" are more than overbalanced by significant weaknesses.

1   A portfolio that is *poor* in overall quality. There are major weaknesses and few, if any, strengths. A "1" portfolio lacks the redeeming qualities of a "2." It is usually characterized by brief pieces that are unoriginal and uncreative in content and style. The portfolio seems to have been put together with very little time and thought.

RESOURCE C

Guidelines for Self-Study to Precede a Writing Program Evaluation

One month before the WPA consultant-evaluators are scheduled to visit your campus, you should send them a self-study. The purposes of this self-study are, through the process of writing it, to help you understand more clearly the reasons for the visit and to acquaint the consultants with your institution.

Ideally this self-study will be prepared by a team including the writing program administrator at your institution and others who are directly involved in your writing program, not by one individual.

The self-study should be largely a narrative report focusing on the main concerns you have about your writing program. The questions below are intended to help you think of all the possible facets of your program you might want to describe in your self-study. You need not answer all these questions and they are not intended as an outline for your report.

The final self-study should be about ten pages in length, not including any supporting documents.

Note: These guidelines were prepared by the Council of Writing Program Administrators and published as a draft—for comments and revision—in *WPA: Writing Program Administration,* 1993, *17* (1-2), 88-95. Reprinted by permission.

I. General Background
   A. Focus of the Visit
      1. What are the program's current concerns?
      2. What changes in the program are being contemplated?
      3. What issues would you like the consultant-evaluators to address?
   B. Current Institutional Conditions
      1. What specific institutional changes are affecting your writing program?
      2. What specific characteristics of your student body affect your program?
   C. Missions
      1. What is the mission of your institution?
      2. What is the mission of your writing program?
      3. How does the mission of your program support the mission of your institution?
   D. Philosophy and Goals
      1. What are the principles or philosophy of the writing program(s) at your institution?
      2. What are the goals of your program?
      3. How do these goals reflect the program's philosophy?
      4. How do your program's practices enact the philosophy and goals?

II. Curriculum
   A. Philosophy and Goals
      1. What are the philosophy and goals of the writing program(s) at your institution?
      2. Do the goals of the writing program(s) accord with the goals of the institution as a whole?
      3. How are the philosophy and goals communicated to the teachers, to the students, and to the appropriate administrators?
   B. Courses and Syllabi
      1. What writing courses are currently taught in your institution? By what departments are they taught?
      2. How are these courses sequenced or otherwise re-

lated? Which courses are required, and of whom are they required?

3. If your institution identifies some students as "basic writers," how are their needs addressed?

4. Are the syllabi for the courses uniform, or different for each teacher? (Or do some teachers follow a uniform syllabus, while other teachers follow their individual syllabi?) If the syllabus is uniform within each course or for several sections within each course, who is responsible for developing it?

5. If the syllabus is uniform within each course, what opportunities do individual teachers have for experimentation with the syllabus? If the syllabi are individual, what ties or links make the course cohere across the sections?

6. What is the logical basis for the sequence of assignments within each course? How does that sequence relate to the goals and philosophy of the program?

7. How much writing, and what kinds of writing, must students do for each course?

8. What kinds of **reading** are assigned in the writing courses? What instruction is given to students in the reading of these texts? in the reading of their own drafts?

C. Instructional Methods and Materials

1. What events or activities typically take place in the classrooms of the program's writing courses?

2. What textbooks are used in each writing course? Why is the program using these textbooks? What instructional materials other than textbooks does the program use? How do these textbooks and other materials fit the goals and structure of the course(s)? Who chooses the textbooks and other instructional materials used in the courses?

3. How much time do teachers devote to individual conferences?

D. Responses to and Evaluation of Student Writing

1. At what point(s) in their composing do students

receive responses to their writing? What kinds of responses do they receive? At what points during the course(s) do students receive evaluation of their progress?

2. What procedures do faculty use in evaluating students' writing (e.g., letter grades on each paper, letter grades on some papers only, no grades until the end of the course)? On what bases (standards) do faculty evaluate papers?

3. What processes are used to assure consistency across sections in evaluation of students' writing? How does the program assure that the bases for evaluation cohere with the goals of the program?

4. How does the evaluation of students' work reflect their achievement of the stated goals of the course?

E. Assessment

1. What tests and testing procedures are used in the writing program for such purposes as placement, exemption, determination of readiness to exit from a course or from the program, determination of eligibility to enter a more advanced program? What procedures are used to correct errors in placement? How do these procedures relate to the goals of the program?

2. Under what conditions are the assessment procedures conducted? Who conducts them? Who interprets and uses the results? What training do those who conduct the assessment have? If tests are scored by humans (i.e., not machines), what training do the scorers have?

3. What methods are used for continued monitoring of the assessment instruments to assure their current reliability and validity for the students and the purposes they are to serve? How frequently is the monitoring conducted?

III. Faculty

A. Status and Working Conditions

1. What percentage of full-time faculty at each rank,

of adjunct faculty, and graduate students teach
writing? How many writing courses do faculty at
each rank or status teach? What percentage of the
writing courses are taught by faculty at each rank
or status?

2. What are the qualifications for writing faculty and
how are they established? What training and experience in teaching writing do the writing faculty
have? What professional organizations do they belong to? What is their record of research, publication, conference participation, and professional
activity in composition and rhetoric?

3. What are the salary ranges by rank and category?
How do these salary ranges compare to comparable
departments? To neighboring, comparable institutions?

4. How are teaching, administration, and research in
composition rewarded in terms of salary, promotion, and tenure?

5. How are adjunct faculty appointed? By whom?
When in relation to the opening of a term? How are
they evaluated? What is the length of their appointment? How are they reappointed? What percentage
have multiple-year contracts? How are the adjunct
faculty compensated in terms of salary and benefits? Are there step raises or cost of living increases
for adjunct faculty? Are adjunct faculty compensated for preparation if a course does not fill or is
covered by a full-time faculty member? Is there a
departmental policy on percentage of part-time faculty? Do adjunct faculty attend department meetings and writing program meetings? Serve on departmental or writing program committees? What
opportunities exist for adjunct faculty to develop
curriculum, choose textbooks, formulate policy
and procedures? What arrangements are made for
office space, telephones, mailboxes, and clerical
support for adjunct faculty?

B. Faculty Development
   1. How is faculty development defined as a goal of the institution, the department or administrative unit, and the writing program? What are ongoing plans for faculty development in teaching writing?
   2. What courses, speaker programs, workshops, teaching awards, etc., does the writing program offer or support to encourage excellence in teaching writing?
   3. What opportunities for faculty development in teaching writing already exist? Who uses them? How do faculty find out about them? In what ways are faculty encouraged to avail themselves of these opportunities?
   4. Are these opportunities available to adjunct faculty and teaching assistants?
   5. Are issues of race and gender addressed in faculty development?
   6. What financial resources are available for travel to workshops, conferences, and institutes related to teaching writing?
   7. What avenues exist for writing faculty at each rank and status to design, implement, and evaluate faculty development programs best suited to their needs and interests? How are faculty encouraged to develop their skills in composition research and teaching writing? What opportunities exist for learning about faculty development programs in writing at other institutions?
   8. Does the department or institution support faculty development by offering paid leaves or sabbaticals for further education in composition studies and rhetoric, by publishing journals, by developing software or other media for use in teaching writing?
   9. What support does the department or institution give for development of institutional and individual grants to improve writing instruction and curricula and for released time, overhead, and other support to carry out the grant?

IV. Program Administration
   A.   Institutional and Program Structure

1. What writing programs are there on campus (e.g., first-year composition, writing across the curriculum, technical writing)?

2. What is the size and make-up of each of the departments or administrative units in which these programs are housed? What is the governing structure of each? How are these related administratively?

3. What are the internal governing structures of the writing programs? Are there writing program administrators (e.g., director of first-year composition, composition committee chair, director of the writing center)? If so, what are the WPAs' administrative relations to other levels of administration? To whom are the WPAs responsible?

4. If there are night school, continuing education, or nondegree programs, who determines how writing is taught in those programs? How is control exercised? Who is responsible for the teaching of writing in other departments or colleges within the institution?

5. How are the teaching and tutoring of writing funded? Who controls these funds? On what are these funds spent? How does the funding of the writing programs compare to the funding of other programs on campus?

6. Are institutional grant funds available for program development (e.g., curriculum development and assessment)? If so, have WPAs applied for and been awarded any of these grants?

7. Who hires, promotes, and tenures the writing faculty throughout the institution? Who determines their salaries and assigns courses to them?

8. How are new teaching positions determined and by whom?

9. Who determines such things as class size, curriculum, and teaching load in the various programs?

10. How are internal problems solved? Who decides on syllabi, testing procedures, textbooks, etc.? What procedures are in place for full-time faculty, adjunct faculty, teaching assistants, and students to shape policies?

11. What permanent or *ad hoc* committees related to writing programs exist? How are these committees appointed? Who serves on them (e.g., full-time faculty, adjuncts, students)? What do these committees do?

12. What are the procedures for negotiating student and faculty complaints about grading, teaching, harassment, learning atmosphere, and administrative processes and policies?

13. What administrative, clerical, and technical support is there?

14. How are the writing programs' histories documented (e.g., annual reports, status reports on progress toward multi-year development plans)? Who writes these histories and who reads them? How are they used?

B. Writing Program Administrators

1. How are the WPAs chosen and what are the lengths of their appointments?

2. What are the terms and conditions of appointments of the WPAs? Are these terms in writing?

3. What are the academic and professional qualifications of the WPAs? What are the WPAs' ranks and tenure statuses? Who decides the WPAs' tenures, promotions, and salaries?

4. What are the WPAs' teaching loads and how do they compare with other faculties' loads?

5. How much and what type of research are WPAs expected to do? To what extent are the WPAs' efforts in program development and institutional research considered scholarship?

6. How and by whom are WPAs evaluated? How are WPAs rewarded?

V.   Related Writing Programs and Instructional Units

In many institutions the English Department's composition program is not the only place where writing instruction takes place.
Others sites charged with teaching writing may include many of the
following: writing centers, reading centers, learning centers, testing
centers, disabled student centers, Writing-Across-the-Curriculum
Programs, ESL and bilingual programs, tutoring services, corres-
pondence and extension courses, telecommunications and long distance learning courses and programs, high school bridge programs,
writing proficiency programs and exams, and discipline-based writing programs in colleges of education, business, nursing, law, and
engineering.

     Please address the relationships with the programs that are
most pertinent to this visit. (Also include relationships that may
become significant in the immediate or long term.) Briefly tell how
you perceive the relationships between your program and the other
academic units charged with writing instruction.

    A.   Administration
       1.   To what extent do services offered by the writing
         program and other units overlap?
         a.   Do their common goals and procedures rein-
           force each other or conflict?
         b.   In what formal and informal ways (through
           scheduling, a coordinating committee, etc.) is
           each unit related to the writing program?
       2.   How is each unit funded?
       3.   How does each unit follow up on students who
         have used its services?
       4.   How is credit determined for work in these units?
       5.   What arrangements exist for the evaluation of each
         unit?
    B.   Curriculum
       1.   How many students and faculty are associated with
         each unit?
       2.   What is the profile of the students?
       3.   How are students placed in or referred to each unit?

4. What kinds of materials (books, computers, television) and techniques (tutoring, workshops) does the unit use?
5. How do students learn about the unit?

C. Personnel

1. What are the job descriptions for the director and teaching staff of each unit? How are the director and staff selected?
2. What is the institutional status (faculty, full-time, part-time, graduate student, etc.) of unit personnel?
   a. How are they compensated for their work?
   b. How is their work evaluated?
3. What provisions exist for training and professional development of unit staff?

You may not want to overwhelm consultants with background materials, but you may want to include the following in an appendix to the narrative report.

- Statistical information for the previous and current academic year: enrollments, class sizes, composition of the teaching staff, final grade distribution.
- A description of each course within the program(s) to be evaluated (objectives, syllabi, texts, placement and exemption procedures, grading criteria).
- Copies of evaluative instruments.
- Materials pertaining to teacher training (both faculty and graduate students or adjuncts), including orientation meeting agendas, workshop descriptions, and syllabi for training courses.
- School catalogues, department handbooks, and departmental student materials.

Evaluation of the Writing-Across-the-Curriculum Program: Minnesota Community College System

GOAL 1: Increase the Amount and Types of Student Writing Done Across the Curriculum

GOAL 2: Improve Faculty Attitudes Towards the Use of Writing in Instruction

Evaluation Devices for These Goals

Faculty Evaluation of the WAC Program: End-of-year Likert-Scale survey of all WAC faculty
Hour-Long Interviews of a random sample of WAC faculty

GOAL 3: Increase the Quality of Student Writing

Holistic Rating of Student Essays gathered in a random sample of WAC classrooms; essay ratings will be correlated with participation in WAC classes

Note: This WAC program evaluation was prepared by Gail Hughes and funded by a grant from the Bush Foundation, 1985–1994. Reprinted by permission.

GOAL 4: Increase Student Attainment of Subject Goals Through Instructional Writing

Quasi-Experimental "Matched Classes" Studies (in most cases, two sections of the same class; use of Holistic Subject Rating to score essay exams)

GOAL 5: Improve Student Attitudes Toward Writing

Course Evaluation Survey by students in both Experimental and Control classes
Student Evaluation of Writing Activities Survey by students in Experimental classes

GOAL 6: Provide Information for Organizing WAC Workshops

Workshop Checklist: All participants complete a survey in which they rate workshop sessions
Short-Answer Questionnaire completed by workshop participants several weeks after returning to their campuses

GOAL 7: Provide Information for Organizing Follow-Up Activities

Background Characteristics Survey (reasons for attending and previous experiences with writing activities)
Writing Issues Survey (short pre- and post-workshop survey)
Information Needs Survey (short end-of-workshop survey)

GOAL 8: Provide Diagnostic Information Which Will Enable Faculty to Be More Effective in Their Use of Writing Activities

Teaching Strategy Form by Experimental teachers
Writing Activities Diagnosis Form by Experimental teachers

References

Adelman, C. (ed.) *Performance and Judgment: Essays on Principles and Practice in the Assessment of College Student Learning.* Washington, D.C.: Office of Educational Research and Improvement, U.S. Department of Education, 1988.

Allan, R., Nassif, P., and Elliot, S. (eds.). *Bias Issues in Teacher Certification Testing.* Hillsdale, N.J.: Erlbaum, 1988.

Anson, C. *Writing and Response.* Urbana, Ill.: National Council of Teachers of English, 1988.

Barth, J. *The Friday Book.* New York: Putnam, 1984.

Belanoff, P., and Dickson, M. (eds.). *Portfolios: Process and Product.* Portsmouth, N.H.: Boynton Cook, 1991.

Belanoff, P., and Elbow, P. "Using Portfolios to Increase Collaboration and Community in a Writing Program." *WPA: Writing Program Administration,* 1986, *9*(3), 27–40.

Belanoff, P., and Elbow, P. "Using Portfolios to Increase Collaboration and Community in a Writing Program." In Belanoff and Dickson (eds.), *Portfolios: Process and Product.* Portsmouth, N.H.: Boynton Cook, 1991.

Bizzell, P. "What Can We Know, What Must We Do, What May We Hope: Writing Assessment." *College English,* 1987, *49*(5), 575–584.

Blackmur, R. P. "Toward a Modus Vivendi." In *The Lion and the*

Honeycomb: Essays in Solicitude and Critique. Orlando, Fla.: Harcourt Brace, 1955.

Bloom, B., and others. *Handbook on Formative and Summative Evaluation of Student Learning.* New York: McGraw-Hill, 1971.

Bloom, L., and White, E. *Inquiry: A Cross-Curricular Reader.* Englewood Cliffs, N.J.: Prentice-Hall, 1993.

Braddock, R., Lloyd-Jones, R., and Schoer, L. *Research in Written Composition.* Urbana, Ill.: National Council of Teachers of English, 1963.

Breland, H. *Group Comparisons for the TSWE.* Research Bulletin RB-77-15. Princeton, N.J.: College Entrance Examination Board, 1977a.

Breland, H. *A Study of College English Placement and the Test of Standard Written English.* Research and Development Report RDR-76-77. Princeton, N.J.: College Entrance Examination Board, 1977b.

Breland, H., and Gaynor, J. "Comparison of Direct and Indirect Assessments of Writing Skill." *Journal of Educational Measurement,* 1979, *16*(2), 119–127.

Breland, H., and others. *Assessing Writing Skill.* New York: College Entrance Examination Board, 1987.

Britton, J. *Language and Learning.* Coral Gables, Fla.: University of Miami Press, 1970.

Britton, J., and others. *The Development of Writing Abilities (11–18).* New York: Macmillan, 1975.

Brossell, G. "The Effects of Systematic Variations in Essay Topics on the Writing Performance of College Freshmen." *College Composition and Communication,* 1989, *40*, 414–421.

Brossell, G. "Writing Assessment in Florida: A Reminiscence." In E. White, W. Lutz, and S. Kamasukiri (eds.), *The Politics and Policies of Assessment in Writing.* New York: Modern Language Association, forthcoming.

Bruner, J. *The Process of Education.* Cambridge, Mass.: Harvard University Press, 1960.

Burt, F., and King, S. (eds.). *Equivalency Testing.* Urbana, Ill.: National Council of Teachers of English, 1974.

Comprone, J. J. "Literary Theory and Composition." In G. Tate (ed.), *Teaching Composition: 12 Bibliographical Essays*. Fort Worth: Texas Christian University Press, 1987.

Connolly, P., and Vilardi, T. *New Methods in College Writing Programs: Theories in Practice*. New York: Modern Language Association, 1986.

Connors, R. "Composition Studies and Science." *College English,* 1983, *45*, 1-20.

Cooper, C., and Odell, L. (eds.). *Evaluating Writing: Describing, Measuring, Judging*. Urbana, Ill.: National Council of Teachers of English, 1977.

Cooper, C., and Odell, L. (eds.). *Research on Composing: Points of Departure*. Urbana, Ill.: National Council of Teachers of English, 1978.

Corbett, E.P.J. *Classical Rhetoric for the Modern Student*. New York: Oxford University Press, 1965.

Cronbach, L. J., Rajaratnam, M., and Gleser, G. "Theory of Generalizability: A Liberation of Reliability Theory." *British Journal of Statistical Psychology*, 1963, *16*, 137-163.

Daiker, D. A., Sommers, J., Stygall, G., and Black, L. *The Best of Miami's Portfolios*. Oxford, Ohio: Department of English, Miami University, 1990, 1991, 1992.

D'Angelo, F. J. "Aims, Modes, and Forms of Discourse." In G. Tate (ed.), *Teaching Composition: 12 Bibliographical Essays*. Fort Worth: Texas Christian University Press, 1987.

Davis, B. G., Scriven, M., and Thomas, S. *The Evaluation of Composition Instruction*. (2nd ed.) New York: Teachers College Press, 1987.

Derrida, J. *Of Grammatology*. (G. Spivak, trans.) Baltimore: Johns Hopkins University Press, 1976. (Originally published 1967.)

Diederich, P. *Measuring Growth in English*. Urbana, Ill.: National Council of Teachers of English, 1974.

Elbow, P. *Writing Without Teachers*. New York: Oxford University Press, 1973.

Elbow, P.. and Belanoff, P. "Portfolios as a Substitute for Proficiency Examinations." *College Composition and Communication*, 1986a, *37*, 336-339.

Elbow, P., and Belanoff, P. "State University of New York at Stony Brook Portfolio-Based Evaluation Program." In P. Connolly and

T. Vilardi (eds.), *New Methods in College Writing Programs: Theories in Practice.* New York: Modern Language Association, 1986b.

Elbow, P., and Belanoff, P. *Sharing and Responding.* New York: Random House, 1989.

Emig, J. *The Composing Processes of Twelfth Graders.* Urbana, Ill.: National Council of Teachers of English, 1971.

Faigley, L., and others. *Assessing Writers' Knowledge and Processes of Composing.* Norwood, N.J.: Ablex, 1985.

Fish, S. *Is There a Text in This Class? The Authority of Interpretive Communities.* Cambridge, Mass.: Harvard University Press, 1980.

Flower, L. "Writer-Based Prose: A Cognitive Basis for Problems in Writing." *College English,* 1979, *41,* 19–37.

Flower, L. "Cognition, Context, and Theory Building." *College Composition and Communication,* 1989, *40,* 282–311.

Flower, L., and Hayes, J. "The Dynamics of Composing: Making Plans and Juggling Constraints." In L. Gregg and E. Sternglass (eds.), *Cognitive Processes in Writing.* Hillsdale, N.J.: Erlbaum, 1980.

Flower, L., and Hayes, J. "Plans That Guide the Composing Process." In C. Frederiksen and J. Dominic (eds.), *Writing: The Nature, Development, and Teaching of Written Communication.* Hillsdale, N.J.: Erlbaum, 1981.

Freedman, S. W. *Response to Student Writing.* Urbana, Ill.: National Council of Teachers of English, 1987.

Gere, A. R. "Empirical Research in Composition." In B. W. McClelland and T. R. Donovan (eds.), *Perspectives on Research and Scholarship in Composition.* New York: Modern Language Association, 1985.

Gere, A. R. *Writing Groups: History, Theory, and Implications.* Carbondale: Southern Illinois University Press, 1987.

Godshalk, F., Swineford, E., and Coffman, W. *The Measurement of Writing Ability.* Princeton, N.J.: College Entrance Examination Board, 1966.

Gould, S. J. *The Mismeasure of Man.* New York: Norton, 1981.

Greenberg, K., Wiener, H., and Donovan, R. (eds.). *Writing Assess-*

ment: Issues and Strategies. White Plains, N.Y.: Longman, Inc., 1986.

Hamp-Lyons, L., and Condon, W. "Questioning Assumptions About Portfolio-Based Assessment." *College Composition and Communication,* 1993, *44*(2), 176–190.

Haswell, R. *Gaining Ground in College Writing: Tales of Development and Interpretation.* Dallas: Southern Methodist University Press, 1991.

Haviland, C., and Clark, J. M. "What Can Our Students Tell Us About Essay Examination Designs and Practices?" *Journal of Basic Writing,* 1992, *11*(2), 47–60.

Henry, J. *Culture Against Man.* New York: Random House, 1963.

Hillocks, G. *Research on Written Composition.* Urbana, Ill.: National Council of Teachers of English, 1986.

Holland, N. *Five Readers Reading.* New Haven, Conn.: Yale University Press, 1975.

Hughes, G. "The Need for Clear Purposes and New Approaches to the Evaluation of Writing Across the Curriculum Programs." In E. White, W. Lutz, and S. Kamasukiri (eds.), *The Politics and Policies of Writing Assessment.* New York: Modern Language Association, forthcoming.

Hughes-Wiener, G., and Jensen-Cekalla, S. "Organizing a WAC Evaluation Project: Implications for Program Planning." In L. Stanley and J. Ambron (eds.), *Writing Across the Curriculum in the Community College.* New Directions for Community Colleges, no. 73. San Francisco: Jossey-Bass, 1991.

Iser, W. *The Implied Reader: Patterns of Communication in Prose Fiction from Bunyan to Beckett.* Baltimore: Johns Hopkins University Press, 1974.

Kinneavy, J. *A Theory of Discourse.* Englewood Cliffs, N.J.: Prentice-Hall, 1971.

Kitzhaber, A. R. *Themes, Theories, and Therapy: The Teaching of Writing in College.* New York: McGraw-Hill, 1963.

Koenig, J., and Mitchell, K. "An Interim Report on the MCAT Essay Pilot Project." *Journal of Medical Education,* 1988, *63*, 21–29.

Kohlberg, L. *The Meaning and Measurement of Moral Development.* Worcester, Mass.: Clark University Press, 1981.

Krashen, S., Scarcella, R., and Long, M. (eds). *Child-Adult Differences in Second Language Acquisition.* Rowley, Mass.: Newbury House, 1982.

Larson, R. L. "Review: *Research on Written Composition.*" *College Composition and Communication,* 1987, *38*(2), 207–211.

Lawson, B., Ryan, S., and Winterowd, W. R. (eds.). *Encountering Student Texts: Interpretive Issues in Reading Student Writing.* Urbana, Ill.: National Council of Teachers of English, 1989.

Lederman, M. J., Ryzewic, S. R., and Ribaudo, M. *Assessment and Improvement of the Academic Skills of Entering Freshman Students: A National Survey.* New York: Instructional Resource Center, City University of New York, 1983.

Leitch, V. "Two Poststructuralist Modes of (Inter)Textuality." *Critical Texts,* 1982, *2,* 3–5.

Leitch, V. "Deconstruction and Pedagogy." In G. D. Atkins and M. Johnson (eds.), *Reading and Writing Differently.* Lawrence: University Press of Kansas, 1985.

Lindemann, E. *A Rhetoric for Writing Teachers.* New York: Oxford University Press, 1987.

Lloyd-Jones, R. "Primary Trait Scoring." In C. Cooper and L. Odell (eds.), *Evaluating Writing: Describing, Measuring, Judging.* Urbana, Ill.: National Council of Teachers of English, 1977.

Meyers, G. D. "The Phenomenology of Composition: Applications of Reader-Response Criticism to the Teaching of Writing." Paper presented at the annual meeting of the Conference on College Composition and Communication, San Francisco, March 1982.

Mitchell, K., and Anderson, J. "Reliability of Holistic Scoring for the MCAT Essay." *Educational and Psychological Measurement,* 1986, *46,* 771–775.

North, S. *The Making of Knowledge in Composition: Portrait of an Emerging Field.* Portsmouth, N.H.: Boynton Cook, 1987.

Ong, W. J. "The Writer's Audience Is Always a Fiction." *PMLA,* 1975, *90*(1), 9–21.

Orwell, G. "Politics and the English Language." S. Orwell and I. Angus (eds.), *The Collected Essays, Journalism and Letters of George Orwell,* Vol. 4, *In Front of Your Nose (1945–1950).* New York: Harcourt Brace, 1968. (Originally published 1950.)

Perl, S. "The Composing Process of Unskilled College Writers." *Research in the Teaching of English*, 1979, *13*, 317-336.

Perry, W. G. *Forms of Intellectual and Ethical Development in the College Years: A Scheme.* Troy, Mo.: Holt, Rinehart & Winston, 1968.

Piaget, J. *The Language and Thought of the Child.* (M. Gabain, trans.) New York: New American Library, 1955. (Originally published 1926.)

Porter, J. "The Reasonable Reader: Knowledge and Inquiry in Freshman English." *College English*, 1987, *49*, 332-344.

Rose, M. *Writer's Block: The Cognitive Dimension.* Carbondale: Southern Illinois University Press, 1983.

Ruth, L., and Murphy, S. *Designing Writing Tasks for the Assessment of Writing.* Norwood, N.J.: Ablex, 1988.

Sanders, S., and Littlefield, J. "Perhaps Test Essays Can Reflect Significant Improvement in Freshman Composition: Report on a Successful Attempt." *Research in the Teaching of English*, 1975, *9*, 145-153.

Sapir, E. "The Status of Linguistics as a Science." In D. G. Mandelbaum (ed.), *Selected Writings in Language, Culture, and Personality.* Berkeley: University of California Press, 1963. (Originally published 1928.)

Schorer, M. "Technique as Discovery." *Hudson Review*, 1948, *1*(1), 67-87.

Scriven, M. "Goal-Free Evaluation." In E. R. House (ed.), *School Evaluation.* Berkeley, Calif.: McCutchan, 1973.

Shale, D. "Essay Reliability: Form and Meaning." Paper presented at the annual meeting of the American Educational Research Association, San Francisco, April 1986. Revised version in E. White, W. Lutz, and S. Kamasukiri (eds.), *The Politics and Policies of Writing Assessment.* New York: Modern Language Association, forthcoming.

Shaughnessy, M. *Errors and Expectations: A Guide for the Teacher of Basic Writing.* New York: Oxford University Press, 1977.

Skinner, B. F. *Beyond Freedom and Dignity.* New York: Knopf, 1972.

Smith, M. *Reducing Writing Apprehension.* Urbana, Ill.: National Council of Teachers of English, 1984.

Sommers, N. "Responding to Student Writing." *College Composition and Communication*, 1982, *33*, 148–156.

"Teaching and Learning the Art of Composition: The Bay Area Writing Project." *Carnegie Quarterly*, 1979, 27(2), 7.

White, E. M. *Comparison and Contrast: The California State University Freshman English Equivalency Examination.* Vols. 1–8. Long Beach: California State University, 1973–1981. (Available through ERIC, 1111 W. Kenyon Road, Urbana, IL 61801.)

White, E. M. "Holisticism." *College Composition and Communication*, 1984a, *35*, 400–409.

White, E. M. "Post-Structural Literary Criticism and Response to Student Writing." *College Composition and Communication*, 1984b, *35*, 186–195.

White, E. M. *Developing Successful College Writing Programs.* San Francisco: Jossey-Bass, 1989.

White, E. M. "Change for the Worse." *AAHE Bulletin*, November 1990, pp. 1–4.

White, E. M. "Shallow Roots or Taproots for Writing Across the Curriculum?" *ADE Bulletin*, 1991, *98*, 29–33.

White, E. M. *Assigning, Responding, Evaluating: A Writing Teacher's Guide.* New York: St. Martin's Press, 1992.

White, E. M. "Assessing Higher-Order Thinking and Communication Skills in College Graduates Through Writing." *JGE: The Journal of General Education*, 1993, *42*(2), 105–122.

White, E. M. *Creative Composition.* Englewood Cliffs, N.J.: Prentice-Hall, forthcoming.

White, E., Lutz, W., and Kamasukiri, S. (eds.). *The Politics and Policies of Assessment in Writing.* New York: Modern Language Association, forthcoming.

White, E. M., and Polin, L. *Research in Effective Teaching of Writing: Final Report.* NIE-G-81-0011 and NIE-G-82-0024. Washington, D.C.: National Institute of Education, 1986. (Document number ED 275 007, available through ERIC Document Reproduction Service.)

White, E. M., and Thomas, L. "Racial Minorities and Writing Skills Assessment in the California State University and Colleges." *College English*, 1981, *43*(3), 276–283.

White, J. "Who Writes These Questions, Anyway?" *College Composition and Communication,* 1988, *39,* 230–235.

Whorf, B. L. "Science and Linguistics." In John B. Carroll (ed.), *Language, Thought, and Reality: Selected Writings.* Cambridge, Mass.: MIT Press, 1956. (Originally published 1940).

Williamson, M., and Huot, B. (eds.). *Validating Holistic Scoring for Writing Assessment: Theoretical and Empirical Foundations.* Cresskill, N.J.: Hampton Press, 1993.

Winterowd, W. R. *Rhetoric and Writing.* Needham Heights, Mass.: Allyn & Bacon, 1965.

Witte, S., and Faigley, L. *Evaluating College Writing Programs.* Carbondale: Southern Illinois University Press, 1983.

WPA Board of Consultant-Evaluators. "WPA Self-Study Guidelines." *WPA: Writing Program Administration,* 1993, *17*(1–2), 88–95.

Yancey, K. *Portfolios in the Writing Classroom.* Urbana, Ill.: National Council of Teachers of English, 1992.

Young, R. E., Becker, A. L., and Pike, K. L. *Rhetoric: Discovery and Change.* Orlando, Fla.: Harcourt Brace, 1970.

Index

327